Please
return
materials
on time

D1053027

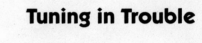

Tuning in Trouble

Tuning in Trouble

Talk TV's Destructive Impact on Mental Health

Jeanne Albronda Heaton
Nona Leigh Wilson

Jossey-Bass Publishers • San Francisco

Substantial discounts on bulk quantities of Jossey-Bass books are available to corporations, professional associations, and other organizations. For details and discount information, contact the special sales department at Jossey-Bass Inc., Publishers. (415) 433-1740; FAX (800) 605-2665.

For sales outside the United States, please contact your local Paramount Publishing International Office.

 Manufactured in the United States of America on Lyons Falls Pathfinder Tradebook. This paper is acid-free and 100 percent totally chlorine-free.

Library of Congress Cataloging-in-Publication Data

Heaton, Jeanne Albronda.
    Tuning in trouble : talk TV's destructive impact on mental health
/ Jeanne Albronda Heaton and Nona Leigh Wilson. — 1st ed.
      p.   cm. — (Jossey-Bass social and behavioral science series)
    Includes bibliographical references and index.
    ISBN 0-7879-0106-7 (alk. paper)
    1. Talk shows—United States. 2. Television—United States—
Psychological aspects. I. Wilson, Nona Leigh.
II. Title. III. Series.
PN1992.8.T3H43 1995
791.45'6—dc20
                                                95-16261
                                                 CIP

FIRST EDITION
HB Printing   10 9 8 7 6 5 4 3 2 1

with love to David, Michael,
midnight tea parties,
and the girls on the 8th grade bus to Washington

Contents

Acknowledgments

This project seemed insurmountable, but was eventually finished with the support and encouragement of many. We would like to thank those whose special contributions made this all possible.

First and foremost we appreciate the seed that was planted by Alan Rinzler, our editor, who had the courage to take us on, the inspiration to keep us going, and the knowledge to make it happen.

There are people who made special contributions we wish to acknowledge: John Berglund of Journal Graphics, who tirelessly responded to our endless requests; Rodney Sanders, Karen Williams, Kerry Chevalier, and Amy Shepherd, who helped with library searches and retrieval; Tom Mantey, who taped hundreds of hours of Talk TV so we could watch and keep working; and Traci Sittason-Stark, who was our "expert" consultant on the talk of TV.

We interviewed many people who generously gave of their time. We would especially like to thank: Vicki Abt, Leslie Accoca, David Allen, Larry Balter, Robert Cabaj, Gilda Carle, Rex Crawley, Christopher Darryn, Gayle Delaney, Ron Drach, Stuart Fischoff, Tim Fisher, Doug Fizel, Rob Freeman-Longo, Willard Gaylin, Joshua Gamson, Cecilia Garcia, John Garriques, Michelle Gibson, Marcia Gillespie, Stan Jones, Charlotte Kasl, Courtland Lee, Edward Liska, Richard Majors, April Martin, James Masterson, Robert McCall, Ellen McGrath, Catherine Odette, Tom O'Neill,

Thomas Parham, Ruth Peters, Patricia Priest, Elayne Rapping, Laurel Richardson, Howard Rosenberg, Sandra and Guadalupe Sanchez, Jenny Sayward, Nancy Steele, Kendall Stewart, Barbara Schwartz, Caroline Silby, Chris Taylor, James Windell, and Phil Workman.

In a more personal way, there are others we want to acknowledge. Jeanne would like to thank: my husband, David Heaton, for his love, encouragement, and support; my mother, Mildred Albronda, who has always been the inspiration in my life; my father, Henry Albronda, whose memory I cherish; my children, my stepchildren, and their families, who give me meaning—Shannon and Kevin O'Leary, Chris and Janet Heaton, John and Anna Heaton, Carrie and Alan Waddell; and all those who gave me the glue to keep going while they listened to more about Talk TV than they ever wanted to know—especially, Margie Wolf, Karen Williams, Sue Apple, Sheila Mark, Cindy Birt, John Garske, Fred Weiner, Jim Gleason, Sheila Williams, Vicki Brenner, and Eric Albronda.

Nona would like to thank: Michael Keller for bringing new love and happiness into my life, and for his support through many months of talking about Talk TV; Tom Mantey, my long-time companion, for encouraging my early efforts at writing and for always being there for me; Anne Blackhurst for a beautiful friendship and for her unfailing ability to say just what I need, just when I need it; Joan and Joe Wilson, my parents, whose love is always with me.

Tuning in Trouble

Introduction

Television is at the heart of American culture: its power and influence are unparalleled. Approximately two-thirds of Americans report that they get most of their information about the world from TV. Though influential, this phenomenon is relatively new. In 1956, only 4.6 million homes in the United States had television sets, and no programming was available during many hours every day. By 1990, there were 92.1 million homes with TVs and the average viewer could select from approximately thirty channels. The number of homes with TVs keeps rising. There are now more homes in the United States with televisions than with running water. There is never an "unprogrammed" hour, and in the majority of homes, the television is on for more than seven hours each day.

From its inception, television has offered a combination of news and amusement. It is not surprising, therefore, that daytime talk shows, the ultimate blend of information and entertainment, are claiming increasingly more time and earning top ratings. At the time of this writing, there are over 30 syndicated "strip" talk shows in production. Syndicated strips appear every day of the week in the same time slot. The result is that viewers can choose from at least 150 daytime talk shows per week. And, as if that weren't enough, in July 1994, *America's Talking* began as a new cable station airing only talk shows twenty-four hours a day.

While the market seems secure enough, individual shows are

frequently dropped and new ones added. Decisions about what to cancel and what to keep are important, because popular shows can draw upwards of fifteen million viewers. In the November 1992 sweeps, Oprah earned a 12.2 rating and 32 share. What that means in plain language is that one-third of the TV sets in use at the time were tuned to her. Or, put another way, one-eighth of all the TV sets in the United States were tuned to *The Oprah Winfrey Show.*

Clearly, there is no mistaking that daytime talk shows have the country's attention—and that has ours.

On any given day, television talk shows provide opportunities to hear about everything from the most mundane details to the most prurient aspects of life. Consider, for example, May 6, 1994. Viewers could tune in Oprah Winfrey for a look into "Viewers' Homes," Phil Donahue to find out what it's like to be "Abducted by a Serial Killer," Jane Whitney for advice on "Promiscuous Teen-Daughters," Sonya to learn about "Women Who Love 'Bad Boys,'" Geraldo to find out about "Women Who Marry the Men Who Rape Them," or Leeza for a "Prom Makeover." Americans seem to have acquired an endless appetite for public disclosures of private matters. Anything personal will do, but the broad spectrum of human misery is particularly popular: trauma, conflict, struggle, betrayal, humiliation, pain. And television talk shows don't just air this misery—they produce it.

The industry claims to be providing useful information. Producers and hosts say they have helped create a more sensitive and educated public. Many of those who have appeared as guests say doing so changed their lives. Many who watch feel the same, and even suggest that these shows help them to live better lives. From this perspective, the shows are a needed and worthy endeavor. They are responding to a widely felt desire for personal information.

Undoubtedly, Phil, Oprah, Sally, Geraldo, and the others have helped uncover hidden trauma and liberate a lot of suffering people. The shows have been instrumental in disseminating previously taboo or unavailable information, such as the difficulty of being a homosexual teenager, the shame felt by men who are raped, the continuing struggle of early childhood abuse, or the trauma of battered wives. And when certain guests or viewers report that the shows have changed their lives, their assessment is not only heartfelt, it's accurate. Television talk shows are, in fact, responsible for giving a lot of people a lot of information they otherwise would not have. There is no gain in denying the service the shows provide. But neither is it helpful to ignore the cost of that service.

It is important to remember that talk show producers, and even the hosts and guests, are not primarily mental health advocates, nor are they particularly concerned with educating the public. The subject matter for these shows is chosen because of its ability to generate ratings and therefore revenue. Mental health issues make for interesting shows that attract viewers, and viewers produce profit. And profit is the overriding goal of talk shows, not good mental health.

Consequently, in order to appeal to a large viewing audience, these shows must employ tactics that will heighten their entertainment value. A "talking head" explaining complicated mental health problems does not make for dramatic viewing. The problems must be transformed into entertainment. To achieve that alteration, the shows adopt the following strategies:

- Present all problems (from dealing with a questionable date to the murder of a family member) as equally urgent. Create an air of expectancy, a sense that a secret is going to be revealed.

- Highlight pain and conflict, underscoring the idea that something "real" and of consequence is happening.

- After spending the better part of the show establishing that the issue of the day is damaging and life-altering, shift gears and provide a solution. End on a positive note and reinforce the idea that useful information has been provided.

The final product distorts real problems: the production staff either magnifies simple ones or abbreviates complex ones. For example, we can tune in and watch as a young girl describes in lurid detail how she was neglected by her alcoholic mother whom she has not seen for several years. In response to a truly traumatic childhood, the girl's pain appears great. Then the host tells her, and us, that the mother is in the studio. The mother walks on the stage and says, "I'm sorry" and the daughter replies, "I love you." That's it. That's the resolution.

We all know that is not how real problems are resolved, but a more appropriate treatment of such deep conflicts and the wounds they produce would never fit the show's format. So the production staff, the host, the guests, and even the studio audience conspire to create an entertaining version of real-life problems. Doing so requires a careful orchestration of details so that what is actually a very controlled production can appear spontaneous and real.

Production staff carefully select topics that will be lively and then use theatrical techniques to keep them hot. Directors and assistant producers question and then coach the guests on what to say. If the guests fail to respond as expected, the hosts know how to redirect the conversation or make a quick break for a commercial. The audience can be brought in specifically for the day's topic or can be primed by the production staff to help out. Home viewers are invited to join in by calling with their comments, which of course are prescreened and edited.

At minimum, these shows are a backdrop to our lives; voices chatter away without being the focus of our attention. Certainly, many viewers do not think television talk shows are a very good way to learn about mental health issues. But even as background noise, the shows are a source of information for millions of people. By presenting these performances as unrehearsed and unstaged discussions, producers encourage viewers to believe that their own lives can come undone and be repaired quickly and repeatedly. Furthermore, the involvement of mental health professionals lends the illusion of credibility to that notion.

It is our contention that, in their current form, talk shows contribute to and even create more problems than they solve. We are not denying that, for many people, the shows feel helpful. We *are* asking, at what price? We suggest that the cost is high for the general public—a cost that includes immediate ramifications for the mental health profession. Some of the problems the shows create include:

- Promoting a distorted view of what it means to have mental health problems, or for that matter what it means to be "normal."

- Encouraging viewers to use guests as a reference group, thereby creating a "that's me" copycat syndrome. Viewers overidentify and then "discover" that they have a multiple personality or an attention deficit disorder, or "remember" that they've been molested.

- Diminishing viewers' compassion for troubled people by exhausting them with attention-seeking guests who champion distasteful causes (such as hating one's wife because she is fat, being proud of a big ego, or being committed to dating only married men).

- Promoting a false sense of what is therapeutic. The shows present unrealistically simple solutions that can leave viewers either laughing in disbelief or frustrated with their own efforts to solve real problems.

As mental health professionals, we are concerned about how information regarding typical problems, as well as serious psychological disorders, is conveyed to the general public. We believe that talk shows create a formidable problem for our culture by turning real-life concerns into television spectacles. More specifically, we believe the shows make a mockery of the mental health profession. It is our concern that the profession is in considerable danger of losing its credibility as daytime talk shows become associated with mental health information and the profession is reduced to the level of sound-bite sensation.

Furthermore, we believe that the danger escalates as the profession allows itself to be increasingly drawn into the circus atmosphere created by talk shows. While it's understandable that mental health professionals want to use talk shows as a forum for providing information, once on the air they have little control over what happens. Talk show hosts, guests, and audiences routinely identify and describe problems as well as offer solutions. The mental health professionals who appear validate not only the shows' authority to do so, but the manner in which they do it. When this happens, mental health professionals condone the exploitation of real people and real issues for the sake of entertainment. We think the profession as a whole needs to reconsider its stance in regard to television talk shows.

It is our goal, in writing this book, to offer information to viewers and mental health professionals about how television talk shows are created and to raise questions about their consequences. This book can be thought of in three major sections. The first four chapters present an overview of the Talk TV industry's development and a detailed examination of the common components: hosts, guests, and experts. They provide a conceptual framework for understanding how the shows have come to be what they are and how the individual components work together to create the desired effect. From this section we want readers to gain a more informed understanding of what is involved in putting together a talk show.

The next three chapters offer a closer examination of the shows' results. We will explore the effects they have on viewers, the on- and off-camera consequences for guests, and the resulting troubles for the mental health profession. From this section we hope readers will develop a greater awareness of the potentially harmful aspects of television talk shows.

Having examined the shows and described the problems they cause, we will then suggest strategies for improvement. The last chapter is devoted to recommendations—modifications at the production level, initiatives the mental health profession should undertake, and changes in viewing habits. From this chapter, we hope readers will come away with a better sense of what can be done to minimize the negative consequences of television talk shows.

Notes

P. 1, *two-thirds of Americans report:* Rapping, E. "Daytime Inquiries," *Progressive*, Oct. 1991, pp. 36–38.

P. 1, *by 1990:* Nielsen Media Research. *1990 Nielsen Report.* Northbrook, Ill.: Nielsen, 1990, p. 8.

P. 1, *seven hours each day:* Nielsen Media Research. *1990 Nielsen Report.* Northbrook, Ill.: Nielsen, 1990, p. 6.

P. 2, *12.2 rating and 32 share:* Reuven, F. "On Television Talk, Talk, Talk," *New Leader*, Feb. 8, 1993, p. 20.

1

A Brief History

With audiences approaching fifteen million per show and revenues of over $150 million a year, shows such as *Donahue*, *The Oprah Winfrey Show*, *Sally Jessy Raphael*, and *Geraldo* have taken a dominant position in American culture. These shows and their many imitators, however, didn't just turn up overnight. Such broadcasting has evolved over many years from early radio, late-night television talk, and early daytime talk. The competition between them as they fought for viewers led producers to tap into whatever "talk" seemed most appealing to viewers. The formula for success has been: viewers equal ratings, which in turn equal revenues. In pursuit of ever greater profit, the shows have changed dramatically over time. Tracing those changes provides an interesting perspective on today's shows.

Early Radio Talk

Some very important influences came from early radio shows that originated during the Depression. *Ted Mack's Original Amateur Hour*, a homespun talent show, had enough appeal to get over ten thousand applications a week for the twenty or so available opportunities to "make it" on radio as a performer. And whereas Frank Sinatra got his start on the show, most never even got an audition.

This show foreshadowed the opportunity for the audience to participate by becoming guests and maybe even stars.

Truth or Consequences, a game show that aired first in 1940, attracted an audience by ridiculing its contestants. Participants selected from the audience had the opportunity to answer questions that listeners had mailed in. Listeners also suggested "consequences" for those who did not answer "truthfully." If the contestants guessed correctly they won $15. If they missed, they suffered a consequence, such as having to recite "Little Bo Peep" while eating an apple suspended from a string. As a consolation prize, they also received $5 and five cakes of Ivory soap from the sponsor. By suggesting questions and providing consequences, the audience became an integral part of the show. The willingness of guests to risk being humiliated in order to achieve celebrity was an important element in creating the spontaneity and liveliness of both the *Amateur Hour* and *Truth or Consequences*.

Another early radio show that engaged the general public was *Vox Pop*, which began in 1932 and continued very successfully until 1947. This show consisted of on-the-street interviews in Houston and was enormously appealing because the encounters stayed fresh as a result of spontaneous, unexpected responses from average people. The show increased its popularity by touring to new locations. Oprah, Donahue, and others use the same technique to this day to expand their audiences and markets.

The call-in format for radio began when disc jockeys invited listeners to phone in comments, which were then paraphrased on the air. Barry Gray of WMCA New York has been credited with having invented the overnight call-in show in 1945. Gray replaced periods of music with conversation between himself and celebrity guests. Talk eventually took over the show and celebrities were replaced with "ordinary" people. He discovered that his audience loved eavesdropping on regular conversation. The show was a hit and its success broke new ground; other radio hosts copied the format.

By the 1960s, call-in radio shows were syndicated in much the same way TV shows are now. Joyce Brothers, Ph.D., a psychologist who gained fame by answering questions about boxing on *The $64,000 Question*, hosted a syndicated call-in show offering information and advice about personal problems. In doing so, she stirred up some early controversy among professionals over the ethics of giving advice over the air without knowing the details of callers' lives. Regardless of the controversy, imitations appeared and were equally successful. *The Bill Ballance Feminine Forum* and San Francisco's *California Girl* became known as "topless radio" because the callers—mostly female—were willing to expose intimate details of their lives and fantasies over the airways.

These early shows had to walk the line between finding spontaneous callers and rehearsing the show so as not to bore the audience. Producers learned early on that if they allowed older voices to dominate, the show wouldn't attract the younger audiences sponsors were seeking. They also noticed that boring monologues by people with axes to grind (or who were obviously "crazy") caused listeners to switch stations. In order to polish on-air dialogue, the production team had to screen calls and provide air-time delays.

The interview and call-in show has remained a staple of radio programming. Not surprisingly, these talk-radio shows have been the source of several of Talk TV's main personalities, such as Sally Jessy Raphael and Sonya Friedman (of *Sonya Live*). Early shows involved the general public as potential "stars" and set the stage for TV to provide the picture image of what was only suggested by the voice of radio.

The Early Days of Talk TV: A Cultural Monologue

The 1950s and the early 1960s was a time in our country's history best characterized by control and conformity. There were clear and commonly articulated rules about the proper role and place for both things and people. There was a great sense of decorum, putting the "right face" on public issues, and playing by the rules. It was also a time marked by separation: men from women, whites from blacks, intellect from emotion, public from private. The separations were also hierarchical, with all that was associated with white, male, intellectual, and public factors occupying a superior position. The "conversation" taking place in the country was in accordance with these distinctions.

Discussions of "real" issues, meaning public matters of work and politics, were reserved for white men. White women were relegated to conversations about home and family, which were generally considered to be of little importance and even less interest. Blacks and other minorities had even less of a voice. Thus, the national "conversation" of the time was more like a monologue issuing from the white male voice.

Shows like Edward R. Murrow's *Person to Person* and *Mike Wallace Interviews* provided a forum for a strong male host to focus on a single person or issue. And generally, the rules of our culture regarding who should talk, what should be talked about, and the manner in which it should be discussed were followed by television programming. But some of the men of late night talk shows began to change at least some of the rules.

In the 1950s and early 1960s, the basic elements of Talk TV were introduced. Sylvester L. "Pat" Weaver Jr., an NBC-TV network executive, launched a new concept in television programming. On May 16, 1950, he introduced *Broadway Open House*, an hour-long show that aired nightly at 11 P.M. Don Hornsby, a comedian, was the first host, but he died of polio two weeks after the start of the show and was replaced by Jerry Lester. Along with Lester came a cast of regulars, including Dagmar, TV's prototype of the "dumb blonde" female sidekick. This loosely scripted program centered around casual conversation and comedy intermixed with skits and song and dance routines. The show was only on the air for about a year, but it broke important ground by indicating that late-night audiences were open to the looser, more spontaneous entertainment that erupted from the chemistry of people talking and joking with one another. Once tried, these late-night talk shows became a regular feature of television programming.

When *Broadway Open House* went off the air, it was replaced by

The Steve Allen Show, which premiered in August 1951. This show also marked new territory. Guided by Allen's personality, the show established a new style of talking, with even greater spontaneity. The show and its host were light, breezy, and chatty in a way that had not been tried before. The new approach was a great success and, recognizing its potential, Pat Weaver made Steve Allen the host of *Tonight!* at its premier in September 1954.

In only two and a half years, Allen established a late-night format that was to become tradition: the opening monologue, the host's desk, and a series of guests seated to the right. *Tonight!* fell apart when Allen left the show and various unsuccessful hosts were tried and replaced. However, by then the late-night audiences had grown accustomed to its presence and NBC brought the show back with a new and even more successful host: Jack Paar.

On July 29, 1957, when the show returned, it came back with not only a new name, *The Tonight Show,* but with an entirely new style. In what was to become a regular feature of his tenure, Paar was direct, honest, emotional, and uncontrollable. Within several minutes of the show's going on air, Paar appeared distracted and lost. He told the viewers that he wasn't up to doing the show and the screen went black. The show was over. Paar went on, over the course of approximately five years, to rant and rave on camera, to attack his critics, and to walk off the show. He even wept on air. He was a different breed and generated a great deal of interest and attention. His openness and personal approach to the show were truly unheard of at the time, but certainly played a significant role in introducing emotion and personal disclosure to Talk TV.

In addition to changes in the host's demeanor, Paar also introduced "serious" guests to the late night world and carried on conversations about political events during an "entertainment" show. His unpredictability, emotional outbursts, and discussion of controversial topics proved to be a compelling combination that attracted a great number of viewers. Both Jack Paar and Mike Wallace were willing to ask personal questions of their guests. Mike Wallace, who is known for asking personal and probing questions on *60 Minutes,* a long-running news show, began this trademark style on his interview show in the 1950s. One early incident involved the interrogation of Hugh Hefner, the originator of *Playboy* magazine, about his personal response to playboy centerfolds. The style of questioning introduced by Paar and Wallace opened the door for more personal disclosures from the guests.

Jack Paar left *The Tonight Show* in 1962 for a more lucrative prime-time slot. Several hosts were considered, including Merv Griffin, who had been a substitute for Paar. But Johnny Carson was selected and Griffin was given a daytime show as a consolation. Carson was a cool, comic contrast to Paar. He moved away from the personal and political to a lighter, faster-paced style. But Carson also made changes that helped set the stage for today's shows. He introduced a number of behind-the-scenes techniques to improve the quality of on-air interactions while maintaining the illusion of spontaneity. Carson eliminated time allotments for each guest, so that if things got boring he could move on to something else. He also initiated "coaching" sessions for guests before the show to reduce the likelihood that the conversation would drag. By the end of the 1960s, Carson was drawing over four million viewers and earning tremendous revenues. His success firmly established the talk format as one of the most lucrative programming options.

1950s–1960s Talk: Women's Talk

Unorthodox behavior was not yet considered suitable for daytime viewing. The early daytime shows were geared for a female audience and so remained more conventional and conservative. But talk shows found their way into this arena as well. Women's talk was not considered as hard or provocative, but it most certainly was establishing some very enduring and important traditions of its own. Two key features were introduced right away: even the earliest women's talk shows focused on domestic life and encouraged increased personal disclosure.

In 1954, again under the guidance of Pat Weaver, *The Home*

Show premiered. Hosted by Arlene Francis, the show offered advice about home decorating and child rearing. Like most of the women's talk shows to follow, *The Home Show* was softer, lighter fare, representing not only the appropriate topics (recipes and celebrity gossip), but reinforcing the proper disposition for women (always nice and pleasant). *The Dr. Joyce Brothers Show* was an early success that featured talk about personal problems. She was described in the *Reporter* in February 1962 as having "a flair for making private areas public without being embarrassing or offensive." In the early 1970s, Dinah Shore continued the tradition with *Dinah's Place*, complete with living room and kitchenette. Still, the content would center around cooking, cleaning, decorating, or friendly chats with celebrities. This homey, helpful approach is indelibly imprinted upon women's talk. In both the larger culture and on television, women were being told to focus their energies on home life and to be friendly and pleasant while doing so. Even the men who hosted daytime talk shows in the 1960s, such as Merv Griffin and Mike Douglas, were congenial, cheery "chatters" who made guests feel comfortable and at ease. On the air, they interviewed celebrities, tried out their cooking skills, and sustained a pleasant complacency.

Two other shows of this era are particularly noteworthy: *Queen for a Day* and *Stand Up and Be Counted!* Utilizing a kind of game show format, both programs required women to compete by telling personal accounts of hardship, with the audience helping to determine who should "win" based on who had suffered the most. In his book *All Talk*, Wayne Munson perceptively points out that these shows substituted personal suffering for the usual skill and knowledge used by male game-show participants, reinforcing the idea that experience and feelings are what women know best. Additionally, these shows rewarded their female guests with prizes for having aired their unresolved conflicts on national television for the viewing audience's amusement. The core components of these two shows have played an increasingly significant role in daytime talk.

As daytime talk shows evolved, their decidedly "female" quality remained. Not only did the shows continue to focus on concerns traditionally considered of interest to women—such as home, family, and relationships—but they did so in a personal, subjective, "female" way. Women's conversations have long been portrayed as more personal and less hierarchical, and regardless of whether or not such characterizations are accurate, Talk TV has embraced and promoted them. Even in the very early daytime talk shows, these elements were visible. *Stand Up and Be Counted!* presaged today's talk show in the use of audience participation and placed the audience in a helper role. This more democratic, participative aspect has increased as the talk show industry has grown.

The final point we want to make about early talk shows is that, as with other aspects of life at the time, there were few choices. People did not have the viewing options that we have today, and in the absence of competing "conversations," television talk repeated the same "monologue" that was occurring in the nation.

A Whole New Way of Talking: The Donahue Years

By the mid 1960s, the control and conformity of the 1950s gave way to questioning and rejecting traditional authority. Long-held beliefs about everything from God and country to family, sex, and happiness were no longer secure. The "proper face" that had been so carefully put on in the 1950s was ripped off in an attempt to find what was really underneath. People and views that had never been heard before were interrupting the easy stream of the previous monologue. They demanded a place in the national conversation and found their way in through an invitation to talk on TV.

In 1967, the *Donahue* show aired in Dayton, Ohio, as a new daytime talk alternative. And alternative it certainly was. Phil Donahue, a former newscaster, did not offer the customary "women's fare." On Monday of his very first week, he interviewed the nationally known atheist Madalyn Murray O'Hair. Tuesday, his show featured single men talking about what they looked for in women. Wednesday, he showed a film of a baby being born, from the obstetrician's point of view. On Thursday, Phil sat in a coffin and interviewed a funeral director. And by the end of the week he had held up "Little Brother"—an anatomically correct doll without a diaper. When Donahue asked viewers to call in responses, the Dayton area phone lines jammed from all the calls.

Daytime talk was instantly changed. There were numerous other local shows, but Donahue maintained exclusive claim to the top national spot. In fact, for eighteen years—until Oprah premiered in 1985—daytime talk was *Donahue*. Over the years, the show served as a model and opened the door for all other daytime talk shows that followed. Any attempt to understand the dynamics and influence of today's talk shows, therefore, must center on *Donahue*.

His early guests reflected the issues of the time—Ralph Nader on consumer rights, Gloria Steinem on women's issues, Jerry Rubin on free speech, Bella Abzug on feminism, even Joe Frazier, from a remote location at the Ohio State Penitentiary, on violence. Never before had such socially and personally relevant issues been discussed in such a democratic way with daytime women viewers. Further, Phil Donahue broke with time-honored talk convention and did not have a desk to sit behind, nor did he keep his guests removed from the audience. He even encouraged local viewers to call in. But his most revolutionary contribution to daytime talk, the one that truly established him as having a conversation with women, did not come immediately, nor was it a preplanned addition.

Donahue had inherited his television audience from *The Johnny Gilbert Show*, which had previously aired in his spot. There were two weeks of advance tickets already sold when that show went off the air, so there they sat, the new Phil Donahue audience. During commercial breaks, Phil interacted with these women. He credits them with providing bright, insightful questions for him to ask. As with most of the country, it had not yet occurred to Phil to let the women speak for themselves. One day, however, during a station break, a personal exchange began between an audience member and the guest, Gunilla Knudsen (a Swedish model who won fame by saying, "Take it off . . . take it all off" in a Noxema Shave commercial). When the show came back on the air, the woman from the audience was on stage braiding Gunilla's hair. The response was electric. From that moment on the audience was an integral part of the show's format. Talk TV would never be the same. Like so many others in America, the women watching Donahue finally had a place in the conversation, and they were determined to be heard.

Donahue says of his audience at the time that when the "red light went on, they stood and said what they had to say. And they were smart." The chance to interact with him and his guests brought a lot of women to the show. The positive response of his audience made the show an immediate hit locally. Based on that success, Donahue was able to move into other markets, and by 1969 was airing on all of Avco's Ohio stations.

The show provided useful information and dialogue that had been largely unavailable to house-bound women. It afforded them the opportunity to voice their opinions about everything from politics to sex, and even the politics of sex. The show's revolutionary changes were certainly a reflection of the times: the country was in the midst of civil rights protests and the Vietnam War. Conflict was everywhere.

A typical exchange, as seen on Donahue, involved differences of opinion about protests against the war. For example, one of Donahue's guests was a woman whose daughter was in jail because of her participation in a protest. The guest was not supportive of her daughter's actions and was called to defend her position by an audience member:

AUDIENCE: What if she dies?

GUEST: If she dies, she dies.

AUDIENCE: You have an obligation to her.

GUEST: You have an obligation to the men coming home dead from this war.

As we can see, there was a shift away from a purely "objective" examination of the issue. What was relevant was what was personal, but at this point the discussion was still primarily about issues. This marked the first step in a series of moves toward an increasingly personal point of reference.

The show's emphasis on more subjective knowing was more than the traditional relegation of women to talking about "feelings." It reflected a movement in the country as a whole toward a position of distrust concerning impersonal knowledge and authority. The nation was getting a broader view of what was happening behind all that "proper front" of the 1950s. People felt increasingly disillusioned. They felt angry and they felt they had a right to know what was going on "for real." Donahue's success was largely a result of his skillful appropriation of these counter-culture concerns into the show's format.

Donahue's training as a journalist taught him the drawing power of conflict and trauma. He explained his approach in his book, *My Own Story*, by stating, "Journalists don't care about house fires, they care about fatal house fires. If it's a house fire in which children die, it is (Lord have mercy on me!) a better story. The worse is better mentality takes hold early in a career and grows as the journalist grows."

He also understood the conflicts of the 1960s and the drawing power of watching people argue about issues. He deliberately created conflict on the show, when he staged explosive fights between anti-ERA activist Phyllis Schlafly and National Organization for Women President Eleanor Smeal; or between General Motors president Edward Cole and consumerist Ralph Nader; or between self-confessed rapist Eldridge Cleaver and feminist Susan Brownmiller. He drew in the audience with, "Come on, help me out here"—a request that became his trademark. What he discovered was the power of on-air audience participation and conflict, which drew even greater attention to his show.

Donahue described his formula for success in an interview with Jane Hall of the *Los Angeles Times:* "We got lucky because we discovered early on that the usual idea of women's programming was a narrow, sexist view. I'd been the host of a radio show, and I'd seen what lights up the phones. We found that women were interested in a lot more than covered dishes and needlepoint. . . . When we put a gay man on the air in the 1960s we got irate mail from people who were afraid their kids would 'catch' being gay, how dare we. . . . These were issues that people cared about." *Newsweek* magazine credited his early success to the exploration of topics such as impotence, incest, abortion, malpractice, reversal of sterilization, bereaved parents, breast augmentation, children of alcoholics, faith healing, unwed motherhood, and transvestitism (a show for which Phil gained notoriety by wearing a skirt). This same article pointed out that "Ever since 1967 . . . Donahue has been tackling topics that would send play-it-safe executives reaching for the Di-Gel." The determining factor for Donahue was "Will the woman in the fifth row be moved to stand up and say something?" It was no longer enough to tell a shocking story that affected real people, those people needed to be involved in the telling.

Thus, although the mass media of the 1960s were being indicted as part of the "system" causing the nation's problems, Donahue was able to tap into that suspicion. He featured hot issues and then aligned himself with "the people" by letting them speak. The show adroitly used the angry resistance to mass culture to create yet another feature of mass culture. At the very same time that the nation was railing against the vapidness of commercialism and excessive consumption, the television talk show succeeded in turning listener calls and audience participation into a consumable and lucrative item on the market. Human pain and conflict became a commodity. This is not to say it was deliberate (and given the way Donahue discovered audience participation, it probably wasn't), but simply that it was one of the unavoidable realities of personal talk on television. Once discovered, however, the usefulness of the country's conflict was not ignored. The sentiment of the talk industry was perhaps best summarized by the words of a 1960s Metromedia guide for talk hosts, which warned, "remember, we are broadcasters first and world savers second."

As the political conflicts of the early 1970s began dying down, the talk show had to find a new source of controversy to fuel viewer interest. That controversy was readily found in the personal lives of "average" people. The conflict over the war had thoroughly shaken the country and left everything a little looser, including the rules about personal conduct. Experimentation was the new order and provided plenty of topics for Phil Donahue. But Donahue was not the only one turning attention from political to personal issues, the change was happening throughout the culture. The clear separations between personal and public no longer held. "Full disclosure," a concept that originally applied to public matters, was beginning to encroach on private life as well.

The Louds: A Family's Disclosure

Perhaps the television event that most solidified this new direction was the 1973 PBS broadcast of "The Louds: An American Family." In a PBS experiment, a television crew moved into the Loud household to film "typical" American life. During the initial episodes, the show was criticized for being boring and mundane. But before the crew had left, the Loud family had become America's premiere dysfunctional family. Lance, the oldest son, paraded flamboyantly before the camera in lipstick and scarves. Pat Loud confronted her husband Bill with his infidelity and, by the end of the show, the family had split up.

The show created the illusion of being able to peek into a window and see the Louds as their truest selves. The country was still very naive about the power of television and there was the erroneous assumption that because the show was not scripted, there was nothing "staged" about it. But the Louds knew America would be watching and it was their opportunity to showcase their concerns, to make an impression. Twenty years later, some of the family at least acknowledged that the presence of the camera heightened the intensity of interactions and that things might have gone differently if they weren't being filmed.

The significance of the show was that it contributed to the

growing interest in exposing whatever could be exposed. Television had always been best at covering live spectacles, but *The Louds* was something altogether new. As the cameras turned to personal life, privacy eroded, and what was taking its place was an appetite for more unveiling.

Donahue Moves: Talk Without Interruption

Despite his local popularity and creative efforts to attract big-name guests to his show, the Dayton location was hurting Phil Donahue. By 1973, the year of *The Louds*, he had lost some stations and realized that in order to make it, he needed to move the show. So that year Donahue went to Chicago. Dinah Shore's show was failing because it was "just too nice" for a public who wanted peeks into forbidden zones, so the only competition for Donahue came from local productions. Donahue continued to emphasize controversial topics in a public forum. He also let the country in on his own problems with divorce, which only endeared him even more to his female viewers.

In 1976, the show was sold. Multimedia Corporation of Greenville, South Carolina, bought it for $425,000 and things began to heat up. He won a national Emmy Award for Outstanding Talk/Service or Variety Series, his salary jumped to $500,000, and he signed a six-year contract with Multimedia. His show aired in two hundred cities and was watched by approximately eight million people. One appearance on *Donahue* was estimated to be worth as many as fifty thousand book sales.

Donahue was firmly established in the national market and had secured a loyal following among women. Discussing Donahue's success, his one-time neighbor and early guest Erma Bombeck said that Donahue was "every wife's replacement for the husband who doesn't talk to her. They've always got Phil who will listen and take them seriously." Ralph Nader pointed out that "Phil is a kind of First Amendment in action. He has celebrities on the show, but his great contribution is the participation of ordinary people." By the mid 1980s, his contributions earned him eighteen Emmy Awards and many commendations from women's organizations.

Looking back, we can see that despite all its changes, *Donahue* maintained at least some aspects of the older customs. There was still a white male leading the conversation, determining the topic, and setting the pace. Donahue explored personal issues, but he did so in a largely investigative, cerebral fashion. Finally, there were still few choices. If viewers wanted this kind of information and discussion, *Donahue* was virtually the only option. But all of that was about to change.

Getting in on the Conversation: A New Voice

In the mid 1980s, there were 85.9 million households with televisions, over 57 percent had more than one set, and viewers watched an average of 7.7 hours a day. Donahue was enormously popular, and earning high revenues, but he was not yet among the top twenty syndicated shows.

There was, however, a growing interest in daytime talk and a number of smaller local shows were doing well. One such show was *Telling Secrets with Sonya*, which began in 1982 on the *USA Network*. With training as a psychologist, Sonya Friedman had, like many other talkers, started out in radio. In 1978, Sonya hosted *Radio Crisis Intervention* as "the shrink-behind-the phone" on WXYZ in Detroit and was then offered a spot on television. But despite shows like Sonya's or other smaller local talkers, no real competition in the Talk TV market emerged until 1984.

But emerge it did. Oprah Winfrey took over the failing *AM Chicago* show but was hardly encouraged to do so, in part because the show was slotted against *Donahue*. "They said I was black, female and overweight. They said Chicago was a racist city." But there was something about her presence that really worked, because within two months of being on the air, *AM Chicago* outranked

Donahue in the Chicago market. Roger King, chair of King World Productions, which distributes *The Oprah Winfrey Show*, credited *Donahue* for her success. He said that Phil "paved the way for Oprah in many ways. He aired topics that nobody touched before him, that people wouldn't talk about on the air, like incest and abortion. Phil really opened the door for everybody." But in contrasting her with Phil Donahue, Richard Zoglin of *Time* magazine pointed out that while Donahue's show was an obvious model for Oprah, there were some important differences. "What she lacks in journalistic toughness, however, she makes up for in plainspoken curiosity, robust humor, and above all, empathy. Guests with sad stories to tell are apt to rouse a tear in Oprah's eye or get a comforting arm around the shoulder. They, in turn, often find themselves revealing things they would not imagine telling anyone, much less a national TV audience. It is the talk show as group-therapy session."

Oprah's appeal for more intimacy was a ratings winner. She did the same topics Donahue had done but with a more therapeutic tone. She conveyed a desire to help. Over the years, her concern about issues that are largely psychological in nature has extended to her willingness to talk about her own problems with sexual abuse, with weight control, with cocaine, and with relationships.

There was also more "intimacy" on the radio, and this began to find its way to television. Ruth Westheimer, with a Ph.D. in education and a background in early sex education, had been very successfully hosting *Sex on Sunday* on WYNY-FM. She was then asked to do a night time TV talk show, which included explicit sexual information and descriptions of sexual situations. In 1984, she began *Good Sex with Dr. Ruth Westheimer* on Lifetime Cable Network with Larry Angelo as her co-host. The series used video segments, called *Ask Dr. Ruth*, during which people on the street could ask questions. It also used actors to reenact case histories. Later, to heighten the realism and viewer interest, celebrity guests came on to pose their own sexual questions.

Dr. Ruth was often described as the Joyce Brothers of her time.

Although her show was cashing in on the sensation of sex-talk, Dr. Ruth did abide by some important ethical guidelines. She didn't bring her own clients on the show and only used reenactments of already successful cases. She made some attempt at providing disclaimers for on-air diagnosis, yet she was still criticized by some mental health professionals for pandering to media hype. Many mental health professionals, however, felt she opened the door for people to talk about sex in an era when such talk was needed.

In the meantime, Donahue took note of the new competition from Oprah and pressed on to promote his own show. He moved the production to Rockefeller Center in New York City, where it continues to be produced today. The new location afforded a more aggressive and outspoken audience and Donahue claims it brought a new energy to the show. Donahue continued to be attracted to political issues and in 1985 teamed up with Vladimir Pozner from Russia for the first-ever, live-by-satellite discussion between American and Russian audiences.

Oprah continued to succeed and the AM *Chicago* show was quickly renamed after her. By 1986, *The Oprah Winfrey Show* went national. Again the change in daytime talk reflected what was happening in the broader culture. The nation had been talking about inclusion for a long time but marginal progress had been made. The push for a more democratic society finally penetrated daytime talk. Not only did Oprah talk about the relevant issues, she embodied them. As a member of one of the most oppressed groups, black women, Oprah led a new kind of "Talk." She appeared more open, available, and revealing to her audience. She made more physical contact. She seemed warmer, softer than Phil. Phil was driven to uncover and explore. Oprah came to share and understand.

The intimacy of Oprah became her claim to fame, and she helped heighten the notion of "bonding" between viewers and hosts. Over the years, Oprah increasingly disclosed details of her own life, much as a real friend does when a friendship grows. It was on her show, while interviewing a guest, that she went public with her experience of sexual abuse. "Winfrey cried, then spoke of the horror she had concealed for more that 20 years. 'I wanted to say I understand,' she recalls. 'The same thing happened to me. I hadn't planned to say it. It just came out.'"

In 1987, *The Oprah Winfrey Show* surpassed *Donahue* by becoming the first syndicated Talk TV show to be ranked among the top twenty syndicated shows. Not only was it in the top twenty, but it came in at number four with a 10.5 rating, which meant that 31 percent of the televisions in use while the show was on were tuned to *Oprah*. This was a quite a feat, considering that there were 88.6 million households with television sets. But 1987 wasn't only an important year for *Oprah*. "Talk" was heating up all over.

Other Voices: Lots More Talk

Phil and Oprah made it easier for those who followed; their successors were able to move much more quickly to the top. And that's exactly what they did. In 1987, Sally Jessy Raphael and Geraldo Rivera entered the talk market. In just one year Sally won an Emmy, beating out Donahue and Oprah. Meanwhile, Geraldo earned a spot in the top twenty syndicated talk shows. The pace had clearly picked up. The enormous success of both Sally and Geraldo indicated some interesting dynamics about what was happening in the talk market.

Sally was actually discovered by Donahue when he was on vacation in Mexico. She was hosting a talk radio show out of Albuquerque and Donahue suggested to Multimedia that she might be good as a Talk TV host. Burt Dubrow, a producer with Multimedia, offered her a TV host position in St. Louis, saying, "You want to be Mr. Rogers for adults, right?" Sally confirmed, "That said it all, I would talk directly to the audience at home, not just to the guests. That way the viewers would be drawn into the show as participants." Audience participation was nothing new, neither was her show's format, or even her style of hosting. But what her show did say, loud and clear, was that America was ready for more talk even if it was just more of the same.

Sally had some difficulty making the transition from radio to television, but that was easily taken care of: "On radio I was a friendly voice of authority. On TV I sounded too strong, and strong doesn't sell, at least not for long . . . over the long haul the hosts with the greatest staying power on television have been people who are comfortable to watch. . . . So I had to learn to tone down my voice and my opinions if I wanted to make it on television. I had to come across as warm, comfortable, and feminine, the kind of friend you'd like to chat with over coffee." The earliest prescription for female success was still working: Be Nice!

Meanwhile, psychologist Sonya Friedman, of *Telling Secrets with Sonya*, had managed to publish several best sellers in the pop-psych market including *Smart Cookies Don't Crumble* and *A Hero Is More Than Just a Sandwich*. With an increased following, she was offered a new Talk TV show in 1986, *Sonya Live in L.A.* She also graduated to a $750,000 annual salary. Her two-hour show included news features, weather, business reports, and live phone calls. She considered herself "a serious news person. If you compare me to Oprah Winfrey, my producer will bite you." She was also compared to Joyce Brothers and likewise came under the same criticism. "The notion of a psychologist-turned-talk-show-host does raise questions about the methods Friedman may use to extract pithy answers from her guest." In response, Sonya said, "I think any interviewer uses skill to get into people's heads." Her show was never listed in the national ratings, but held a steady position. Sonya was labeled the "Queen of Lunchtime Cable" until the fall of 1994, when the show was cancelled.

Sally Jessy Raphael moved to New Haven and within a year went on to New York. While she was working to be sisterly with her viewers, the new man on the scene was out for sensation. Sensation wasn't exactly something new to daytime talk, but Geraldo Rivera did bring a new intensity. And the market was ready. Just when

Oprah and Sally were appealing to viewers' softer side by pushing for greater sensitivity and warmth, Geraldo countered with a show full of hostility. Viewers loved it.

Geraldo's show may have come by all the anger and conflict honestly. Consider its origins. Geraldo had just lost a $3 million contract with *20/20* as a result of being uncontrollable and headstrong. He found another job: to open Al Capone's vault. He was embarrassed to do it, but went ahead with a tremendous amount of hype and bravado. Of all the Americans watching television at the time, 34 percent watched him do it. The vault was empty. Geraldo said, "What can I say?" The show was a record-breaking success. A big empty vault surrounded by fanfare—no better metaphor exists for what Geraldo went on to do with Talk TV.

Geraldo possessed none of the interpersonal charm or savvy that Phil and Oprah exuded. Eric Sherman, reporting for *TV Guide*, indicated "Rivera seems ill at ease with the talk show format. A man who possesses the personality of canned ham, he appears to be unsure of himself, mumbling, as he roams through the audience, occasionally forgetting the name of a guest. He's been known to bark commands at audience members ('Stand up!') and panelists ('No, I don't want you to answer that question, you just answered the last one'). But what he lacked in facilitation skills he more than made up for in excitement and energy."

Geraldo took viewers on an emotional roller coaster. One minute he would be literally fighting with guests, the next minute he would be crying over a guest's story of personal tragedy. He did both with the same unabashed enthusiasm, and audiences loved it. Sherman described Geraldo's love of exaggeration by suggesting that Geraldo would say, "Criminals aren't just punks, they're vicious, cowardly thugs."

Issues on Geraldo's show took on the same exaggerated proportions as his language and emotion. Geraldo selected young women in thong bikini bottoms and bras to dance as strippers on the show as a good way to "explore" the issue of mothers who disapprove of their daughters' professions. Although Phil and Oprah had covered outrageous topics and pulled their share of media stunts, Geraldo set a new tone. The emphasis was entertainment. He didn't so much explore issues as promote them. His ability to do so successfully was a sign of the times as well as of the talk market's strength. Producers learned they really could "put their money where their mouths were."

By 1988, Oprah purchased her show in full and began HARPO Productions. Phil Donahue also maintained a considerable share of Multimedia, contributing significantly to the company's profits. In a 1989 article in the *New York Times*, Nan Robertson reported that *Donahue*'s share of the morning audience had grown to 31 percent, up from 27 percent, and *The Oprah Winfrey Show* ranked number one in the afternoon with 30 percent of the market, a rating she had kept since 1986. This success led to an audience of nine to ten million viewers and gross salaries for the hosts of $8 million a year. They had earned a place among the forty highest-paid entertainers in the country.

Troubled Talk: Competition and Sensation

The growing competition between these four shows during the late 1980s served to fuel the market even more. Long accustomed by now to conflict, controversy, and turmoil, daytime talk viewers seemed ready for even more. And more of it is what they got. Syndicators discovered that they could air the shows back to back, with the shows serving as lead-ins to one another, and garner even higher ratings. Although some media experts speculated that the market was saturated and that there wasn't enough to talk about, they were wrong.

Talk shows continued uncovering even more shocking details about the private life of the American public and Talk/Service became known as "bizarre talk." Lena Williams, in an article headlined "It Was a Year When Civility Really Took It on the Chin" for the *New York Times*, noted that 1988 "may well be remembered as the year when nastiness came into its own and became a commodity." Morton Downey Jr.—who called his guests and studio audience "slime" and "sleaze" and told them to "zip it"—was perhaps the best example.

The power of Talk TV to gain and hold an audience was clear as sensation became the established method for success. Producers were highly motivated to win the market and the resulting competition led to low-brow tactics and topics. Sally Jessy Raphael's top-rated shows from 1983 to 1989 were:

Mothers Who Hate Their Daughters' Boyfriends (1/25/89)

Cross Dressers, Transsexuals, and Female Impersonators (2/12/88)

People with Countless Lovers (12/21/88)

Jim and Tammy Bakker (12/19/88)

Teen Sex (1/23/89)

Divorce: When Wives Win and Husbands Lose (1/16/89)

It appeared that having opened the door to private life, nothing was sacred and everything was up for grabs. Geraldo, still the most sensational, managed to have his nose broken during a segment on "Hatemongers" and drew still more attention to his show. While the shows were fighting it out, they were also beginning to draw increasing criticism, not only of their tactics but their motivations.

In a 1987 article in the *Los Angeles Times*, Oprah attempted to distance herself from the sensation-seekers by saying that what moved her to cover certain topics "isn't the trauma or the tragedy. It's that this woman had everything go wrong in her life and yet she survived—no she triumphed."

The problems began to go beyond the shows themselves. Their exaggeration or trivialization of real concerns led others to get in on the game. There was a growing sense that the shows were ridiculous and that they had covered just about every truth, leaving fakery as the only option to make things even wilder.

In 1989, for example, Tami Freiwald (an out-of-work actress) successfully tricked three talk shows. First she appeared on *Sally Jessy Raphael* as Rebecca, a sexual surrogate. With her was another actor, Wes Bailey, who pretended to be a young and impotent married man. Bailey appeared with his "wife," who was yet another actress. Freiwald ("Rebecca") then appeared on *Geraldo* as a sexual surrogate who had initiated a thirty-five-year-old virgin. . . . Guess who? Wes Bailey. Not wanting to leave *Oprah* out, Freiwald also came on as Barbara, a woman who hated sex after fourteen years of marriage. (Maybe it was all that sexual surrogacy.)

Viewers, not producers, caught Freiwald and the shows found out about a new problem in America: talk show fraud. Geraldo threatened to sue, Oprah didn't say much, and Sally, in true talk tradition, invited Bailey back on the show so she could let him have it in public. This kind of incident, to be repeated several times, indicated not only a new exploitation of the talk shows but how, once again, the shows were able to tap into that energy and make it their own. Any controversy made for good "talk"— even if it was generated by the source bringing it to the viewer.

Although mental health problems had become the main course of Talk TV, with many professionals appearing on the shows, the mental health profession showed no real interest in the phenomenon. And when asked to respond, the profession was greatly divided, with some warning about numerous potential dangers as others rallied to support the positive outcomes of bringing so much information to the public.

In this third phase of Talk TV, new voices entered the conversation and some important steps were taken that increased diversity and made the shows even more democratic. But the same problems that plagued the country as it strove to include more voices also arose in Talk TV. Inclusion and sensitivity co-opted by a competitive and self-serving industry produced some unsightly results. As a result, contradictions that were always present in Talk/Service rose to the surface.

The Nineties: An Avalanche of Talk

By the 1990s, the cable market had greatly expanded the number of available channels. The regulation of the cable industry helped secure the position of local stations as a necessary staple of the cable market. The need to fill in with programs that were easy and economical to produce left considerable space for more talk shows to be created. The opportunity was there for both local stations and syndicators to develop similar programs. The market was enormous: 92.1 million U.S. households, 98 percent of the total number of households in the country, had at least one television set.

Talk TV was doing very well. The 1990 Nielsen ratings showed *Oprah* at the top with a 35 percent share of the audience. Her show appeared in 98 percent of the available markets. *Donahue* came in second with a 28 percent share of the audience and also appeared in 98 percent of the available markets. *Sally* followed with a 24 percent share and aired in 87 percent of the markets. *Geraldo* finished with an 18 percent share and was available to 93 percent of the markets.

Money came with the markets. In 1992, Oprah Winfrey's show earned $157 million in revenues by capturing 32 million viewers each show. Donahue's show was estimated to earn $90 million and Sally's about $60 million. These numbers only tell part of the story. The other part is that the shows cost very little to produce in comparison to other types of shows. A talk show costs approximately $150,000 to $200,000 per week to produce, or about $10 to $20 million a year. This figure can be contrasted with anywhere from $700,000 to $1.8 million for each weekly episode of action drama. The enormous profits, the ease of production, and the availability of markets all led to a proliferation of new shows in the early 1990s.

Regis and Kathie Lee, which began in 1991, captured a small share of the national morning market and earned a 4 percent rating. The show maintained a steady place in the ratings and its success is quite interesting. In the midst of all the emotional gore and catharses going on, a chatty, early-morning flashback to the 1960s appeared.

Talk TV is often a binge-purge proposition. Just as Oprah and the other "softies" had stuffed the market with kindness, then Geraldo came along and changed the pace, so did Regis and Kathie Lee enter a madhouse of high-voltage talk with an easy-listening version. They came at just the right time and offered something "different": celebrity guests and low-key conversation. Only it wasn't something different, it was a repeat of what Dinah and Merv had found so successful. If you talk long enough, you're bound to repeat yourself.

Also in 1991, in a stellar demonstration of the market's ability to sustain all kinds of conversations simultaneously, Maury Povich was recruited from his successful evening tabloid news show, *A Current Affair*, to host his own daytime talk show, *The Maury Povich Show*. He was an immediate controversy and, therefore, success. Joining Regis and Kathie Lee and Maury Povich, was newcomer Montel Williams. Williams, a former naval officer, was discovered by Viacom while he was doing motivational speeches about the danger of drugs. Jenny Jones, a stand-up comic, chimed in as well after appearing on *20/20*. Warner Brothers Domestic Television decided, based on her appearance, that she'd be a good talk show host.

Late-night talker David Letterman joked that he was one of the lucky hundred people to have their own talk show. And in fact, it was beginning to seem as if all hosting a talk show required was an interesting name and a mouth that moved. Added to the list was Rolonda Watts with *Rolonda* and Mo Gaffney with *The Mo Show*.

The number of hours of Talk TV available between 9 A.M. and noon leapt from 6.5 hours in 1990 to 10.5 hours by 1992. Everyone was aware of Talk TV—even the president. George Bush was the last president who had to be told about talk shows. In fact, President Clinton knew that enormous numbers of citizens tune in daily. He chose to appear on *Donahue* as a means of clearing up issues about his role in the Vietnam War. As part of his campaign, candidate Clinton used a talk show format, in what he called "town meetings," to defeat George Bush. The power of Talk TV was noticeably increasing and a lot of shows tried to break in on the action.

Some succeeded, many did not. Les Brown, Vicki Lawrence, Ron Reagan Jr., Chevy Chase, and Whoopi Goldberg all tried shows but lost out in the ratings wars. Local broadcasters look for shows that will provide profits, which means the shows need to have a rating of at least 2. Successful shows, such as Oprah Winfrey's with a rating of 12.5, keep viewers from changing stations and thereby serve as a lead-in to the next show or as a lead-out for the preceding show. Local news broadcasters depend on syndicated shows to capture an audience by keeping viewers tuned in. In order to be attractive to local stations, syndicated TV talk shows are often given to local stations in exchange for advertising time. This system of exchange (known as "barter syndication") means that shows with ratings less than 2 would not provide adequate lead-ins or lead-outs for either the local broadcasters or the syndicator to profit financially.

In 1993 came *The Ricki Lake Show*, featuring the formerly over-weight actress from *Hairspray* and *China Beach*. Ricki, only twenty-four years old herself, addressed issues of interest to a young, female audience. She also lost a lot of weight, something that has traditionally captured young women's attention. By January 1994, *Ricki* had a rating of 4—which meant that it had captured an audience of 3,768,000. Richard Bey joined in and won ratings by crying, complaining about his own life, and finding guests with problems bigger than his own. He insults his guests with great regularity and is popular for doing so. Jerry Springer, who was a news anchor for WLWT-TV and former mayor of Cincinnati, was enlisted by Multimedia, along with Rush Limbaugh, for shows that are still running. Added to the already long list in 1994 was Gordon Elliott.

As early as 1987, media critics were speculating that America was all talked out. They were wrong. By 1993, there were between twenty and thirty (the number changed frequently) syndicated talk shows on the air. And just in case a viewer missed something, or wanted to see something again, Entertainment Television introduced the immediately successful *Talk Soup*, which summarized the day's believe-it-or-not highlights. By talking about what's already been talked about, *Talk Soup* seemed the epitome of the Talk TV mentality.

In 1994, talk shows were still very cheap to produce, costing about $50,000 for a single episode, and continuing to yield enormous profits: $400,000 per show. With that kind of profit, expansion was probably inevitable. And in July 1994, the crowning glory of Talk TV (to date) began: *America's Talking*, an all-talk cable television channel. Available in 10.5 million cable homes—with fourteen hours of live original talk—this single channel offers more hours of talk to more homes than all programs on all channels provided when Talk TV began only forty years ago. Roger Ailes, president of CNBC (the channel's owner), said, "We think there's a lot more to talk about than [what's on] the daytime circus." This ought to sound familiar. It's code for "there's still money to be made." Roger Ailes said the channel will focus on "themes." Now that would be something new.

The Talk TV market has enjoyed continuous growth and expansion since its beginnings. And throughout its development it has thrived on contradiction. The shows claim to be providing useful information, but they are actually designed as entertainment. The hosts appear connected to their guests and personally motivated to help, but they interview hundreds of guests a year, most of whom they will only see for the hour on the show, and their "personal motivation" might be the enormous amounts of money they earn. The guests are presented as ordinary people, but have been selected not only on the basis of the extraordinary nature of their problems but also for their audience appeal. The discussion is touted as spontaneous, but tremendous behind-the-scenes effort goes into keeping it lively and fast paced. And the audience is credited with providing "real people" input, yet they've been coached on "helping out" or shipped in for the show. Even the at-home callers, who seem as if they could be anyone, can't really be *anyone*—older people or people with "boring" questions are eliminated. Further, those who are selected are advised about how to ask questions.

The contradictions even extend to our own responses and

reasons for watching. The shows provide information, but along the way there sure are some real thrills and it can be hard to know the reason we stay tuned. The term *infotainment* is used to refer to the blending of information and entertainment into a new entity that no longer allows a clean division between the two. In other words, infotainment seems real only better, and entertaining but also "true" and "useful."

Talk shows epitomize infotainment. On talk shows, trauma disguises itself as amusement and trivia masquerades as noteworthy news. By covering the wide range of our experiences, from intimate to banal, the shows leave no space in our lives uninvaded. This infiltration has led some to believe that these shows need to reflect on what they're trying to accomplish. Marcia Gillespie, editor-in-chief of Ms. magazine, has concluded that talk shows "should be erased right off the air. There needs to be a moratorium on talk [TV] and some serious thought given to the point and purpose of these shows."

Talk shows have embedded themselves in our culture and our consciousness. Everyone makes reference to them, from the Cookie Monster on *Sesame Street* to the President of the United States. Increasingly, those references are harsh. After having used the shows to his benefit, Bill Clinton became known as the "Talk Show President." He then attacked the shows in 1994 for having too much influence and for "lying" about him. In one of their most astounding and enduring maneuvers, the shows simply use the increasing criticism to their own benefit.

The shows have come a long way from the polite chatter of the 1950s. There are now a lot more channels and many more opportunities for enormous profit, because the talk has been extended to confrontation, revelation, justification, and sometimes to outright battles and brawls. Through it all, however, the basics of host, guests, experts, and audience interactions remain the core ingredients. We turn now to explore how those fundamentals are carefully crafted to produce the current version of Talk TV.

Notes

P. 9, *got an audition:* Munson, W. *All Talk.* Philadelphia: Temple University Press, 1993, p. 29.

P. 10, *soap from the sponsor:* Munson, W. *All Talk.* Philadelphia: Temple University Press, 1993, p. 30.

P. 10, *call-in show in 1945:* Munson, W. *All Talk.* Philadelphia: Temple University Press, 1993, p. 36.

P. 15, *women know best:* Munson, W. *All Talk.* Philadelphia: Temple University Press, 1993, pp. 30–36.

P. 17, *jammed from all the calls:* Donahue, P. *My Own Story.* New York: Simon & Schuster, 1979, p. 98.

P. 18, *and they were smart:* Donahue, P. *My Own Story.* New York: Simon & Schuster, 1979, p. 100.

P. 18, *dead from this war:* Donahue, P. *My Own Story.* New York: Simon & Schuster, 1979, p. 100.

P. 19, *the journalist grows:* Donahue, P. *My Own Story.* New York: Simon & Schuster, 1979, p. 122.

P. 19, *feminist Susan Brownmiller:* Waters, H. "The Talk of Television," *Newsweek,* Oct. 29, 1979, 76–82.

P. 20, *people cared about:* Hall, J. "Breaking a News Chokehold," *Los Angeles Times,* Nov. 12, 1992, p. F-1.

P. 20, *reaching for the Di-Gel:* Waters, H. "The Talk of Television," *Newsweek,* Oct. 29, 1979, 98, 76–82; p. 77.

P. 20, *world savers second:* Munson, W. *All Talk.* Philadelphia: Temple University Press, 1993, p. 46.

P. 21, *weren't being filmed:* Horowitz, C., and others. "Reality Check: Twenty Years Later, TV's Loud Family Proves There's Life After Fame," *People Weekly,* Mar. 22, 1993, *39,* 61–62.

P. 22, *eight million people:* Parish, J. *Let's Talk! America's Favorite Talk Show Hosts.* Las Vegas, Nev.: Pierre Books, 1993, p. 117.

P. 22, *worth fifty thousand in book sales:* Waters, H. "The Talk of Television," *Newsweek,* Oct. 29, 1979, *98,* 76–82; p. 76.

P. 22, *take them seriously:* Parish, J. *Let's Talk! America's Favorite Talk Show Hosts.* Las Vegas, Nev.: Pierre Books, 1993, p. 113.

P. 23, *participation of ordinary people:* Parish, J. *Let's Talk! America's Favorite Talk Show Hosts.* Las Vegas, Nev.: Pierre Books, 1993, p. 114.

P. 23, *7.7 hours a day:* Nielsen Media Research. *1986 Nielsen Report.* Northbrook, Ill.: Nielsen, 1986, p. 3.

P. 23, *was a racist city:* Bly, N. *Oprah! Up Close and Down Home.* New York: Kensington, 1993, p. 51.

P. 24, *door for everybody:* Robertson, N. "Donahue Vs. Winfrey: A Clash of the Talk Show Titans," *New York Times,* Feb. 1, 1988, p. C-30.

P. 24, *group-therapy session:* Zoglin, R. "Lady with a Calling," *Time,* Aug. 8, 1988, *132,* 62.

P. 26, *just came out:* Levitt, S. and others. "Not Scared, Not Silent," *People Weekly,* Sept. 7, 1992, p. 48.

P. 26, *drawn into the show as participants:* Raphael, S. J. *Sally: Unconventional Success.* New York: Morrow, 1990, p. 155.

P. 27, *over coffee:* Raphael, S. J. *Sally: Unconventional Success.* New York: Morrow, 1990, p. 155.

P. 27, *my producer will bite you* (and the other quotes in this paragraph): Toepfer, S. "On the Sunny Side of 50, Pop Psychologist Sonya Friedman Has Legs As Talk Babble's New Queen," *People Weekly*, Nov. 16, 1987, pp. 75–76.

P. 28, *the last one:* Sherman, E. "Who's the Best? Donahue? Oprah? Someone Else?" *TV Guide*, Mar. 26, 1988, 36, 26(4).

P. 28, *vicious, cowardly thugs:* Sherman, E. "Who's the Best? Donahue? Oprah? Someone Else?" *TV Guide*, Mar. 26, 1988, 36, 26(4).

P. 29, *became a commodity:* Williams, L. "It Was a Year When Civility Really Took It on the Chin," *New York Times*, Dec. 18, 1988, pp. A-1–2.

P. 32, *one television set:* Nielsen Media Research. *1990 Nielsen Report.* Northbrook, Ill.: Nielsen, 1990, p. 8.

P. 32, *episode of action drama:* Benson, J. "Syndies Overload the Chatter Platter," *Variety*, Feb. 15, 1993, p. 104(2).

P. 35, *$400,000 per show:* Williams, M. "Voices of 30-Plus Exclaim: Can We Talk?" *Advertising Age*, Mar. 8, 1993, 64(10), S-6.

P. 35, *the daytime circus:* Sharpe, A. "Talked Up: Sedate Multimedia Inc., Home of Phil and Sally, Faces Unclear Future," *Wall Street Journal*, May 10, 1994, A-1–5 (2), p. 1.

P. 36, *talk shows "should be erased right off the air":* Marcia Gillespie, personal interview, Jan. 6, 1995.

2

Hosts

The Image and the Reality

There is only one constant in television talk shows' ever-changing parade of characters: the host. Day in and day out, amid the chaos, conflict, and change, the host is a beacon of familiarity. Guests come and go. Topics are discussed and dismissed. And although each day's television talk shows are ostensibly "about" specific guests and topics, the individual guest or topic has little lasting value in the overall scheme of the show. It's the host who captures our attention and sustains it.

Performing the core tasks of interviewing and soliciting participation, the host links together guests, experts, and audience, and thus have the primary responsibility for pulling it all together on the air. The contrast between the control of the host and the chaos that is going on all around them places them in the dominant position. At all times, even when angry and confronting, the host must also appear to be caring and concerned, so that people will want to disclose their problems and feel free to show their emotions. In fact, television talk shows depend on an image of the dedicated, caring host. Both the hosts' behavior and the popular legends created by the media generate a powerful and appealing image. That image draws more viewers and masks the reality of big-business Talk TV.

Creating the Image

Talk TV shows build their identities around their hosts, who are introduced to us as people we want to visit on a daily basis. Promotional spots for daily topics use pictures and clips from the show that encourage us to join in on the fun, information, or problem of the day. But these enticements always include a focus on the host we need to get to know.

First Names, Please!

Donahue, *The Oprah Winfrey Show*, *Sally Jessy Raphael*, and *Geraldo* are all named for their hosts. As new shows have been added, they also have incorporated the name of the host, such as *Ricki Lake*, *Montel Williams*, or *Jenny Jones*. Advertising spots for the shows use the host's first name; like friends, we are asked to join Sally, Geraldo, Oprah, and Phil at the same time every day. The link between show and host is deliberate and accomplishes several important things.

First, there are certain features that are so subtle they hardly seem noteworthy, but in fact contribute a great deal to developing the feeling of a personal connection to the shows. From the very first time people think or speak of a host or show, they do so on a first-name basis, just as they would with friends and peers. Additionally, the shows appear at the same times on the same stations five days a week and in doing so are easily incorporated into viewers' household routines. Whether it's drinking coffee with Regis and Kathie or putting the kids down for a nap with Ricki, or unwinding after work with Geraldo, the hosts are there every day, no matter what. The routine and familiarity can foster a sense of wanting to know what Phil thinks about homosexuality, how Oprah feels when she steps on the scales, or what Ricki will advise about difficult roommates.

The sense of familiarity, the level of intimacy with the host that exceeds our actual connection, is constantly reinforced. This is partly achieved through the show's highly personal content, which often represents the kind of discussions that friends and family find difficult to have. Sally and Geraldo appear to never back away from painful issues. They never change the subject or seem disinterested in what is bothering someone. At times, they must cut to a commercial, introduce a new guest, or wrap up the show. But these are constraints of the format and don't have to be attributed to the host's disinterest or displeasure. As a result, viewers may come to feel over time that Oprah and Phil "have been there" through all sorts of events and may fantasize that the host knows more about what is troubling them or what needs to be done about their problems than do the real people in their lives.

A sense of camaraderie with the hosts is critical to developing a loyal following. The shows depend on the willingness of some people to tell their secrets and others to listen attentively. In fact, the success or failure of shows is often a matter of whether or not viewers like the hosts. So the shows work hard to foster a sense of "friendship" and all that entails—trust, loyalty, consistency, sharing of secrets, and a willingness to overlook flaws. To achieve this, the shows provide plenty of personal information about the hosts.

Hosts with a Mission

There are ample opportunities to learn about what motivates talk show hosts. They routinely describe their intentions in press releases and public appearances. In doing so, they present quite a serious attitude about their work: being a talk show host is more than a job, they suggest, it's a calling. There are, they tell us, important social, political, and moral underpinnings to what they do. Although their descriptions vary and each lays claim to "being different," a popular theme emerges for all, and that is the desire to help. This barrage of information about the hosts' missions becomes the lens through which their on-air actions are viewed.

Oprah Winfrey is perhaps the most intimate with her audience and guests and takes her role beyond that of mere friendly assistant. Hers is the loftiest of all work: spiritual renewal. And she even sets herself apart from other evangelists by pointing out that she does not ask for anything in return. "My show is really a ministry, a ministry that doesn't ask for money. I can't tell you how many lives we've changed—or inspired to change." To accomplish this change she wants to provide viewers with information because "knowledge is power! with knowledge you can soar and reach as high as your dreams will take you."

Sally also wants to help. She told Larry King in a 1994 interview on *Larry King Live* that all shows are "host driven" and that she sees herself on the level of "every man." She is frequently heard to say, "Talk to me about what's bothering you." Ricki Lake compares herself to her therapist, saying, "Basically, I do exactly what she does! I facilitate communication, help bring people together, and bring them to some kind of agreement or resolution. It's wild." Rolonda Watts says, "Our goal is to be 'user friendly.'"

Phil and Geraldo also want to "help," but they take less of a "talk-show-as-therapy" approach. Both men focus primarily on their concerns with covering the issues and their consequences for people, rather than proclaiming their concern for humanity. Donahue has presented himself over the years as an impartial, sensitive, and concerned listener. Geraldo, on the other hand, has maintained his *20/20* investigator role, digging up the dirt and jumping into the muck. Although this may seem to be a minor difference, it does in fact influence how the hosts are perceived and the character of their shows.

Part of the dynamic here is gender related. It is easier for the public to believe and to trust Phil and Geraldo as issue-oriented hosts rather than "best friends." Originally, Phil said he wanted to do shows on important topics, explaining that he does his shows in such a way that the lady in the back row, who never thought about being on television, would want to stand up and say something. His mission, then, was to engage viewers in discussion about important social issues. He still maintains this is his primary goal, but acknowledges that it isn't as easy as it used to be. Now Donahue admits that he has to walk a fine line between imitating Edward R. Murrow and P. T. Barnum—"a balancing act [that] is becoming more precarious with each passing sweeps rating period." He alternates between lamenting that he can no longer do a whole hour around a topic and claiming he really isn't doing anything any different than he ever did.

Geraldo intends to create a "sensational" image and even benefits from the critics who are always saying he is the worst. Statements such as "who else would be so brash as to spell his name with an exclamation point" and "at the rate it's going, Geraldo Rivera's nose should cover his entire face by the time Joey Buttafuoco gets out of prison" only add to his carefully crafted image as someone who isn't concerned with image. The fact that he has had his nose broken several times by irate guests reinforces his sense of purpose: he really cares about the issues, he boils over them. And he cries over them, cries for abused children and gigolos alike.

Geraldo says that his audience expects the critics to say bad things about him. He points out that the advantage is that he can be the perennial underdog so that his fans will defend him from his detractors. He is right, and like friends sticking up for a wayward pal, Geraldo's fans love him both because and in spite of his outrageous antics. So if controversy is the way to get attention, Geraldo is a master. His seven-year run confirms his durability in the Talk TV world. As Geraldo points out, he's "still here" and many of his "critics are gone."

Trying to Be Different

With so many nationally syndicated talk shows currently airing, the competition is intense and breaking into the market can be difficult for new hosts. While basically covering the same material as all the other shows, each must somehow find a niche—not an easy thing to do.

One of the most popular approaches is simply to claim to be

different. This claim requires that the hosts on the one hand acknowledge the underbelly of the market, agree that it is indeed unpleasant, but quickly profess that they will not succumb to the baser side of the industry.

Catching viewers' attention starts with the predictable press releases about what the new host intends to do. Leeza Gibbons, the host of both *Leeza* and the weekend edition of *Entertainment Tonight*, appeared in 1993 with interviews in the popular press. She explained in a 1994 *Today* interview her intention to do something different, because "trash talk has reached the saturation point." On the one hand she claims, "I always wanted to be like Dick Clark. He was the host of hosts." On the other hand, she wants to deal with cutting-edge issues but do so with respect. She clarifies, "I have two children. I run a house. I have a busy career . . . we're busy and we need to be smart, and we want to work through the emotional challenges in our lives. We want to talk about our relationships. So those are the things that I really want to focus on." Likewise, in 1994, Marilu Henner, former star of two successful sitcoms (*Taxi* and *Evening Shade*) and author of her autobiography (*By All Means Keep Moving*), began a new talk show called *Marilu*. She, like Leeza Gibbons, was convinced that motherhood made her "different" from the rest. "I'm probably the only talk show host that's breast feeding," she told Charlie Rose on his show in 1994. "Is that too provocative?"

In a similar fashion, Bertice Berry, whose show began in 1993 and was canceled in 1994, described her program as a show for the 1990s. "We've informed people they were abused. Let's not wallow in it. I don't want to end on an argument and say we're out of time. Let's present options." Ricki Lake, who has really been a leader in the new shows' ratings race, said that she was going to do something different as well. Her change was to consist of an emphasis on a younger audience, youngsters from ages eighteen to forty-nine, that is. She stated, "Our show is funny, it's not exploitive. It's not crude. It's not freaks. We're offering a clearer alternative to people who want to watch talk shows but feel they can't relate to shows on menopause or whatever the older skewing issues (are)." Maury Povich stated, "I hang my hat on my credibility as a journalist. I would not do a show on big breasted women, I won't do a show on six transvestites." Montel Williams added, "Many of these hosts are responsible for creating an audience of voyeurs, my concern is to lead us back from this point to where television can be informational without losing its entertainment value. And you won't see me pontificating like I know it all."

This new group of hosts claimed to be breaking new ground by moving Talk TV away from freak-show deviance. They assured viewers the new shows would be meaningful, helpful, and important . . . just as Phil, Oprah, Sally, and Geraldo claimed when they first appeared.

So there we have it: a group of people concerned with our personal and collective welfare, interested in addressing issues and helping viewers. But despite their perpetual pronouncements, the hosts alone could not possibly manage to create the larger-than-life image demanded by their jobs. Fortunately for them, they don't even have to try. The popular media keep Americans informed of the "intimate" details of the hosts' lives. By reading and hearing about their personal lives, we are drawn even closer to them. They become more than just hosts. They become real people, "just like us."

Using the Media

The mass media afford the hosts and their production staffs a variety of avenues for creating and maintaining desired images. The ups and downs of the hosts' lives are opened to viewers so we can celebrate or cry when a host gets married, or gains and loses weight, has a baby, or loses a child. Autobiographies, magazine features, tabloid headlines, and revealing stories work in unison to keep the hosts and their shows in the forefront. Public relations specialists promote each show, which usually translates into promoting the host. Pieces such as "Talk Show Hosts Tell All!" provide opportunities for the hosts to share personal details about themselves or offer helpful tips such as make-up strategies for working women. Kathie Lee Gifford's manicurist was interviewed about Kathie's nails. Leeza revealed that she likes to do Hip Hop Animal Rock Aerobic exercises with her daughter Lexi. Sally discussed colors she uses for certain topics like black and red (strong colors) for heated topics or to give advice, neutral and taupe for emotional issues, and blues and greens for celebrities, but of course, everything must go with the red glasses. Rolonda said she changes her hairstyle with changes in her life. A recent *Redbook* article even included information on how Oprah's bra size went from 44D to 36C.

Although sharing information about personal habits does a lot to create a sense of familiarity and intimacy with the hosts, mundane details like these do not provide an adequate basis for believing the hosts are safe people to tell our secrets to. The hosts' images are constructed to tie the viewer to them. The strength of that tie, as we shall see, depends on certain key features of the image that stimulate audience disclosure.

Hard Work

Understanding how hard the hosts work contributes to the overall idea that important work is being accomplished. We read about how Oprah comes to her HARPO Studios at six in the morning and then works out in the fitness room before going to makeup. The first show is taped at 9 A.M., then she spends close to an hour saying good-bye to the audience, a practice shared by Donahue. She then must change clothes and be ready for the next taping at 11 A.M., followed by another hour of saying good-bye to that audience. After that she does promotional spots for television markets. She has a cafe at her studio called "Harpo Cafe," where she can eat before meeting with the staff of various departments on production ideas. She has paperwork to do and phone calls to make. After all this, she does another workout and is home by 8 to 9 P.M., where she has scripts to read and numerous other projects to review.

Leeza Gibbons reports being burdened with similar responsibilities. "It's a killer schedule," she said during her *Today* appearance. "I mean, the challenge with a family, you know, your priority clearly is your husband and your children. But sometimes I whirl around so fast I can't even get my focus. . . . It can't go on forever." Reports of these kinds of schedules link the hosts to their hardworking viewers and establish how very dedicated they are.

The Power to Give

Part of the hosts' image is the power they achieve from the wealth they accumulate. Fans feel a sense of participation because they have helped make them so successful. The more wealth hosts have the more celebrity status they acquire. Oprah's estimated net worth is $250 million, making her one of the richest entertainers on television. Discussions of Donahue's houses, video tours from Oprah's lavish vacations and descriptions of gifts to her staff, and accounts of all their incomes leave no doubt that the hosts have "made it."

When hosts have truly made it big they often use their power to do useful things. Oprah was personally involved in getting Congress to pass a bill that requires a national register for child molesters. The bill was even called the "Oprah Bill" and she was pictured with President Clinton when the bill was signed into law. Montel Williams began his media career as a motivational speaker. He has donated many hours to speaking to groups of teenagers about the dangers of drugs and unprotected sex. In addition, he has talked extensively about the problems experienced by black men. He took a public stand when he walked out of the Friars Club because he was offended when Ted Danson showed up in blackface at a roast for Whoopi Goldberg. The publicity around these events is used to demonstrate that the hosts are making significant contributions to their communities.

The media are also frequently invited to events at which hosts donate large sums of money to important causes. Oprah is probably the league leader here with a million dollar donation to Tennessee State University and another million to Morehouse College. She gave Chicago Academy for the Arts High School $500,000 and another $1 million to an inner-city Chicago high school. She also raised $150,000 for Chicago's Hull House by inviting two thousand of her fans to a benefit sale of nine hundred dresses and other items from her wardrobe. After doing a show about the 1989 San Francisco earthquake, Geraldo gave $10,000 personally and his show gave another $10,000 to the recovering victims at the Marina school.

With all this wealth to give back, the celebrity status of the hosts makes even more people want to be associated with them. Their power makes more viewers want to share in the limelight surrounding these stars. When guests feel that Oprah pays attention to their pain, they share her status at least for the moment.

Sharing the Pain

Since the centerpiece of Talk TV is personal problems, disclosures by the hosts that chronicle only success and hard work would hardly encourage guests and viewers to air their pain and misery. People feel more at ease telling secrets, and can better trust advice they hear, when talking with someone who knows what it's like. As a result, the hosts need to establish a common bond with guests and viewers. And that bond is based on mutual suffering.

Through books, magazines, and other media, the hosts share intimate details—not just personal grooming habits—that signal their credibility. But even more than simply alerting us that they understand, their disclosures instruct us as well. By revealing their traumas, joys, and struggles so openly and freely, the hosts establish a standard of behavior that fosters the kind of disclosures that ultimately benefit their shows. Further, because their star status confers power and authority, their followers are likely to take their cue from them. And the hosts encourage public disclosure of personal information.

Various books and articles work in tandem to create a seamless image of the host as "one of us." Autobiographies represent the closest thing in print to direct communication with these stars. Through them, the hosts reveal their secrets. By immersing ourselves in their "voice" for an extended period of time, an illusion of intimacy is created: we "know" them.

Donahue's autobiography, for example, is called *My Own Story: Donahue*. In it he recounts how he had problems with the Catholic Church, got a divorce, and reared his sons as a single father, all the while missing his only daughter, who lived with her mother. Likewise, Sally's book highlights her early career problems, her difficulties with her first marriage, her divorce, her devotion to her second husband, and her problems with her ailing mother. Her story is titled *Sally: Unconventional Success*. Geraldo's autobiography, *Exposing Myself*, reveals a long series of affairs with famous women and describes his career battles. By reading these works, we learn that Phil, Sally, and Geraldo have struggled, if not with the very same issues we have, at least with the same feelings. Additionally, the titles of their books encapsulate the dominant image of each of the authors, while hinting at some underlying struggle.

Although Oprah canceled the debut of her autobiography, her comments about why she did so reinforce her already well-established image as an optimistic and resilient survivor. She explained that the book wasn't positive enough and the attention to her childhood abuse didn't cast the light she hoped to create in an autobiography. In addition, there have even been two biographies of Oprah done for children, outlining her triumphs over adversity. Drawing on the power of association with the star, Oprah's cook's cookbook, *In the Kitchen with Rosie*, quickly became a best-seller.

In the periods when an autobiography is not available or up-to-date, interviews in magazines continue to describe the personal dilemmas of popular hosts. Each of these popular articles adds just a bit of something new, creating the impression that a new revelation has been made and keeping viewers poised for more. For example, a newspaper article about why Oprah canceled her book

contract revealed some intimate details the autobiography was supposed to contain, which wouldn't otherwise have been known.
Readers got new details about recurrent issues in the Oprah image:
in reference to her weight loss struggle, it was revealed that "the
pounds represented the weight of my life" and that her sexually
active adolescence was not enjoyable. "It wasn't because I liked
running around having sex. It was because once I started, I didn't
want the other boys to be mad at me." Readers learned that her
troubled romantic life was rooted in low self-esteem, "I was in relationship after relationship where I was mistreated because I felt
that was what I deserved." These are issues that without a doubt
create a common bond with many, many viewers. Her willingness
to share such information heightens respect for her ability to
achieve what she has and also increases viewers' belief in her as a
credible confidant.

The almost-fatal traffic crash of Sally Jessy Raphael's son in January 1992 was described graphically in newspaper articles. "J. J., her
son, lost control of his car, smashed into a tree and hurtled down a
ravine. He underwent seven hours of surgery and lay in a coma for
seven days while his mother kept a bedside vigil. He is still recovering." Three weeks later her daughter Allison was found dead of
respiratory failure in her sleep. In a touching account of her devastation, Sally explained, "I never want to live through another year
like this again. I don't think I could. I'm trying to find out how to
live without an answer. It's very tough. I think it's a random universe." These accounts clearly show that she has been through
enormous pain and leave no doubt about the suffering it caused.

Phil Donahue maintains his position in middle America by
focusing on troubles of home life and child-rearing. In a magazine
interview, he disclosed his concern about his sons' interest in mar-
ijuana. He told how he had to go to the police station and that "At
home afterwards, I did my share of yelling" and then privately
hoped that "if I could just get them through high school using pot
alone—no harder stuff—I'd be very fortunate." Again, readers can

take comfort in knowing that even for Phil Donahue things are not perfect, that at times he loses his cool, doesn't know what to say, and makes mistakes.

Each host has a story to tell. By telling theirs, they encourage others to do the same. The books, interviews, magazine articles, and headline newspaper stories represent their part in an ongoing conversation of increasingly personal disclosures. Between the images created in the media and the reality of who they are, is the show. There, they are seen doing what they were ultimately hired to do. The host's role is crafted and yet real, and it is what we observe daily as we "visit them on TV."

Show Time

The images promulgated by the popular media act as gift wrapping—encircling the shows, catching our attention, and alerting us to what kind of treat we might expect. But it is largely the hosts' performances on the shows that determine whether or not we'll come back for more.

At times, it might appear that all the host has to do is listen and occasionally ask some questions, but there are a number of challenging tasks the host must successfully execute in order to pull the package together. As with any skilled worker, the host's success often lies in making it look as if there's nothing to it. As a result, some dimensions of their role are often overlooked. A closer examination of what the hosts do on the air will help clarify how their images are created and maintained.

Setting the Stage

Hosts must first and foremost appear to be people we would like to talk to or even argue with. The media help establish this character, but in the studio hosts have to contend with the added dimension of overcoming audience concerns about speaking out in public. The hosts' basic task is to establish either enough safety or enough out-rage to bring people to their feet. Donahue points out that the audi-ence is often fearful, "Your mother is watching, you'll say the wrong thing, we'll make a fool out of you, you'll look fat, you'll stutter, you won't remember your questions. There's a lot of anxiety here." Demonstrating an understanding of these problems and trying to provide the necessary reassurances to get the audience to respond is one of the hosts' responsibilities.

To ensure that there will be sufficient participation, the hosts often start warming up the audience before the show. During this time, the hosts answer questions and provide the reassurance that audience members need in order to get them to join in. Donahue reports that his role during preshow warm-up is to tell them, "This is a television studio, and it's an uncomfortable, unfamiliar place to the audience. . . . So the idea is to let them know that I care, that I won't abandon them, that I hold the record for stupid questions."

Some hosts take as much care in clearing the stage as they do in setting it by staying after each show to meet the audience. Each day, Donahue and Oprah remain in the studio after each show and shake hands with the 250 people in the audience. They let fans take all the pictures they want. Not all hosts apply this personal touch, but it creates a heightened sense of connection and loyalty when it is used.

Camera Ready

For most of us, the show begins and ends with the camera's action. "Show time" is when we get to see and hear the hosts in action. They must be polished and prepared, yet appear natural and spon-taneous. The irony of television performance is that if the host is successful, we will forget about the camera. And in order for that to happen, the host must appear to have forgotten it—while remain-ing acutely aware of what it will present to the viewers.

Previous work experience in front of a camera certainly helps hosts know how to use the camera to their benefit. Phil Donahue,

Oprah Winfrey, Geraldo Rivera, Maury Povich, Leeza Gibbons, and Rolonda Watts all had established TV careers before they began to host talk shows. Others such as Sally Jessy Raphael, Montel Williams, Jenny Jones, and Ricki Lake also had ample radio, acting, or public speaking experience, which helps ensure their comfort and ease in front of an audience.

Camera poise depends on the hosts' abilities to remain relaxed and apparently spontaneous while juggling a variety of demands: responding to guidance from the floor director, attending to guests, monitoring audience response, stretching out or condensing segments, answering phone-in callers, and being prepared for the unexpected. These often-conflicting demands require that hosts be able to think on their feet and react in ways that will move the show in interesting and entertaining directions.

Being able to speak comfortably and effectively is the necessary first step, but it is by no means sufficient. Talk shows aren't monologues; the host has to inspire others to add their voices so a conversation is created. That, of course, means getting people personally involved.

Making It Okay

Although many of us have been taught that watching people suffer and gossiping about their misfortunes is inappropriate, such activities are the very heart of television talk shows. This conflict could potentially present a major problem for Talk TV, so the hosts must help us bypass any concerns by establishing their awkward topics as appropriate and acceptable subjects for discussion.

The most popular strategy is to remind us of the value of open discussion and to appeal to our understanding of what it's like to be wronged or excluded. Even the raunchiest of human perversities are of some interest and there are all sorts of legitimate reasons for being drawn to them. We might be curious or concerned, we may have experienced the issue ourselves or wish to understand those who have.

For example, Oprah has admonished, "These sex confessions seem bizarre to you, but they're not bizarre to someone who's lived through them. And if sex is a concern for lots of people, then let's do a show on it—and find a way to do it in good taste."

All the hosts rely heavily on such socially minded rationales but add some levity and keep it "real" by occasionally conceding that we all get a thrill from other people's peculiarities. Oprah adds, "It's okay to titillate if in the process you help someone."

A recent *Ricki Lake* program featured an on-air debate about the merits of dieting. The participants were a group of contented fat women, who were shoveling pizza into their mouths six slices at a time, and a group of fat women who were dissatisfied with being fat. Ricki did not present this scene as a spectacle for our amusement, in which stereotypes about women, food, and sex converged. Instead, she told us this was a serious issue, and worked to draw us in on that level. (Ricki has some credibility here because we know that she has struggled with these issues in her own life.) Once we'd entered the conversation as serious participants, Ricki signaled an understanding of the other basis of appeal for this topic: that people are strange and outrageous. She could laugh and roll her eyes with us and with them, and in doing so allowed us to feel okay about doing the same at home.

Sally Jessy Raphael also wants us to believe, or to at least agree to pretend, that our interest in the Siamese twins on her stage is educational. She uses a lot of pseudointellectual jargon, such as calling them "co-joined," and a serious tone of voice to elevate the conversation to a level of professional concern. In this way she, and we, can feel justified in asking things that might otherwise seem rude or intrusive, such as how they go to the bathroom or if their necks get tired being in that position.

With both of these shows, and many more, we could, if we wanted to, poke fun at guests from the start. But the shows are framed in such a way that if we do so we're on the outside of the conversation, doing something other than what was going on in the studio. And in that case the transgression is our own. The hosts offer sanction for watching, discussing, and even laughing. But we must do so on their terms: for educational, moral, social improvement.

Even after overcoming concerns about our own participation, however, ethical questions remain about what is happening to the people on stage. Do they really want to be there? Is it okay to ask them questions? The hosts must assure us that their guests want to be there and the guests in turn must confirm this. Again, the value of open discussion is offered; not only will we be educated but the guests will be able to tell their stories and therefore reap cathartic benefit. If that is not enough to persuade us that all is acceptable, the hosts remind us that the guests will receive free advice on the shows by the experts and assistance afterward if needed.

Uncovering Details

Having set the stage for massive public disclosure, the host must be able to draw out secret information. Hosts have to probe for details and encourage the audience to do the same, without appearing to blatantly turn a guest into a specimen on display. The hosts must keep the shows moving, and preferably moving deeper.

The host must convey interest in hearing more. Rolonda Watts reminds her audience, guests, and viewers that her philosophy— "It's worth talking about"— extends to everything. Ricki Lake reiterates the fact that she "cares" and Geraldo tells us that he "loves" all his guests. Typical hosts balance questions and attentive listening, dotted with encouragement and supportive responses.

The hosts frequently acknowledge the difficulty of what guests are trying to do, which serves to increase their own credibility with both the guest and the audience as people who understand. This tactic often prompts more disclosure. Hosts often express their own bewilderment, saying things such as "That really happened to you?" They voice concern with the issue at hand, and in that way maintain a personal connection to the guest. "I'm so sorry, gosh that must be difficult." Such statements are often accompanied by some sort of disclosure on the part of the host—sometimes even something as shocking as "I used crack cocaine during a past relationship with a man." Again, this kind of reciprocity encourages continued disclosure.

When guests are struggling or hosts are finding it difficult to know what to say next, the audience or phone-in callers are useful in keeping the conversation moving. The hosts must know how to get the audience involved and how to use them to prompt further revelations. Ricki and Jenny, and others as well, frequently instruct the audience to applaud the guests. Ricki does this by saying, "We're rooting for ya, aren't we?" and the audience confirms with a round of applause.

No matter what comes out during the show, the host must convey a desire to hear more of it. Often this results in some rather difficult situations. For example, when Jenny Jones invited guests on her show to talk about "revenge," what came out were such ugly, painful details of human cruelty that even Jenny's lip was curling as she listened. One woman gleefully described how she had called the mother-in-law and friends of the woman her husband had had an affair with and let them know what had happened; if someone didn't believe her, she put her husband on the phone to confirm it. The guest also put flyers to a similar effect on the cars parked at the church where the woman taught Sunday school and sent her black flowers that she could use in "the funeral she was going to give to her reputation since I killed it."

Having introduced the show with a personal disclosure that some of her favorite movies are those where people get revenge, Jenny had set a tone that encouraged both guests and audience to revel in the details, no matter how distasteful. When the guest paused, and her unfaithful but obviously fearful husband sat silently squirming next to her, the camera turned to Jenny, who appeared equally uncomfortable and embarrassed by it all. Yet, having asked for this, all she could say was, "And what did you do next?" Of course, there was more. There were other guests that day with other stories of revenge: bulldozing houses or pouring Nair hair remover over friends' heads. And through it all, our host Jenny asked for more.

The Reality

The images of hosts emerge from a blend of fiction and fact. But behind those images are some very important realities about talk show personalities and the roles they play. The hosts claim to be providing a service. The hosts appear to be deeply concerned with the welfare of their guests and audience. We only have to watch them in action, however, to know that what they are most concerned about is maintaining their status and keeping their ratings high. There are a variety of on-air techniques that reveal their commercial motives.

Instigating Conflict

The tone for each segment is set by the hosts and is a reflection of their personal style, mode of expression, and manner of questioning. The hosts can set a provocative tone by asking antagonizing questions or a sympathetic tone by using expressions of empathy and concern. But their choices about whether to be provocative or sympathetic have little to do with the subject or guest and much more to do with what will produce excitement and achieve higher ratings.

To create drama and entertain, the hosts provoke conflict, then purport to solve it. Geraldo invited John Bobbitt to the show. Bobbitt is well known as the man who had his penis reassembled after his wife cut it off. Using Bobbitt, Geraldo was able to construct a one-hour show around this man's penis. Bobbitt, now divorced, brought on his co-stars—Ms. Tiffany Lords, Ms. Jasmine Aloha, and Ms. Letha Weapons—from the pornographic movie he made about his marriage.

Geraldo questioned Bobbitt and the others about the details of the many conflicts in his relationship to Lorena. At one point during the show, Geraldo disingenuously asked if John was "still in love with his wife Lorena." "Yes," John said. Geraldo then assumed that Lorena was watching and asked John to look into the camera and apologize. John faced the camera and said, "I'm sorry for everything that happened in our relationship."

Believing that conflict to be resolved, Geraldo rolled on to the next one. Ms. Tiffany Lords announced to Bobbitt, and to a whole nation of TV viewers, that she was pregnant with his child. The three porn stars then got into an argument about Ms. Lords' veracity. About which Bobbitt said simply, "Oh, wow."

Geraldo, with consummate sensitivity, then drew listeners back to the centerpiece of the show. "So, from the film, it appears as if it works," he said. "It's a little funky-looking, but it works." The film he was referring to was, of course, *Uncut and Uninhibited*, which viewers could order by calling the 1–800 number appearing on the screen.

The show ended with the same level of decorum with which it began:

> GERALDO: "I didn't expect it to end the way it has. John, you know there'll be headlines about this one . . . What are your intentions vis-a-vis Miss Tiffany Lords?"
>
> JOHN: "We'll have to decide what we're going to do about this matter."
>
> TIFFANY: "I'm too young to have a child and I'm starting out my career."
>
> GERALDO: "Thanks for watching, everybody. See you next time."

Another common talk show tactic is to provoke conflict between mothers and daughters over the way one or the other dresses. Sally's show on "Nude-Dancing Daughters" or Geraldo's "Shocked Parents of Daughters" each brought on sets of feuding mothers and daughters. On both shows, after some discussion of how the daughters felt confined by their mothers' bad opinions and the mothers' accounts of their daughters' outrageous outfits, the hosts signaled the daughters to strip down to bras and thongs. The cameras went back and forth between the daughters' gyrations and the mothers' dismayed expressions. The hosts asked thinly veiled questions of concern in order to prolong the spectacle and give viewers their money's worth.

What is most amazing about the hosts' questions is how they seem to have no direction or point other than to provide an opportunity to elicit more outrageous behavior or to demonstrate how "wise" the hosts are. When Geraldo asked a man convicted of molesting his daughter why he did it, the man said, "I don't know."

Geraldo continued probing with, "Were you attracted to her?"

The man answered, "I don't know, not really."

"As you lay on top of your eight-year-old daughter, Walter, did you not have at least a twinge of conscience, sir?" We're not really getting information that helps us to better understand the guest. But we are getting information that is intended to help us better understand Geraldo. We're learning that Geraldo doesn't approve of molesting children and that he knows what is moral. The hosts get to use guests as springboards for declaring their own values.

Montel Williams presented the same moralistic routine when he brought on a man who said he was a serial rapist. (A claim that was later revealed to be highly questionable.) Without checking his authenticity, but asking questions designed to demean the man, Montel got to come on strong and let viewers know he's against rape.

The hosts know, however, that if they are too aggressive and attack the guests, the audience will turn against them. Even if the studio audience is coached by a director to applaud or cheer, the host must play to the most basic reactions expected from a real audience. The hosts can ridicule only when it is supported by public reaction. Geraldo has perfected the ability to straddle this fence. He deliberately brings on guests with ridiculously provocative claims, which then allow him to play both the fed-up citizen and the concerned host.

For example, on his "Killer Kids" show there was a panel of

teenagers who collectively claimed to have murdered hundreds of people for money or thrills. One boy, referred to as "Ghost," claimed in all seriousness to have murdered over five hundred people. At this point the show was headed in the direction of being seen as totally ridiculous. In order to maintain any credibility, Geraldo needed to indicate disbelief in his own topic yet keep the discussion going. Without missing a beat, he simply responded, "Now that's just not true, is it?" By doing so, he was able to ease the frustration of audience and viewers. He responded as we would expect, making sure that we all knew he understood that the guests his show had selected were exaggerating. Of course, he expected them to create the exaggerations that drew his criticism.

Similarly, Sally did a show focusing on people who steal. She brought on a family that had even stolen the bride's wedding dress. During the question-and-answer period of the show, the hotel manager where the guests had been put up by the show called in. The manager revealed that the guests had stolen the hair dryer from their room. Sally confronted her quests while at the same time saying, "I can't believe you would do this! I am really shocked." The guests continued to deny that they had stolen anything from the hotel until Sally brought out their suitcases from backstage. She dug through the luggage until she came up with the missing hair dryer. All the while, she maintained that this was a great surprise and that she was very disappointed that guests she had invited on her show would steal from the hotel she had paid for. The fact that they were invited on because they steal was lost in Sally's righteous indignation.

In a similar vein, the shows often create surprises which involve bringing out people from former conflicts in a guest's life. Revealing something on air that had not been previously known to another, often startled, guest is also quite popular. On Oprah a husband described to his surprised wife that he was still involved with his mistress and that the mistress was pregnant. Oprah defended herself, saying she was also surprised. "I wouldn't do that [intentionally] to anybody." What's surprising is Oprah's naïveté, since such shows are about getting people to talk about subjects for which they've not been prepared.

Even shows that are billed as information are often just opportunities to show violent, gruesome scenes with painful consequences. The title serves as a code to inform viewers of what type of victim will be the day's feature. For example, Oprah's "Safety Proofing Your Home" gave viewers an hour-long dose of child-disfigurement. The show included very graphic descriptions of how an eighteen-month-old child had been strangled in miniblinds. The mother's pain was given much more air time than the expert who was supposedly there to explain how to childproof a household. Another mother, whose child drowned in a five-gallon tub while she was washing the car, was brought on to describe her agony. Making sure the emotion was graphic enough, Oprah included the 911 tape of the mother screaming about her dying child.

As if this wasn't "informative" enough, Oprah also included some children who had been seriously injured by doing "dumb things" like riding a bike without a helmet, or car surfing, which involves hanging onto the bumper of a moving car. Oprah focused on photographs of these horrible injuries and probed for descriptions of anguish from her unfortunate guests. Even though some helpful information was included, there can be little doubt that the feature attraction was gore, not information.

Ed Glavin, now a producer with Donahue but formerly with Morton Downey Jr., summed it up quite well when he said "What guests don't realize is that the host is in total control. If he wants you to look like a good guy, you look like a good guy: if he wants you to look bad, he can make you look bad."

Larger Than Life

The emphasis on the personal and the helpful masks the fact that this is big business. Phil, Oprah, Sally, and Geraldo are not just four people, they are the cornerstones of major industries. Their shows are not just about people talking, but are also about making millions and millions of dollars. And it is the blend of both these aspects that is intriguing: the something "personal" but also larger than life. Thus, the image of "just like us" hosts doesn't quite square with the actual lifestyle the hosts can so easily afford.

The reality is that no one except the rich and famous could afford the lavish lifestyle nationally syndicated hosts can live. When Oprah showed up at a party given by billionaire Donald Trump in a $200,000 sable coat, we ought to have realized she was running in very different circles than "us folks." In 1992, she purchased a $3,000,000 log and stone home, complete with a ten-seat Jacuzzi, in the ski area of Telluride, Colorado. She has a condominium on the fifty-seventh floor of the Water Tower Place in Chicago. In addition, she has a 160-acre farm in Rolling Prairie, Indiana. She owns her own jet, estimated to be worth $18,000,000. She owns a restaurant in Chicago called "Eccentric," which opened in 1989. Her staff, friends, and family are regularly treated to expensive trips and gifts. Likewise, Donahue took his staff to France to celebrate twenty-five years in the business. Donahue said of his move to New York, "New York is a biiiig turkey. Lucky I can afford it, but I know it's not for everybody."

True to form, Geraldo angered his millionaire neighbors at the Kittansett Golf Club by landing a helicopter on his front lawn, which is across the way from the 17th green. The Riveras also are reported to have a very expensive Chinese shar-pei dog called Connie Chung, which they had shorn and dyed with spots like a leopard. Golfers complained that the dog relieved herself on the greens, so the club had to purchase an electric fence.

Sally went from rags to riches. Her salary is in the millions and she owns an apartment in Manhattan, a bed-and-breakfast in Bucks County, Pennsylvania, and a country home in Montrose, New York.

The hosts' wealth and lavish lifestyles demonstrate the success hosts must have to attract more advertisers and viewers. This success and schmoozing with celebrities makes the hosts look good on magazine covers, which further attracts the attention of print media and tabloid reporters. In addition, most hosts not only receive a generous salary but also own at least portions of the production companies that produce and profit from the shows.

Running the Show

Producing a show that runs every day, five days a week, requires tremendous coordination of the many people involved. Hosts appear to provide the sense of direction for the shows, but as Sally said, "It is the producer's job to orchestrate a show from start to finish." Producers prepare the topics, arrange for the guests, and then provide the host with the summarized information on the topic.

Lori Antosz Benson, a senior producer for *Donahue*, said, "Preparing Phil isn't like preparing other talk show hosts. He reads constantly and watches a lot of news on TV, so he's really well informed. What we end up doing, usually, is writing our own perspectives on the topics we've chosen, and he'll take that perspective and add it to his own." Whether well-prepared or not, the hosts rely on the production staff to keep them informed on guests, topics, and technical details. Therefore, hosts must maintain good relationships with their production staffs.

Both Donahue and Oprah pride themselves on having had their major producers with them from the beginning. In July 1994, however, Oprah accepted the resignation of Debra DiMaio, who had been with her since Baltimore. In fact, DiMaio even went to Chicago first and then recruited Oprah to come on as the host for *Chicago* AM. They were often depicted as twins and talked affectionately about each other. Insiders report that it was DiMaio who was the "bad guy," leaving room for Oprah to always be the "good twin." One report on the breakup pointed out that it was DiMaio who yelled at the staff and who fired those who didn't resign first. This allowed Oprah to maintain her role as the "good one."

It is hard to know what the true relationship is because it is largely applause and compliments that are reported in the press. But despite hosts' attempts to say that the producers "run the show," the reality of having to balance obligations, and to maintain communication so that things run smoothly on the air, rests with the host. It is the host who gains power as the show succeeds. As a result, hosts' relationships with staff are never equal.

There is no doubt that in each talk show the focus is on the host for whom it is named. The benign image created in the media and enhanced by their performance on camera masks the calculated reality of their control. Writing about Oprah's enormous wealth and power for *Ladies Home Journal*, Melina Gerosa said, "She may be the most powerful woman in the country."

A daily forum in which the hosts are given the focus and control affords them great power and makes all the other players second string and easily replaceable. Of all the aspects that make up Talk TV—guests, production crew, audience, and experts—none commands more ability to control what is happening than the hosts. Every other part of the show is really geared to keeping the hosts' image forefront and compelling.

Notes

P. 44, *"My show is really a ministry"*: Goldstein, P. "Oprah Winfrey on the Tightrope of Good Taste," *Los Angeles Times*, Calendar sec., Dec. 20, 1987, pp. 7, 8.

P. 44, *"knowledge is power"*: Moore, T. "How *The Oprah Winfrey Show* Helps People Live Better Lives," *JET*, Apr. 18, 1994, p. 57.

P. 44, *"I do exactly what she does"*: Marrel, M. "Ricki . . . The Movie Actress Turned Talk Show Host Who Is Turning on a New Generation," *Interview*, Jan. 1994, p. 108.

P. 44, *"Our goal is to be 'user friendly'"*: Davis, P. "Rolonda . . . Something Worth Talking About," *Michigan Chronicle*, Apr. 3, 1994, p. 1.

P. 45, *"a balancing act [that] is becoming more precarious"*: Benson, J. "Syndies Overload the Chatter Platter," *Variety*, Feb. 15, 1993, 350(1), 104(2).

P. 45, *"spell his name with an exclamation point"*: Clark, K. R. "Exclamations Are Still the Point for Geraldo! at 20," *Chicago Tribune*, Sept. 25, 1990, sec. 5, p. 1.

P. 45, *he's "still here"*: Clark, K. R. "Exclamations Are Still the Point for Geraldo! at 20," *Chicago Tribune*, Sept. 25, 1990, sec. 5, p. 1.

P. 46, *"Let's present options"*: Arkush, M. "Upstarts Want to Break the TV Talk-Show Mold," *Los Angeles Times*, Sept. 4, 1993, pp. 1, 3, and F-1.

P. 46, *"Our show is funny, it's not exploitive"*: Perner, D. "At Dinner with Ricki Lake; Half the Weight and On the Rise," *New York Times*, Nov. 24, 1993, pp. C-1–C-4.

P. 47, *"I hang my hat on my credibility"*: Roberts, R. "Povich Talks About TV, Trash, and His Wife," *Houston Post*, Aug. 3, 1993, p. 1.

P. 47, *"Many of these hosts"*: Boyd, H. "A Male Oprah Winfrey with a New Spin," *New York Amsterdam News*, July 27, 1992, p. 23.

P. 48, *changes in her life*: Fears, Linda. "Talk Show Hosts Tell All!" *Ladies Home Journal*, June 1994, *111*(6), 38–44.

P. 48, *44D to a 36C*: Landman, B. "Oprah Winfrey: How She Does It," *Redbook*, Sept. 1994, pp. 100–101; p. 101.

P. 52, *"It wasn't because I like running around"*: Randolph, L., "Oprah Opens Up About Her Weight, Her Wedding, and Why She Withheld the Book," *Ebony*, Oct. 1993, p. 130.

P. 52, *"J. J., her son, lost control"* (and the other quote in this paragraph): Rader, D. "How to Live Without Answers," *Washington Post*, April 25, 1993, p. 4.

P. 52, *"I did my share of yelling"* (and other quotes in this paragraph): Jahr, C. "Behind the Scenes with Phil Donahue," *Ladies Home Journal*, Dec. 1985, pp. 28–29, 135; p. 28.

P. 54, *"Your mother is watching"*: Hofacker, K. J. "An Analysis of the Don-ahue Show from 1967 to 1978," unpublished doctoral dissertation, Dept. of Speech, University of Michigan, 1979, p. 119.

P. 54, *"This is a television studio"*: Hofacker, K. J. "An Analysis of the Donahue Show from 1967 to 1978." Unpublished doctoral dissertation, Dept. of Speech, University of Michigan, 1979, p. 119.

P. 56, *"These sex confessions seem bizarre"* (and the quote in the following paragraph): Goldstein, P. "Oprah Winfrey on the Tightrope of Good Taste," *Los Angeles Times*, Calendar sec., Dec. 20, 1987, p. 7.

P. 58, *"I used crack cocaine"*: Gaines, P. "How Oprah's Confession Tumbled Out," *Washington Post*, Jan. 13, 1995, p. B-1; "Hope Oprah's Words Help Others Beat Drugs," *Chicago Defender*, Jan 16, 1995, p. 1.

P. 62, *"I wouldn't do that"*: Fisher, L. "In Full Stride," *People*, Sept. 12, 1994, pp. 84–88; p. 88. (Bracketed interpolation appeared in that source.)

P. 63, *"What guests don't realize"*: Newman, Judith. "Are They Crazy? Why Do People Tell All on Talk Shows?" *Cosmopolitan*, Aug. 1992, pp. 215–219; p. 218.

P. 64, *"New York is a biiiig turkey"*: Jahr, C. "Behind the Scenes with Phil Donahue," *Ladies Home Journal*, Dec. 1985, p. 28.

P. 64, *an electric fence*: Robinson, J. "Geraldo's Showboating Makes Waves in Buzzards Bay," *Boston Globe*, Aug. 2, 1994, p. 58.

P. 65, *role as the "good one"*: Reynolds, G. "The Oprah Myth," *TV Guide*, July 23, 1994, pp. 8–14; p. 14.

3

Guests

The Heart of It All

Guests are the heart and soul of television talk shows. Without the incest survivors, the unhappy couples, the kids embarrassed by their mothers, the dads who dress in women's clothes, or the hundreds of other people willing to show and tell all, there could be no Talk TV, plain and simple. The host may represent the show in the minds of viewers, but, in fact, it's the guests who make it all possible. They are the source of the drama. Without them, there would be nothing to talk about.

Their private stories and personal pain have been turned into a lucrative but expendable commodity. Lucrative because millions of Americans tune in daily to catch the latest revelation. Expendable because each story will only sustain the business for one hour, maybe two. The audience is not drawn to the individual guests but to the stories themselves, and the emotion, trouble, sharing, explanations, and justifications that they provoke.

Aware that today's topic, no matter how riveting, will not sustain tomorrow's viewers, the shows use "bumpers" appearing at the end of each program to announce what new guest and problem is awaiting us on the next episode. Requests for guests with particular problems also appear before and after commercial breaks during the show. Thus viewers are continuously drawn into the show not only by the current guests and their problems, but by future guests and our own potential to become guests. Without a doubt, guests are what these shows are about. And while the primary role of individual guests is to tell us all about themselves, the guests as a whole reveal a lot about the shows that present them.

Getting the Guests

Talk TV requires a steady supply of new guests and problems. Phil Donahue, for example, needs about thirty guests each week. His show has been airing for over twenty-five years, which means that, even allowing for repeats and holidays, *Donahue* alone has had to find tens of thousands of people to appear. There are now over sixteen nationally syndicated television talk shows, all vying for new and interesting guests. With such high demand, assistant producers have to have effective strategies for getting guests. These strategies fall into two broad categories: screening volunteers and actively recruiting for specific kinds of people. It is easy to see that locating and securing guests in such a competitive market is very hard work indeed.

Who Finds These People?

In order to ensure a constant supply, each show maintains a team of workers who identify, locate, and select guests. Additionally, these workers often compile a briefing paper for the host and submit potential questions. In other words, they can be responsible for just about everything except conducting the on-air interview. In order to pull this off, each show employs at least one executive producer who supervises the people who do the behind-the-scenes work of getting guests. Individual staff members wear various titles for much the same job—assistant producers (the most common title), "bookers," talent coordinators, talent executives, segment producers, field producers.

Assistant producers as a whole have developed quite a reputation within the business. Joanne Kaufman, of the *New York Times*, summed it up: "Bookers must have the instincts of a bloodhound and the tenacity of a terrier." Most assistant producers have grueling job requirements in a horrifically competitive field. Most of the hosts tape two shows a day three days a week, and the assistant producers typically have only twenty-four to forty-eight hours to make all the final arrangements and conduct preshow interviews for each show, with little or no break between finishing with one guest and finding and interviewing the next. Gail Evans, vice president for network booking at CNN, says that to succeed at all this, "You have to be an inch deep and a mile wide." In other words, skimming a whole lot of surface without going under.

The extent of their persistence and the accuracy of their instincts for what will catch the public attention have a profound effect of the overall success of a talk show: assistant producers can make or break a show. So understanding the way assistant producers approach their work yields important insight into how the shows view guests.

Screening

Given the inherently solicitous nature of television talk shows, it should come as no surprise that thousands of people write or call the shows asking to appear and suggesting ideas. All of the shows extend an open and continuous invitation to viewers to write or call—and those invitations are productive. Oprah Winfrey reports that her show receives over four thousand letters a calendar week. Of those five thousand, only twenty to thirty are needed for a typical broadcast week, so producers have a lot of screening to do. People who are eliminated, however, can become eligible for shows about rejected ideas for shows. Donahue's producers, for example, did a show about rejected guests that included George Reiger (and his 190 Disney tattoos), Roberta Bergman (who wanted to talk about good posture), Shantha Swany (a gingerbread house expert), and Jacqueline Gatzenviel (the inventor of a self-closing toilet seat lid). But even with the option of making it on as a reject, most volunteers will never get onto the show.

Volunteers always think their stories are great ideas, but producers want topics and guests that are "hot." The distinguishing feature is really quite simple: audience appeal. Mary Duffy, supervising producer for *Montel Williams,* says, "Thirty seconds—Bing! Bang! Boom!—And I can tell whether a guest is going to be any good." Without a doubt, what Ms. Duffy is summing up so quickly is not the value of the experience a potential guest wishes to share, but rather the guest's camera readiness and ability to attract viewers.

The shows defend their quick summations of people by claiming that audiences are more demanding than ever. Pat McMillen, the executive producer for *Donahue,* pointed out that "any sensationalistic show you do doubles any other serious show in the rating. It's viewer voyeurism, I guess." After years of exposure to lesbians, transvestites, rape survivors, and child molesters, viewers are no longer riled by such run-of-the-mill topics and will only tune in for more exciting and unusual guests. And it is, according to producers, the viewers' appetites that force the shows to "get the guests."

But by publicizing the fact that they are looking for whatever keeps the viewers tuned in, the shows are indirectly acknowledging that the primary screening factor is entertainment value. Potential guests know that they must be unusual to get attention. Producers concur that the more unusual the people are, and the stranger their problems, the more interest the show will have in considering them as potential guests.

Indeed, we can more clearly understand what is of interest by noting what is not. Serious issues—retardation, schizophrenia, loneliness in the elderly, depression, low-IQ children in foster homes with no hope of rejoining their parents or being adopted—rarely show up. Talk TV almost never brings us ordinary housewives and stressed-out, hardworking men and women. Producers aren't interested in such stories because they don't play well with audiences. They offer little hope of resolution, they're boring, or they're too hard to tackle. They aren't particularly outrageous or zany, and their themes can't easily be presented tongue-in-cheek.

Clearly then, volunteers are screened on the basis of their ability to provide material that will draw a crowd and maintain interest. And the deciding variables are most often thrill-factor and potential for creating an attention-grabbing spectacle on the air. The shows are looking for variety, human interest, catchy issues with eye appeal, violent or potentially violent conflicts, revelations about what will help viewers lose weight or win their lovers back, or anything that will keep ratings high. These same standards, of course, apply to those who are specifically recruited by the shows.

Recruitment

Assistant producers certainly can't rely on volunteers alone. Getting the really hot stories demands more aggressive recruitment efforts. Every possible avenue must be explored. Newspapers, tabloids, television news shows, private detective agencies, experts, friends, bartenders, and parties are all possible sources for locating guests.

Producers scour the pages of the tabloid magazines and newspapers for stories they think will make for good talk. And since sex, violence, and oddity tend to make the headlines, print media are a kind of prescreening device, helping to alert assistant producers to potential topics. When a story such as the Menendez murders breaks, the shows go in hot pursuit of anyone even remotely associated.

Geraldo, for example, brought on a woman identified only as "Mary" who stated that when she was a child she knew José Menendez, the father who was killed. She reported that her father had employed José. She described what, in her opinion, was a "famous story" and therefore "no secret." She said that her father had gone on a business trip to Germany where he and José went to a nightclub. There José "started to perform various explicit things with women on the stage in front of my dad and his associates. . . . My dad was so mortified that he literally came close to fainting." This little bit of twenty-year-old gossip was used as the launching pad for her main point, which was to inform viewers that "José never touched me. He never tried anything. It was just a visceral vibe that I got—yucky!" An entire show called "The Menendez Murder Trial Examined: Did the Boys Kill out of Fear or for the Money?" was built around her brief appearance and remote connection to the Menendez spectacle. The question posed by the title was, of course, never answered. But when producers think a topic is hot, anyone or anything that will garner ratings is fair game.

In addition to scanning print media, assistant producers also use the shows themselves as a source for recruiting more guests. Most shows advertise specific upcoming topics and request calls from viewers who have experienced those particular problems or feelings. Other shows emphasize that they do not advertise for particular problems. Geraldo, for example, is adamant that his show does not recruit on air for specific problems. That is true. The show does, however, suggest that viewers call a 1–900 number with suggestions for future shows. Thus, Geraldo is not asking for people with specific problems to come forward; rather, he is getting the public to pay his show to give their ideas and possibly be considered as future guests. But regardless of the degree of specificity, all shows use their own broadcasts as an avenue for soliciting future guests.

Articles about the shows appear in women's magazines and are often accompanied by advertisements for guests. One such advertisement in *Woman's World* informed readers that the shows rely on calls, letters, and articles in newspapers and magazines to find the "perfect idea and the perfect guest." The ad went on to state that the shows are "looking primarily for women with a compelling story that would interest a national audience" and for people "who know how to express themselves."

An even more specialized method of locating guests is the National Talk Show Guest Registry, a computer database that contains information on approximately 2,200 potential talk show guests. This service was started in 1993 by Christopher Darryn, who has been assisting television talk shows since 1986. His Reseda, California, company, The Research Department, is designed to help talk shows complete the background research for topics they are covering.

Darryn explained how the idea for the Registry evolved, "Talk shows would contact The Research Department about topics they were interested in covering. Our company would then search for experts and guests, and often once experts were located they could then be used to identify potential guests or bring their own clients." Darryn's company would also search for materials on the subject in order to construct questions for the show.

The Encyclopedia of Associations is yet another method for recruiting guests. It provides contact information for representatives of groups such as the North American Swing Club Association (NASCA). Robert McGinley, president of NASCA, says that bookers frequently call him seeking guests from his organization's membership. And while he will provide names of members willing to appear, he says he is skeptical about their appearances: "Talk shows aren't interested in educating anybody." Nonetheless, he is willing to supply names and some preshow advice to "cut down on postshow disappointment." "Besides," he adds, "when we send our members to appear on a talk show, it means they are going to get a free trip to Chicago or New York City. They're going to be put up in a nice hotel and have their dinner paid for. It's kind of a thrill, and they're entitled to that."

Using Guests to Get Guests

An extremely fruitful and popular strategy for obtaining guests involves using those who have already successfully passed the screening process. Guests are frequently used as leads to other guests. When Geraldo did a show about "Sex in the Forbidden Zone," the producers asked at least one of the guests to supply the name of the man who had abused her, so that show personnel could contact him to appear on the same show. They also asked this guest to call family members and request that they go on as well. And when the selected guest didn't want to make calls to get the additional guests, the show's producers said that they were willing to pursue those people once the names were provided.

In a similar fashion, professional experts, who are a special type of guest, are frequently asked to recruit for the shows they will be appearing on. In fact, before the guest registry began, Christopher Darryn relied heavily on experts to find guests for the shows that contacted his agency. Because mental health experts come into contact with people who have trouble, experts are a particularly efficient resource. Clients, former clients, therapy groups, discussion group members, workshop participants, or people interviewed for books are all prime choices. For that reason, even with the professional recruiting services now available, experts are still a fast and effective way of getting guests. They are so useful, in fact, that they are sometimes even asked to solicit guests for shows to which they themselves have not been invited.

If a topic is really hot, guests and experts can also be recycled. Guests who are proven ratings getters are often called back, as are popular experts. All the shows have cashed in on the opportunity to invite former guests back to their shows. The returning guests are celebrated, treated as dear friends, and brought on with a great deal of fanfare. Geraldo calls them "Stars." Like long-lost friends, these guests give viewers an update on how their lives are going. Invariably, repeat guests are positive and point out how great it was to be on the show, even if "everything" isn't solved.

This recycled version of talk further entices viewers with the promise of an update on a problem that wasn't quite solved. "Montel Gets Help For Former Guests" was the title for Williams's version of this classic Talk TV tradition. On this show, viewers were reintroduced to Shawna, who had previously informed viewers that she had beaten up her mother over a hundred times, and to her mother, who was also a guest. Montel then introduced Alvin Jackson by saying, "And when we come back we're going to meet the man who did this miraculous turnaround, again, Mr. Alvin 'Boom Boom' Jackson who volunteered to help the former guests with their abusive behavior." Viewers never learned anything that would help explain this "miraculous turnaround," or for that matter anything about Boom Boom's credentials. Instead, guests were introduced with a few summary statements about how things had improved for them.

Their appearance was followed by Barbara, a woman introduced only as a mother who disapproved of her daughters, but who was then reintroduced along with the two daughters, Tunisha and Trina. To provide viewers with a taste of the original rift, a video clip was shown of an argument between the mother, her daughters, and Cindy, the lesbian lover of one of the daughters. Much of what was said had to be deleted because it was too profane to broadcast. Then the therapists who provided them pro bono counseling were introduced. They were allotted a few minutes to say, "They're definitely on the road to recovery, a very short-term therapy model."

Then the next returning guest, Eugene, was brought on. Eugene, who had appeared on "I'm Tired of Watching My Friends Die" as a former gang member, came back this time with his therapist, Ms. Bonnie Elseman. Ms. Elseman came with her own equally vague label, "counsels former gang members," and was there to confirm that Eugene had turned his life around.

What made these returning guests "Stars" the first time around was the extent of their difficulties. It pays to stick with a winner, so to speak. The fanfare surrounding their lightning reappearances creates the illusion that these people were helped by the shows, but all the audience really gets is another dose of their misery. Thus, although the shows invite these guests back under the guise of being interested in what has happened since their first appearance, the new invitations are actually just another opportunity to rehash all the trouble and strife that increased the shows' ratings before.

Competition for Guests

As the market has grown, competition among shows has necessarily increased. Martin Berman, executive producer of *Geraldo*, points out that "It's not that the shows have to get more bizarre to compete, they have to get better." What *better* means, according to Berman, is "For a show on rape, it used to be enough to interview the victim. Now you need the victim and the perpetrator. You need her to come face-to-face with her rapist, which is very therapeutic."

It is generally agreed that the pressure increases as a show's relative standing decreases. Thus, assistant producers for such shows as Oprah's or Phil's are spared the really nasty competition because those shows have clout and can attract guests more easily. But regardless of the shows' standings and the degree of competition, it's clear that all assistant producers are under the gun to produce guests, and to do it quickly.

Another important dynamic to understanding guest selection is the fact that assistant producers are highly motivated to advance their own careers. When assistant producers bring in particularly sensational guests, they're likely to be recruited by other shows offering promotion or higher pay. A former booker from A Current Affair was quoted in Newsweek as saying staff members will do anything to get a sought-after individual, "fly them, screw them, just get the guest." Clearly, in such an atmosphere the adrenaline charge of beating the competitors becomes a driving force and affects every aspect of their interactions with guests. In fact, it all too often turns people's lives into a source of "sport."

A classic illustration of the sporting mentality involves Liz Frillici, who was lured away from Sally Jessy Raphael to work for Maury Povich. Frillici openly admits that her biggest coup was getting Marilyn Beers to appear. Beers is the mother of a Long Island girl who was imprisoned beneath the garage of a family friend. Frillici states that "the biggest joy of the story was when they told me that a caravan of cars from the other shows was following her on her way to us. To me, that's fair game, because it's a sport at that point."

Frillici is not the only assistant producer who thinks of the challenge of pulling a show together as sport. Pat McMillen of Donahue admitted that last year the show paid guests for the first time ever. The recipients were two police officers who had beaten Rodney King. They each received $25,000. McMillen was upset by the action, but Donahue responded by stating, "Everyone else is doing it. We aren't in the ballgame if we don't."

Sometimes the competition turns ugly. Less-than-admirable efforts were employed by *The Jane Whitney Show*, *Jenny Jones*, and *Montel Williams* in trying to secure the Spur Posse. The Posse was a group of Southern California boys who received national attention after forming a club that centered on the competition over who could have sex with the most girls. The boys were charged with sexual offenses and as a result were considered prime material for talk shows. What resulted were offers of money, air fare, hotel expenses, and spending accounts, plus some quick phone calls in the middle of the night. *The Maury Povich Show* had put the Posse up, unsupervised, in a hotel. The boys called Jane Whitney's people—who offered more money, picked them up, and moved them to another hotel, this time with supervision that kept them there until show time.

Preshow Preparation

The night before the taping, guests are met at the airport with a limousine to transport them to the hotel. Most shows give vouchers for food. Oprah, for example, issues a standard $75 certificate. The following day, guests are met at their hotel and transported in another limo to the studio where final preshow directions are given. Although the guests have clearly already been selected by this point, the preshow preparation is yet another opportunity to emphasize to the guests what the show wants from them.

Pat McMillen describes the preshow format on *Donahue*: "Usually one of the secretaries goes out to the desk and brings the guests to the greenroom. Their coats are hung up. They are offered a cup of coffee and asked to sign a release form. . . . After they have gotten settled, if it is a show I have booked, I'll go in and say 'hello' and give them a little briefing. . . . The most important thing for them to know is that they aren't just an answering machine, that they are there to talk to the people in the audience as well as to Phil. We want them to know what we expect of them and what they can do on the show . . . I'll tell them that Phil thinks it's good if they're somewhat apprehensive. He thinks they're more alert . . . I tell them that their answers should be as brief and succinct as possible. They should come to their point and then talk around that point."

Phil Donahue himself also meets the guests briefly before the show in order to allay their fears and to establish his expectations. For the last twenty-five years or so, Donahue has been saying things such as, "I will never abandon you. You will never be twisting in the wind . . . I am on your side . . . Please know that I will never be upset with you for showing enthusiasm. You can interrupt me . . . I do not ask you to perform for us. You be yourself . . . but I do ask you, consistent with your own personality, to bring as much energy to this as you can . . . Please know we are only going to get the outer layer of the onion. I want you to anticipate frustration. Just when you start cooking, we're going to have to interrupt."

Guests on the Air: A Performance

Once they are on the air, the people selected to be guests are transformed into the show's topics. They provide the raw material for every aspect of the show. Everything the host does, the viewers watch, or the audience members discuss, begins with the guests. What guests are called upon to do or say as the centerpiece of the show will certainly vary. Regardless of the topic, there are some standard features of all guest appearances.

Make It Interesting

Guests have been selected to appear because their stories seem interesting. Then they're encouraged before the show, by producers and even by hosts, to make it more interesting. But the encouragement sometimes turns into instruction. If things aren't going as planned, guests may be presented with more direct demands.

Allison Rubinstein, for example, appeared on *Geraldo* in 1991 with her husband to talk about the obscene phone calls she had received. Allison reported that she was told that she wasn't crying enough and that the staff encouraged both her and her husband to exaggerate. "Geraldo kept saying to my husband, 'This destroyed your marriage, didn't it?'" In a similar situation, Sandra Sanchez reported that during a commercial break the floor director encouraged her to show more emotion by asking her, "Don't you remember how angry you were?"

Nancy Steele, Ph.D., explained that she had spent considerable time working with a rapist she brought to *Sally Jessy Raphael* about how to remain calm and not lose his composure over audience comments. But the production staff had a different agenda. One of the directors asked him straight out, "Aren't you getting upset? Can't you stick up for yourself?"

Identity: Labels and Disguises

As the focus of conversation, it is important that the guests be easily identifiable—not necessarily as themselves but as specimens for the show's topic. Therefore, instead of merely relying on what guests say to identify who they are and why they are there, the shows label guests for viewers. Much like a label on an item on the shelf or a placard in a zoo, a description frequently appears beneath the guest's face, to identify for viewers what it is they're seeing. The man we are viewing "can't have erections" or the woman is "shot in the neck by husband she still loves" or the girl on the screen is "embarrassed by mother's clothes." The label is a marketing device to remind us about how unusual or deviant the guest is. It instructs us about how to connect or relate to the person on screen. The labels keep the bizarre feature of the guests ever-present, so that even when guests resist the directions to exaggerate and play up the conflict, we only have to read the screen to know that they are actually quite strange.

The idea that the guests are deviant or peculiar is also extended by the occasional use of disguises. Ostensibly, disguises are used when the guests are disclosing some particularly stigmatizing feature of their lives. But often disguises are more ornamental than functional: anyone who knows the disguised guests would still be able to recognize them. For example, Geraldo's "Sex In The Forbidden Zone" featured a young woman who had come on to discuss her sexual involvement with her coach in high school. The show's effort to hide her identity was to place a wig on her head. They apparently did not talk with her about the need to wear something different, because there she sat wearing the same outfit she was known to wear most of the time. The red pants and white shirt were unmistakable to all who knew her. This episode is only one of many failed disguises and reveals one of the real functions of disguises: to increase drama, not anonymity.

The disguises themselves actually decrease the guests' credibility. There is usually little attempt to hide the fact that a disguise is being used or to maintain the guest's dignity. Out come the funny hats, implausible wigs, dark glasses, and scarves. The major accomplishment of such disguises is to create a heightened sense of disbelief and to further depersonalize the guests.

John Garriques, a transsexual from California, discussed appearing with his wife, Sue, on *The Jane Whitney Show*. Both John and Sue decided to wear disguises because they didn't want to be identified. But once in costume, they both recognized that the disguises detracted from the overall message they wanted to convey. John, who had spent years working to accept and value himself, felt it was like going back to "hiding" who he really is. The disguises were also counterproductive to the show's stated purpose: increasing understanding. John wanted to convey to the audience that he was attracted to his wife, Sue, because of her wholesome and caring nature. That point was impossible to make because Sue was dressed up in a dark wig and lots of makeup, and looked like a streetwalker. The disguises weren't effective, moreover; a member of their church knew right away it was them.

Even when the disguises do protect guests' identities, they're still basically exploited to increase ratings. Sally Jessy Raphael recently did a show on people who are stalked by their friends. Despite the fact that the guests were really not in imminent danger, they were kept behind a screen and presented as though the stalker was about to appear at any moment. They kept the guests in silhouette, and viewers were told that these anonymous guests had joined the program via satellite. The cloak-and-dagger atmosphere created by the disguise and satellite connection heightened the sense of danger and drama.

Telling Their Story

There is little room for guests to be presented as complete or complex personalities. Rather, they come representing a particular issue or problem and that is their role throughout the show. Their primary function is revelatory. Guests are invited on because they have experienced some traumatic or unusual circumstance and are expected to tell host and viewers the details of that experience.

According to M. C. Timney, guests get the majority of air time and are allowed the longest responses on average of anyone appearing on the shows. What this means, however, is that guests are allotted about 39 percent of the total show and that their average responses are thirteen seconds long. So guests need to cut to the chase and highlight the most conflicting aspects of their story. Thus guests need to reveal all, but quickly. Guests recognize this. One former guest has even identified the importance of being able to use a "bumper-sticker mentality." This means being able to identify themselves and their problems quickly, with catchphrases such as "Save this husband, steal my wife," "Hug me, I'm desperate!" or "I brake for skinheads."

The rapid pace of the disclosures keeps both the guests and us, as viewers, slightly off balance and that results in a more thrilling ride through the show. The norm is that anything goes. Guests are rewarded by the show and audience for telling everything. The more personal and humiliating the disclosure, the more rewarded the guest is for "sharing" it. And because all shows have the same amount of time, the more complicated a problem is, the more action packed the show will be.

A prime example of this rapid-paced disclosure was a *Sally Jessy Raphael* program featuring a complicated retrospective of a contested shooting. Numerous guests were trotted out, each with a personal version of the event and few in agreement. First came Dwayne, a man who said he was intentionally shot in the neck by his friend, Jeff, when he was in the eighth grade. Both of Dwayne's parents were present to provide confirmation of the story and to describe the agony of dealing with his injuries. But they had only enough time to highlight the trauma because there were still more guests and stories to be heard. We needed still to hear from Jeff, who came on to admit to the shooting but explain that it was an accident. Then came Anthony, Jeff's cousin, who informed us that Dwayne was lying about being paralyzed because he had seen him take three steps at a shopping mall. Thus far, at least, there still seemed to be point to the show. But then out came a friend to complain that not enough people visited Dwayne after the initial furor wore off. And then there was Gena, identified as the possible motive of the shooting, but she simply denied this.

Not surprisingly this compilation of guests produced some very hearty arguing but very meager clarification of the problem, and even less resolution. What was accomplished, however, was a spicy show with a lot of "oohs" and "ahs" from the audience and probably from those of us at home as well. Sally, well accustomed to using her guests in this way, concluded confidently, "This is a good reason for gun control."

Jenny Jones' show on "Women Who Hide Their Pregnancies" was an all-time classic for demonstrating that the primary role of guests is to provide thrills for viewers and not to clarify problems. Four guests and the people they hid their pregnancies from were introduced and given a few minutes to explain their situations. During that time old wounds were reopened and a few new ones were inflicted. The final episode involved a twelve-year-old girl who had hidden her pregnancy from her mother. As she began to describe that her mother was upset with the eighteen-year-old father of her child, time was up for the day and the show's credits rolled over her image. Jenny brought the show to an end by stating "at least the children are healthy." The guests had served the show's purpose and it was time to move on.

Why Do People Do This?

Perhaps the most common response to Talk TV guests is: Why? Why would people agree to bare their souls on national television? It is hard to understand, particularly given the kinds of disclosures that typically take place on talk shows. Humiliating, embarrassing, and traumatizing events are par for the course, and often more is revealed than was originally intended or expected. Regardless, guests are volunteering for this scrutiny and even appear to like it. What seems clear is that many, many people want to do this. But why?

According to the Shows

The shows themselves promote suggestions that viewers and guests are socially isolated and emotionally distraught. In other words, guests were on the edge and lacked the good sense or support to find connection elsewhere. They have a story to tell and no one else to tell it to. It has also been suggested that guests are looking for more than just the opportunity to voice previously unspoken pain. Guests may be seeking assistance from the show in general, or the host or experts specifically.

The shows' producers feed this belief by playing up what they consider the therapeutic benefit of public disclosure. Jeff Erdel of *Geraldo* reports that, in fact, a lot of guests tell him that "it's therapeutic." Maury Povich was quoted as saying that it is the chance for guests to "unburden themselves" that draws them to the shows. His executive producer, Kari Sagin, states that "talk shows work just the way Alcoholics Anonymous works—sometimes it's easier to tell the most intimate secrets to a bunch of total strangers than to your own family." Similarly, Martin Berman, from *Geraldo*, reminds us that "Confession really is good for the soul."

Burt Dubrow, the executive producer for *Sally Jessy Raphael*, believes that people want to reveal a secret they are tired of holding. "Guests put pressure on themselves by going on television. Once they are out there, they know they're going to say something, and they know their mothers are going to find out . . . when they go on television they hope the audience will agree with them. Then they can say to their mothers, 'See, I told you I was right.'"

So viewers are told over and over that the guests want the assistance of the shows, and guests reinforce the idea with repeat performances. Old guests who were in deep trouble are brought back, with another free trip and another opportunity to be on TV, to tell viewers that their troubles are now over, or at least different. The show becomes a serial with a soap-opera quality as we are invited to stay tuned.

According to the Guests

Despite the official claims, there is little evidence to support the notion that guests are in search of help, in a therapeutic sense, from the shows. In fact, there has been little research done to find out from guests what it is that motivates them to appear. The vast majority of explanations, including the shows' accounts, are based either on anecdotal evidence or pure speculation. The most comprehensive effort to date to find out guests' motives according to the guests themselves was conducted by Patricia Priest. Her dissertation in Mass Communication from the University of Georgia in 1992 was titled "Self-Disclosure on Television: The Counter-Hegemonic Struggle of Marginalized Groups on *Donahue*."

Priest conducted extensive interviews with former guests. It is interesting to note that all the major shows, except *Donahue*, refused to help her recruit guests for the study, and *Donahue* would only assist if they could have editorial privilege. She elected to proceed without assistance from the shows. Priest was able to carry out her study on her own and found that, unlike the industry views above, most guests had strong social support. They also were not desperate for human contact. Nor did the guests represent crazed fans who longed to be near the hosts and have them accept them.

Priest found that she could categorize the former guests according to two rather straightforward motives. One group consisted of individuals who, for a variety of reasons, had been marginalized by society and sought the opportunity to educate the public. The second group consisted of people who were mostly interested in the thrill of appearing on television.

Educating the Public

Some guests realize that the shows sought them because of the sensationalized nature of their experiences and knew that the shows would probably use them to hype ratings. But these people also realize that no other avenue exists for redressing social wrongs or sending an impassioned plea to such a large audience.

We interviewed John Garriques, who reported that he agreed to appear on several different programs because it was "important to reach out to others and let them know that people who go through sex changes are normal, that they're not 'freaks of nature.'" John reported that he felt that the more people the shows reached, the more understanding there would be and that through educating viewers, the climate would improve for people like him.

Likewise, Priest reported that many of the guests she interviewed were cognizant of the potential problems with the shows and that they even cited examples of how the shows catered to a taste for the outrageous and ridiculous. But they were also using the shows to achieve their own agendas, which were largely to help inform the public about real problems as best they could given the limitations of the shows. Guests who appeared for these reasons described an increase in self-confidence and overall self-esteem as a result of going on the shows. They were especially pleased by the warm response they got from the studio audience and from strangers who later recognized them as having appeared on television.

Other guests have very immediate and practical messages for

the audience. Three women from the San Francisco East Bay area went on *The Jane Whitney Show* three to four years after their daughters were kidnapped. At the time of their appearance there were no traces of their children anywhere and no suspects had been arrested. A co-worker of one of the women who appeared shared her understanding of why the mother wanted to be on the talk show. She stated that the woman hoped that her daughter was still alive, would somehow see the show, and know that her mother was still looking for her.

Other guests have more self-serving messages. Marion Barry, the recently re-elected mayor of Washington, D.C., decided to go on *Sally Jessy Raphael* with his message. Barry had been convicted in 1990 for smoking crack cocaine in an FBI sting. He appeared on the show with a psychiatrist who was also recovering from alcohol, drug, and sex addiction. Sally introduced them: "Our guests today say they have all brought some measure of shame to themselves and their loved ones. Our first guest will talk for the first time about his addiction to women and sex and how it destroyed his career and probably his marriage . . . so please welcome Marion Barry, the former mayor of our nation's capital." Barry's message was, "You get caught up in it, the ego gets into it and the grandiosity. The con-quests. The women. This disease is cunning, baffling, powerful. It destroys your judgment . . . I lost my spirituality, I now have regained it."

Essentially, Marion Barry succeeded in convincing the public of his transformation and good intentions and, with a new wife in tow, he was inaugurated for the fourth time as mayor of Washington, D.C., in January of 1995. Appealing for divine assistance in his new job, he vowed that his second chance would be different.

"The Thrill of It All"

Sometimes the motivation for appearing has little to do with reworking a painful issue, either for one's own benefit or the enlightenment of others, but more to do with what can be gained from the medium itself: a few minutes of fame and glory. Given the increasingly sensational nature of talk shows, and the mad-dog approach to finding new topics and guests, it should not be surprising that people outside the industry have also identified the shows as a means to personal profit.

The search for a TV endorsement of bizarre behavior might explain the appearance of guest Willie Murrell. Willie went on *The Jane Whitney Show* to tell viewers that he is "so stingy," his wife refuses to have sex with him. To describe just how stingy he is, he told viewers that he splits two-ply toilet paper into two rolls. In an interview following the show, Willie further explained why he went on the show. "Sure I pull toilet paper in half, but the people probably laughed because they've tried to do it themselves. I was nervous being on stage, but I thought I'd be the winner."

Stuart Fischoff, Ph.D., a former president of the American Psychological Association (APA) Media Psychology Division, sums up this latter group by stating that some guests "have nothing to lose" and "some guests want to be neurotic for fun and profit and don't really want help." Fischoff went on to describe a woman who claimed to have been diagnosed as having multiple personality disorder. She wanted him to help get her on talk shows so that she could be noticed and then have a TV movie made about her life. If he couldn't manage to secure a talk show appearance then she wanted him to call on his connections with Warner Brothers.

The woman Fischoff discussed was not completely unrealistic. Some guests do get noticed and do benefit from their appearances. In 1992, for example, Darlene Cates appeared on *Sally Jessy Raphael*. At the time, Darlene had not left her house in five years and weighed five hundred pounds. After that show aired, screenplay writer Peter Hedges showed Paramount Pictures a new script titled *What's Eating Gilbert Grape?* He brought with him the video of the show to demonstrate how fat the character needed to be. Lasse Hallstrom, the director, said that "she was a wonderful personality in this disguise of her own body." Darlene was just what they were looking for in the character "Momma," so she got the part and later got rave reviews.

Some guests are happy with just local recognition, like Bill, a transvestite and talk show veteran. He said, "I enjoy the attention I get. I'll be dressed up in a nightclub, and someone will be staring at me and say, 'Weren't you just on the *Morton Downey Jr. Show* the other day?'" Darlene, and people like Bill, reinforce the fantasy that Talk TV could change our lives. Their success feeds a widespread desire for a chance to be seen.

A Special Sort of Thrill: Faking It

While neither the shows nor many former guests have come forward to suggest that deception might be a motivating force for guests, there are in fact guests who have gotten themselves selected for the shows by purposefully tricking the producers with their stories. With a growing sense that the shows are outrageous, and since they have covered just about every "truth," fakery has become one option for those who want to appear on TV.

Jennifer and Uriel Soto tricked three talk shows in several weeks. First they appeared as married cousins on *Ricki Lake*. Jennifer talked about the spoof to Catherine Crier of *20/20* in 1994, saying that she and Uriel had, in fact, met at a family picnic, but as for being cousins, there isn't a chance. "Uriel is Mexican and has black hair and I'm the opposite." But despite the glaring differences, they conned Ricki Lake. After that, they moved on to *Jenny Jones* and her staff with "Men Who Don't Want Their Wives to Dress Sexy." Then came *Jerry Springer*. That time, they even orchestrated a phone call from the "mother," who accused her "son-in-law" of beating her "daughter." Uriel stomped off the stage in tears. But, of course, he got it together enough to come back and inform viewers that the accusations were lies—which was apparently the only statement that wasn't.

Montel Williams took the prize for showcasing the most grandiose of revelations, and doing so with all "sincerity." Jerome Stanfield was invited for two consecutive shows in March, 1994. Stanfield came on the show as a self-proclaimed HIV-positive serial rapist of prostitutes. He told viewers that he had raped over ninety women and that he was on the show because he wanted to stop. On the second show, Montel introduced Jerome by saying "there have been reports that he may not have been telling the truth but we have no information at this time that leads us to believe that he was not telling the truth. And because of that, we feel it is our duty and our responsibility to broadcast this program out of concern for public safety."

After the second show, Jerome turned himself in to Captain Griffith of the New York City Police Department. Once in custody, Stanfield retracted his statements and the police reported that there was no evidence to suggest that Stanfield had committed such crimes. They said they had no reports to even suggest they should be looking for a serial rapist of prostitutes at that time.

In another episode, Ricki Lake brought on Gwendolyn, who claimed to have infected half of the New Orleans police force with AIDS. Her rationale for lying to the show was printed in the *Times Picayune*: "What is even more shocking is that anyone would believe what they hear on Lake's self-parodying talk-show circus." The shows are adamant that they attempt to verify the truth of what is presented and that they discourage guests from lying. For example, Catherine Crier reported on a 1994 *20/20* program that the *Ricki Lake* show claims to warn guests that it will take legal action against people "who knowingly lie and misrepresent their story" on the program. Regardless of such threats, it still happens. However, they also add that given the nature of their shows, it is difficult to know when guests "conspire to lie." And, in fact, many times it *is* difficult to know if the claims are real or false, and if they're false just who it is that is faking it.

Geraldo, for example, did a show on "self-stalking" in which people reporting to have multiple personalities claimed that one personality "stalks" the others. One woman on this show reported that it was so bad that the stalker personality had made her stab herself during an attack on one of the other personalities. Another guest on the same show claimed to have twenty personalities, which Geraldo attempted to call forth on the show. Whether these guests were actually suffering from multiple personality disorders or not is impossible to know. What is clear is that for the average viewer the claims seem outrageous. The clownish disguises and the host's mocking disposition only heighten the sense that this is a farce and that the show knows it—and even knows that viewers will know it.

From these and many other episodes, it is evident that many of the guests who might be fabricating could not possibly be alone in their efforts to deceive. The utter absurdity and grandiosity of some the claims should, at the very least, prompt the shows to be cautious. Their very nature should suggest that any prudent attempt to deal with them should include efforts to assess their veracity. Given the mad rush to find guests with new, different, and exciting stories to tell, one is left wondering just who it is that is conspiring.

Lies or Truth

TV talk shows emphasize that guests are motivated to appear because talking is supposed to be somehow inherently therapeutic. Guests, on the other hand, downplay the influence of any personal needs in their decisions to appear, other than to educate society or to get a thrill from being seen on TV. But neither the shows' explanations or the guests' own accounts really seem to take in the full picture.

Yes, it can be helpful to talk. But how helpful can it be to do so with five to thirteen million strangers at once? Yes, it is rewarding to educate others. But with so little time and with the circus atmosphere that prevails, the forum isn't educational. Instead, the truly appealing enticement is the opportunity for a huge audience and the joy of national attention. When people have little to lose, free trips and a chance at notoriety seem to be enough to secure an ample supply of the commodity shows seek.

Notes

P. 71, *"the tenacity of a terrier"*: Kaufman, J. "'Hello. Can You Be a Talk Show Guest?'" *New York Times*, May 31, 1987, p. B-25.

P. 71, *"You have to be an inch deep"*: Givens, R. "Talking People into Talking," *Newsweek*, July 17, 1989, pp. 44–45; p. 44.

P. 71, *four thousand letters a calendar week*: Priest, P. *Public Intimacies: Talk Show Participants and Tell-All TV* Cresskill, NJ: Hampton Press Inc., 1995, p. 12.

P. 72, *"Bing! Bang! Boom!"*: O'Neill, T. "Welcome to the Jungle," *US*, Feb. 1994, pp. 78–81, 90–91.

P. 72, *"It's viewer voyeurism, I guess"*: Laskas, J. "What's Happened to Phil Donahue?" *Redbook*, Nov. 1991, pp. 44, 46, 48–50; p. 48.

P. 74, *"perfect idea and the perfect guest"* (and subsequent quote): Bryant, E. "Why Do They Tell All on TV?" *Woman's World*, Aug. 1994, pp. 2–3.

P. 74, *National Talk Show Guest Registry* (and commentary in the following paragraph): Christopher Darryn, personal interview, July 1994.

P. 75, *"they're entitled to that"*: Diamond, J. "Life After Oprah," *Self*, Aug. 1994, pp. 122–125; p. 125.

P. 77, *"For a show on rape"*: Diamond, J. "Life After Oprah," *Self*, Aug. 1994, pp. 122–125; p. 124.

P. 78, *"fly them, screw them, just get the guests"*: Givens, R. "Talking People into Talking," *Newsweek*, July 17, 1989, pp. 44–45; p. 45.

P. 78, *"it's a sport at that point"*: O'Neill, T. "Welcome to the Jungle," *US*, Feb. 1994, pp. 78–81, 90–91; p. 80.

P. 78, *paid guests for the first time ever* (plus Donahue quote in this paragraph): O'Neill T. "Welcome to the Jungle," *US*, Feb. 1994, pp. 78–81, 90–91; p. 81.

P. 79, *in trying to secure the Spur Posse* (and other information on the incident in this paragraph): O'Neill, T. "Welcome to the Jungle," *US*, Feb. 1994, pp. 78–81, 90–91; p. 90.

P. 79, *Oprah . . . issues a standard $75 certificate:* Benson, J. "Show Hoppers Making Hay on Syndie Talkers," *Variety*, Jan. 17, 1994, p. 33.

P. 79, *"one of the secretaries goes out to the desk":* Mincer, R., and Mincer, D. *The Talk Show Book*. New York: Facts on File Publications, 1982, p. 116.

P. 80, *"I will never abandon you":* Mincer, R., and Mincer, D. *The Talk Show Book*. New York: Facts on File Publications, 1982, p. 118.

P. 81, *"Geraldo kept saying to my husband"* Bass, A. "Listening Hard to TV Talk," *Boston Globe*, Oct. 13, 1993, pp. 1, 8, 9.

P. 81, *"don't you remember how angry you were?":* Sandra Sanchez, personal interview, June 24, 1994.

P. 81, *"Aren't you getting upset?":* Nancy Steele, personal interview, Sept. 23, 1994.

P. 82, *a member of their church knew right away it was them:* John Garriques, personal interview, Sept. 1994.

P. 83, *average responses are thirteen seconds long:* Timney, M. C. "The Discussion of Social and Moral Issues on Daytime Talk Shows: Who's Really Doing All the Talking." Unpublished master's thesis, Dept. of Communications, Ohio University, Mar. 1991, p. 42.

P. 83, *"bumper-sticker mentality":* Priest, P. "Self-Disclosure on Television: The Counter-Hegemonic Struggle of Marginalized Groups on *Donahue*." Unpublished doctoral dissertation, Dept. of Mass Communication, University of Georgia, 1992.

P. 86, *"Confession really is good for the soul"* (and other quotes in this paragraph): Newman, J. "Are They Crazy? Why Do People Tell All on Talk Shows?" *Cosmopolitan*, Aug. 1992, pp. 216–219.

P. 86, *"Guests put pressure on themselves"*: Diamond, J. "Life After Oprah," *Self*, Aug. 1994, pp. 122–125; p. 124.

P. 86, *extensive interviews with former guests*: Priest, P. "Self-Disclosure on Television: The Counter-Hegemonic Struggle of Marginalized Groups on *Donahue*." Unpublished doctoral dissertation, Dept. of Mass Communication, University of Georgia, 1992.

P. 87, *"that they're not 'freaks of nature'"*: John Garriques, personal interview, Sept. 1994.

P. 88, *no suspects had been arrested*: Wilson, Y. "Missing Girls' Moms Quiz Kidnap Suspect," *San Francisco Chronicle*, Feb. 5, 1993, p. A-25.

P. 88, *"You get caught up in it"*: Specter, M. "Marion Barry, Airing His Vices," *Washington Post*, May 14, 1991, p. D-1.

P. 89, *"Sure I pull toilet paper in half"*: Diamond, J. "Life After Oprah," *Self*, Aug. 1994, pp. 122–125; p. 125.

P. 89, *neurotic for fun and profit*: Stewart Fischoff, personal interview, Sept. 21, 1994.

P. 89, *"she was a wonderful personality in this disguise"*: Leonardi, M. "Darlene Cates Knows a Weighty Role When It's Offered," *Los Angeles Times*, Dec. 12, 1993, California sec., pp. 28, 32; p. 32.

P. 90, *"on the Morton Downey Jr. show the other day"*: Diamond, J. "Life After Oprah," *Self*, Aug. 1994, pp. 122–125; p. 125.

P. 90, *were lies—which was apparently the only statement that wasn't*: Benson, J. "Show Hoppers Making Hay on Syndie Talkers," *Variety*, Jan. 17, 1994, p. 33.

P. 91, *Once in custody*: Rosenberg, H. "Wanna Confess? Call Montel," *Los Angeles Times*, Mar. 25, 1994, pp. F-1, F-32.

P. 91, *"Lake's self-parodying talk-show circus"*: Lorando, M. "Fake Story Makes Waves on 'Lake.'" *New Orleans Times Picayune*, Nov. 28, 1994, p. 1.

P. 92, *attack on one of the other personalities:* Staff. "Exposing Themselves," *All Talk: The Talk Show Magazine*, Nov./Dec. 1994, pp. 28–30.

4

Experts

The Right Prop

Where would talk shows be without their experts? Counselors, doctors, recovery converts, psychologists, self-help authors, and lawyers are an essential part of the Talk TV tradition. Admittedly, some shows don't use experts and most don't even bring them on until the final few moments, but the "experts" play an important symbolic role, if not a real one, in the entire enterprise of Talk TV.

Experts represent the shows' credibility and commitment to solving tough problems. In fact, the very idea of having experts reinforces two central selling points for Talk TV. First, the problems they are dealing with are so difficult that none of the "average" audience (of course, this includes the host) really knows what to do about them. This is serious stuff. Second, the problems are not obscure issues that affect only a few unfortunate souls. These problems sustain experts and, therefore, entire fields of study. Viewers had better pay attention.

Janet Steele, Ph.D., an assistant professor of communications at the University of Virginia, has suggested that turning to external sources of authority is a common occurrence in television news programming. She stated, "Television speaks with the voice of authority, but television news people don't see themselves as authoritative sources." This problem is intensified on Talk TV, where incredibly complex problems are exposed and are in urgent need of resolution.

Phil Donahue underscored Steele's point when he stated,

"Nobody needs to take a test to be a journalist. Nobody needs to have a college degree. Nobody needs to appear before a board. Nobody needs to have a urine analysis. Nobody has to do anything. Everybody can be a journalist, including *moi*." One could hardly make a better case for needing to call in the experts. And in fact, experts are needed on Talk TV shows because so much of the content centers around complicated mental health issues and none of the current nationally syndicated hosts is a qualified mental health professional.

About 70 percent of talk shows include experts. Most often the experts are professionals from the fields of psychiatry, psychology, counseling, social work, law, and education. Shows also solicit lay experts, who are guests who lack specific professional training, but who have significant personal experience with the problem. In addition there are a large group of motivational speakers and self-help authors who use talk shows for publicity.

The topics covered on the show really dictate who will be considered for expert appearances. Clearly, some topics draw more attention, so talk shows look for people who specialize in hot topics. Experts in the areas of violence, sex, and especially violent sex are likely candidates. Professionals who understand children and family problems are also routinely sought. Producing a popular self-help book makes an expert especially attractive to a talk show.

Not only do experts provide technical information and helpful advice, they also, at times unwittingly, reinforce the legitimacy of the shows, support the image of the hosts, and contribute to the voyeuristic interest viewers have in the guests. A closer look at why the experts are recruited and how they are selected reveals how the shows use experts—both the concept of experts and their actual performance on the shows—to draw in viewers and maintain ratings.

How Do They Get There?

Experts are recruited by the same people who are responsible for securing guests. In fact, the expert and the guests are often sought as a package deal. In addition, the same tight, competitive schedules for finding guests also apply when identifying, screening, and signing experts. After the final decisions on who will be cast have been made, the expert gets about twenty-four to forty-eight hours' notice. Of course, plans may change many times, with shows being canceled, rescheduled, or taken off the air completely at the last minute.

Laurel Richardson, Ph.D., a professor of sociology and the author of *The New Other Woman*, pointed out what she called the "unpredictability principle" in selecting experts. As she defined it, this means that whoever or whatever is most interesting at the moment gets aired, and that can change at any time. With such frantic schedules, producers pursue what they want aggressively. The pressure to get the show on quickly but in an entertaining way also leads to certain priorities in selecting experts.

Becoming the Right Prop

The belief that Talk TV is educational or provides a service is furthered by the use of experts. Experts provide a voice of authority and objectivity in an environment that has been carefully crafted to appear highly democratic and subjective. Emotions rule on Talk TV. Everything is immediate and raw and everyone can have their say, until the expert comes on. The expert is used as a cooling element, introducing the levelheadedness of objectivity, reason, distance, "science."

Experts occupy, at least in theory, an honored place in Talk TV. The expert is there to summarize, clarify, and explain what we've just seen and to offer solutions. We must wait for their arrival or participation, yet we are frequently reminded of their presence. And then, as time is running out, if there is to be any resolution at all, we turn to the expert for answers.

Just knowing the expert is there can increase other participants' sense of freedom to say or ask anything. If a crisis erupts, the expert can handle it. So venting feelings or disclosing hidden traumas—

which often amounts to insulting others and shocking them with embarrassing secrets—heightens the sense that something therapeutic is happening. The expert's presence strengthens the illusion that the shows provide a useful service that benefits viewers.

From the show's perspective, of course, this is a very effective use of experts. Most of a program can be devoted to voyeurism. Then, in the final moments, when viewers may begin to distance themselves as they think of what's coming next, the show provides a taste of what it claims to be all about: information, education. Thus, viewers are left with the sense that it's been a worthwhile hour. In other words, experts are used to give the appearance of authority and credibility.

Even within the limits of hot topics, there are many experts to choose from. When producer Katy Davis went looking for an expert for a show on depression, she told Ellen McGrath, Ph.D., that she had interviewed fifty people before deciding on her for *The Oprah Winfrey Show*. Because McGrath was the author of *When Feeling Bad Is Good* and because she was the head of the American Psychological Association (APA) task force on "Women and Depression," she was an outstanding choice. Had she not accepted the invitation, however, it is likely the producers would have simply found someone else. And viewers would never have known the difference.

What can make the difference between being considered and being selected is "presentation"—how the information is packaged, in terms of the expert's manner of speaking and physical appearance. TV producers do not want a "talking head" that drones on about complexities, contradictions, and competing theories. Yet it is precisely that ability to understand and communicate complexities that constitutes expertise. What producers want, however, are experts who are appealing to viewers, and will provide concise, definitive "answers" that will fit the show's format.

Thus, there is a basic conflict between Talk TV and experts. The shows want experienced professionals, but they want them to be more commercial versions of themselves. That is, the experts must deliver quick and often glib sound bites. While the shows may profess to want state-of-the-art information, the young producers responsible for selecting experts have little understanding of the complexities of the mental health, legal, or educational fields they delve into. Thus to pick the right prop they select what sounds good to them.

Sometimes they select very qualified professionals who can say things succinctly. But producers also solicit pseudoexperts—people who have little or no training in the mental health field but who can speak in sound bites. Some go from show to show with eight-second solutions to everything. One has been on over 250 shows as an expert on everything from young people who murder, to work struggles, to infidelity, saying, "I deal with everything from the boardroom to the bedroom."

The point here is that producers generally care more about making a good show than about the quality of the expertise. In addition, production values and the demands of busy schedules are often at odds with careful preparation. If they happen to get some-one really qualified, that is fine, just so long as the results look good on TV. But first and foremost, producers are hired by the shows to find the right props.

Trying to Be TV Presentable

Talk show producers want experts who can manage well in front of a camera. Like all Talk TV participants, the experts must be enter-taining: quick, witty, and pleasing to watch. Hosts want experts who are personable and presentable, and have television savvy. Experts should, at a minimum, be somewhat physically attractive. The producers are not likely to welcome overweight and over-fifty professionals. They prefer experts to look good and sound good.

Developing scholarly expertise, however, usually does not engender a perky, commercially minded approach to one's subject, nor are experts likely to have the well-toned bodies of teenagers. Thus, there are competing interests from the start in trying to use scholars or experts to meet television industry standards of entertainment. Stuart Fischoff, Ph.D., a professor of psychology at California State University, Los Angeles, a past president of the APA's division of media psychology, and the West Coast correspondent for *Psychology Today*, summed up the problem in this way, "It is hard to find a psychologist who can speak on camera and be other than stunningly boring."

Fischoff is not alone is recognizing this problem. Many professionals are aware of their broadcast deficiencies. Many avoid television, and with good reason. There are plenty of things to be concerned about that have little or nothing to do with having expertise. Relatively trivial issues, like not looking good or not having a quick answer, take on grander proportions when millions of people are watching.

Some professionals are comfortable balancing the needs of the media with their professional expertise. Some are confident that they can do a good job with both their subject and their presentation. Gayle Delaney, Ph.D., the founding president of the Association for the Study of Dreams, is one such example. Delaney has had considerable experience with TV talk shows and is confident that she can provide useful information in a brief form.

"Everyone dreams at night, and I can help them understand a lot about the meaning and how to use that information in less than eight minutes." She described the characteristics she has that make her good on television. "I can help the producer with a hot topic, I know how to keep it lively and to get to the point with great illustrative examples that people can imagine."

Another very experienced talk show "expert" is Rob Freeman-Longo, the director of A Safer Society and an expert in the treatment of sex offenders. Freeman-Longo has a lot of talk show experience and is very clear about what he needs to do to get his message across to viewers: "You have to be highly assertive, willing to cut others off, and able to say things succinctly. You really can't rehearse, instead you have to pay absolute attention and jump in when you can." He wants the public to know that incarcerating sex offenders is expensive both financially and socially. Producers call him frequently. Oprah has even visited his treatment center and videotaped his group treatment sessions. He has learned to keep his message short and to the point. He never brings on his own clients, saying he doesn't see anything therapeutic in "allowing the audience and host to vent their frustrations in a public bashing." With the general public upset about sex offenders, he feels positive about using Talk TV to further his agenda.

Producing the "Goods"

The shows would have us believe, and many casual observers might agree, that the primary role of experts is to provide expertise. But as we can already see, producers prefer experts who can provide succinct, pithy answers that give the impression of expertise without all the bothersome and time-consuming details. They also prefer experts who can provide guests in addition to expertise. In fact, guests, because they are the centerpiece of the shows, can become what the shows most want experts to provide. This is best illustrated by situations such as the one described by Charlotte Kasl, Ph.D., the author of *Women, Sex, and Addiction*. Kasl said the producers for some talk shows asked her to find them guests when they did not even invite her to appear. She is not alone in feeling pushed by the shows to deliver the goods.

Laurel Richardson described the pressure in this way: "These producers know how to manipulate. It must be part of their job descriptions. They are very skilled and will do what is necessary to get what they want. They try guilt, getting angry, and acting horrified when you don't agree to everything they want." Oprah Winfrey's producers wanted Richardson to procure not only nine wives and their husbands, but also the "other women." In exasperation, Richardson turned these requests over to her book publicist (who, of course, benefited from her appearance).

Gayle Delaney was asked to solicit members from her educational dream group for *The Oprah Winfrey Show*. Within two days, the show repeatedly changed the numbers they wanted. It was off-again, on-again repeatedly for the guests who were selected and then told they were not needed. Similarly, when a producer for *Sally Jessy Raphael* called Nancy Steele, Ph.D., for a show on "Wives of Rapists," she was asked to be there in three days and to round up the wives and rapists as well. Steele said, "That is where I should have quit and insisted that I would only go on as a psychologist and not bring on this rapist and his wife. They were really at risk for public criticism and ridicule."

The calls back and forth to potential experts during the selection process introduce professionals to the competitive world of Talk TV. The priorities, motivations, and codes of ethics are quite different for mental health professionals and Talk TV producers. These differences can lead to resentment and dissatisfaction.

Richardson expressed dissatisfaction with Talk TV ethics and cited a particular incident that captures the essence of the problem. She had flown to Boston to do a television talk show and after "waiting for four hours in a room befouled with smoke, I learned I had been displaced by a new and preferred guest, the son of Bob Guccione, the publisher of *Penthouse*. I began to feel like an old Other Woman: entrapped. Waiting for phone calls that did not come, or came when I was not expecting them and had other things to do. My own moral commitments to being on time, following through, and doing what I agreed to do were not reciprocated. I felt expendable, misused, tricked, and angry."

Likewise, Stuart Fischoff described incidents in which he had been called as an expert for the shows, as well as incidents in which he had been contacted afterward to investigate problems that had resulted for guests on shows. What he described are clearly ethical problems for the profession, which we'll discuss in detail in Chapter Seven. We raise the point here simply to note that these problems are evident early in the process of selection, and that some experienced professionals are concerned about the pressure producers place on experts that have in turn led the experts to be "extremely mistrusting and cynical . . . there is no honor among the thieves. They will lie to you and lie to each other."

The initial courting and selection of experts foreshadow what lies ahead in their roles on the shows. Richardson provides an apt description of the process as "infantilization." "Like an infant, on the one hand, the expert is the center of attention, admired, and touted, and on the other, wholly dependent upon others." Separated from major supports and told what to do and when to do it, even fed and groomed by the show, the expert is both the center of the universe and separated from all normal responsibilities.

A Professional Performance

The hosts and guests all "care" about the problems. Caring is a requirement. In fact, they spend most of the show establishing their concern by discussing intimate details of the problems and their consequences. What is missing is some resolution for the problems or some direction for what to do about them. So "experts" are brought on to give us the "answers." Experts are also brought on to contribute to the entertainment value of the show. Together these two functions, providing answers and entertainment, define not only the factors that determine selection, but also how the shows define a professional performance.

Getting Ready

Appearing on television requires special preparation that is typically not a part of graduate training in mental health disciplines. As indicated by the recruitment and selection values, being a TV expert involves much more than academic expertise. Managing impromptu questions with flair, overcoming stage fright, and eliciting even more audience participation and interest—these are all critical skills for performing well under the lights.

After *The New Other Woman* was published, Richardson realized a major book tour required special attention. "Knowing that people are judged more on how they look and talk than on what they say focused my energy during the pre tour period on my presentation of self."

Richardson describes being keenly aware of how she was making herself over to become TV presentable. She began to have dreams about being at a cosmetic counter where a heavily made-up woman insisted on her accepting help with colors and creams. "Looking at the dream-message, I recognized that my fears were more than skin deep: I was afraid that persons I did not respect would reconstruct my persona and my research into their own image. My anxieties were that if I learned how to present myself for the media, I would lose the integrity of self, and that no matter how I tried to control the outcome, the media would 'make up' whatever it chose about me and the content of my research." Richardson's well-articulated fears clearly describe the anxiety of both being media ready and at the same time being true to one's work and oneself.

Most experts report having a respected colleague review and critique their overall presentation on videotape. Some hire other professionals to provide special training and contacts with media producers. James Windell, the author of several books on parenting, including *Eight Weeks to a Well-Behaved Child: A Failsafe Program for Toddlers Through Teens*, received training in how to present himself and his ideas. The firm he consulted, Media Relations, also negotiated contracts for him to appear on morning news, local talk shows, and *Donahue*.

Likewise, Nancy Steele was hired by the National Institute of Corrections in 1990 to train other professionals in how to manage the media. She pointed out that the training was helpful in preparing staff to deal with most media but talk shows present unique and special problems. She contrasted the accelerated pace of *Sally Jessy Raphael* with the five weeks she and Stone Phillips spent preparing information for a show on *Dateline*, a national news magazine program. Her *Dateline* experience led her to believe she would have similar opportunities to shape the presentation of her ideas on Talk TV. She readily admits she was wrong. Her expertise did not make an easy transition to Talk TV shows.

Many experts have extensive teaching and workshop experience that makes them very comfortable with public speaking. But just being comfortable with public speaking is not enough. Likewise, experience with print media or TV news is quite different than going on Talk TV. The fast pace, the unpredictable events, and the limited opportunity to speak all require additional skills. Some professionals with extensive media experience offer specialized training in the specific skills needed to communicate professional expertise to the general public via television. In addition, the APA's Media Psychology Division provides workshop training for interested professionals.

Welcome to the Show

The night before the taping, the expert is usually flown to the city where the talk show originates. A limousine transports him or her to the hotel, where vouchers are provided for all expenses. On the day of the taping, the expert is picked up at the hotel by another limousine and taken to the studio. Show staff are available to "do" the expert's hair and makeup. The assistant producer who arranged the show typically asks and answers any last-minute questions at this time as well.

Immediately prior to the appearance, the expert stays in the greenroom, sometimes alone and sometimes with guests. It is here that the host usually makes a brief appearance to get acquainted and to answer any final questions. Most experts report that the host avoids any conversation about the topic so that everything will seem unrehearsed and spontaneous when the show is taped.

Meeting the Guests

Experts are invited to the show with the presumption that they will supply information about the guests' problems. In order to effectively or ethically do that, experts must know something about the guests' unique situations. The extent of their familiarity with the guests, however, varies widely. This variation is of critical concern in terms of the expert's understanding and accuracy of information (the very reasons alleged for the appearance) and would seem to be important for viewers to know.

Mental health professionals who concede to producers' demands to provide guests often bring current or former clients. This is a questionable practice that we will discuss later; but suffice it to say for now that this routine has the potential to be exploitative. Given the nature of the therapeutic relationship, the expert should be quite familiar with not only the guests' problems but their characteristic style of coping, and what types of interventions are most likely to be effective. This kind of understanding requires not only academic training but a relationship with the person. Unfortunately, the second part of the equation is often ignored by both the shows and the experts.

James Windell was asked to appear as an expert on a Donahue show. The show's producer agreed to allow Mr. Windell to talk with the guests by phone prior to the show. He was assured that these people had important issues to discuss about their children's problems and felt pleased that the producer allowed him to assist in setting up the appearances. As a result, he told the families on the phone that he would be able to help them on the show. Once on the air, however, Windell felt that the agreement he had with the producer about what was going to happen was broken and what he had told the guests prior to the show was sabotaged. The entire *Donahue* show was devoted to uncovering and sensationalizing the problems, with no opportunity for solutions. He was not given the time to give the advice that he had assured the families he could provide. In an attempt to rectify the situation, he wrote them all letters after the show outlining the suggestions he would have provided if the time had been made available.

Some experts meet the guests for the first time on the stage. Barbara Schwartz, Ph.D., who appeared on *Jerry Springer*, met the guests (all parents of children who had been molested) on stage after Springer had riled up the audience with graphic descriptions of their children's abuse. The audience was screaming and yelling about the horror of these children's abuse. Then she was introduced as someone who opposed a new law that would allow communities to know if a sex offender was in their midst. Needless to say, both the audience and the guests were very hostile. Schwartz was set up to be in an antagonistic position with the guests. She had no prior time with these people to establish her understanding of the pain they had been through. Regardless of the fact that she had experience working with victims as well, she was targeted as an abuser and treated as such. Certainly this kind of situation limits the expert's ability to provide useful information to guests or viewers.

Occasionally, experienced experts will demand the opportunity to meet the guests in order to do at least an initial assessment of the problems bringing them to the show. Gayle Delaney described an incident with a producer for *Jenny Jones* that led her to threaten to leave the show right before the taping was scheduled. At the last minute, she was given a written description of a dream one of the guests was going to have her explain. Delaney was afraid the events in the dream may have signaled that the guest had been molested as a child, but she did not feel it was appropriate to get into such material for the first time on national TV.

The producer encouraged her to go ahead with the show despite her misgivings. However, Delaney informed the producer that not only would she not go on but the four other guests she had recruited would also not appear unless she had time alone with this woman before the show. Finally, the producer brought the woman to the greenroom but then didn't want to leave them alone. Again, Delaney insisted and prevailed in her conditions. Since the producers do not routinely set up such arrangements, it was up to this expert to insist on time for a preshow meeting. Most often, however, if the expert has not brought the guest, they have little or no opportunity to meet before the taping. This situation results in even seasoned professionals getting caught in questionable circumstances, such as those described by James Windell, Barbara Schwartz, and Gayle Delaney.

When a compromising incident is discovered, experts rarely refuse to proceed, having already committed to doing the show, and with little or no time remaining before the taping. Moreover, the pace of events is so quick and the situation so overwhelming that experts have to make split-second decisions about rather complicated ethical dilemmas. Thus, they are swept along with the general mode of operation for the show and are not likely to take opportunities to question policies or treatment of themselves or the guests. This step in the process sets the stage for what follows when the expert appears on camera.

Getting Labels

Just like guests, experts are labeled for easy identification. The labels typically identify experts by name and title and a short descriptor of the basis of the expertise, "Opposes sexual predator law" or "Relationship expert" or "Survived Abuse for 17 Years." Additionally, we may be shown book covers or video clips of products the experts are selling at the time. What we typically don't get, however, is any information about academic training, professional experience, theoretical orientation, or approach to working with people—which are, of course, exactly the kinds of things we must know in order to make informed choices about whether or not to trust their opinions and recommendations. But like every other aspect of Talk TV, we are asked and expected to accept what we are told at face value. We are told that those appearing are experts, and we are expected to believe it.

Time to Talk?

So what about the information these experts are supposedly there to present? Most of the experts who agree to appear assume that they will have the opportunity to provide important information. Lawrence Balter, Ph.D., the author of *Dr. Balter's Child Sense, Who's in Control? Dr. Balter's Guide to Discipline*, and *Not in Front of the*

Children, pointed out that most people get their information on how to deal with family problems from watching TV. He says they even get information from watching soap operas. The trick for the professionals is to figure out when and how they can fit in what they want the public to know about a particular issue or problem.

Typically, the experts remain in the greenroom for the first forty to fifty minutes of the show. They are not able to contribute to the ongoing flow of the conversation, let alone make comments that will explain what is going on. That role goes to the hosts, who comment and focus as they see fit. Talk show experts rarely get such an opportunity.

When they do come out, the stage may have nine or ten guests who are in some sort of conflict that most often includes very complicated situations. The experts are then expected to provide a summary and recommendation. If they attempt to do this before the final moments, they can be quickly reminded of their place. Nancy Steele said she tried to interrupt and interject her comments when she was on *Sally Jessy Raphael*. When she did so, Sally stopped the taping, looked directly at her, and said "Look, we haven't introduced you yet. You can't talk."

The average amount of time for an expert comment is thirteen seconds. The total time for all of their remarks takes up only 9 percent of the shows' total time. Compared to the host, who averages seven-second comments but 30 percent of the total time on air, the experts really have very little opportunity to present their points of view.

When It Works

There are times, however, when experts are able to provide some kind of valuable information. Sometimes they are introduced early in the show or are able to interrupt. Charlotte Kasl, the author of *Women, Sex, and Addiction*, said of her many talk show appearances, "You should not be afraid to jump in or else you might never get to talk."

Despite the appeal of Kasl's suggestion, assertiveness is not always sufficient. In fact, there are times when nothing goes unless the host okays it. Ellen McGrath appeared on an *Oprah* episode dealing with "Men Dumped by Pregnant Women." After listening to a family feud involving Becky (a pregnant woman), Becky's mother and father, and Greg, the estranged husband, Ellen McGrath interrupted. She said, "Oprah, if we go back and forth, we're not going to really get someplace with this." To which Oprah responded, "Please, let's get someplace."

On this show, McGrath was not only given permission to interrupt, she was also given the opportunity to explain. So after Becky finished describing why she wanted to "dump" Greg (the father of her unborn child), and after Becky's mother and father described how Greg had beaten and insulted Becky and how he probably wouldn't ever change, Oprah turned to McGrath and said, "I want you to meet Dr. Ellen McGrath; she is a clinical psychologist and author of the book *When Feeling Bad Is Good*. Thank you for joining us to help us out." The audience applauded and Oprah said, "Yes. What is going on here?" McGrath responded, "I think that Becky's really got a problem because Greg's not safe. Greg at this point is still trying to control Becky instead of controlling himself." Oprah: "That's always a problem." Applause, applause. Briefly but insightfully, this expert did get a chance to describe the action.

McGrath described doing another *Oprah* show on "Women and Depression." She said, "Oprah and I worked a partnership that got information out, lots of good information. It was TV at its best." She felt the program was done in a different way because "I was given more air time and I was able to present action strategies to manage depression that I thought were really helpful." She was actually on the stage from the beginning and was satisfied that the show was geared to "getting out good quality information through living stories." She described the focus of the show to be "problem solving instead of sensationalism." She was able to meet the guests before the program to check for vulnerabilities. She was encouraged to stay afterward to make sure questions were answered and referrals were given. Talking about that show with Oprah Winfrey, McGrath said, "We agreed we scored a home run on that one."

Lawrence Balter, a psychologist specializing in children and family, talked about doing an *Oprah* show during the Gulf War. He was on for the whole show and was able to address a wide range of parental concerns, such as worries over children's reactions, the potential for further violence, and the difficulties of families who were separated. He was able to respond to questions from both guests and audience and also felt he was able to make observations that would be useful to the public.

Stump the Expert

In contrast to the above, there often seems to be an almost love-hate relationship between the shows and their experts. On the one hand, shows actively recruit and promote professionals, suggesting that they will defer to their superior knowledge. On the other hand, the shows routinely set up these individuals to look foolish or to be unable to perform the role they have allegedly been assigned.

Before a commercial break on *Jenny Jones*, for example, Gayle Delaney learned of an attempt to surprise her on air. Jenny announced that when they came back there would be a surprise for Delaney. She discovered during the break that one of the guests—Tim, who was a member of a dream group she had conducted in California—had revealed a sexual dream about her during a preshow interview with a producer. The guest had been asked specifically about any sexual dreams he might have had about Delaney. The show sought this information so that Jenny Jones could surprise Delaney on the air. Although rightly irritated with the show's hidden agenda, Delaney decided to use the opportunity for her own purposes. She informed Jenny that she was willing to leave the show right in the middle of the taping unless her guest was comfortable with the revelation of that dream. Once Delaney was assured that the disclosure was all right with the guest, she used the opportunity to inform the public about the ability to have sexual dreams without also having an intent to act on them.

This example demonstrates that the show's basic attitude toward guests and experts is virtually the same: use them to increase ratings. The difference here, however, is that Delaney possessed the skills, assertiveness, and command of the subject to protect herself.

Others have not fared as well. When Laurel Richardson appeared on *Sally Jessy Raphael* to talk about her book *The New Other Woman*, she did not feel that she was able to communicate the message she had intended. She had wanted women to understand that while "other women" may think they are not involved in traditional roles (like waiting for marriage), they still end up in the same long-term traps. Her message emphasized that the strategies used to conceal the relationship increased the woman's dependence and reduced her power within it. The secrecy protected the interests of the male at the expense of the female. Yet in the show Sally "attacked the Other Woman who was sitting, camera front, on the stage. She riled up her Missouri studio audience. One woman, whose husband had six affairs that she knew of, said, 'I fight for what is mine. I kick. I scratch. I bite.' The audience cheered. Another said the Other Woman was mentally ill and needed to find God. Sally Jessy Raphael finally implied I was spearheading a movement of Other Women, or even creating the phenomenon."

Richardson summarized the experience: "I thought the show was dreadful, disempowering and divisive. But my publicist thought it was great—and that I was great—because I handled the conflict in a way which would generate interest in the book." Clearly she was TV presentable and did the job both producer and publisher expected, but the information she had intended was lost in that format.

After having the audience scream and yell at her, Barbara Schwartz felt her experience on *Jerry Springer* was "totally frustrating." "There was no chance to explain anything after Jerry had whipped the audience into a frenzy." She said, "What they wanted were warm bodies to fill up the five chairs on stage so that the audience could have someone to yell at." Even after the show, Schwartz felt concerned that someone from the audience might attack her: she and the attorney who appeared with her scurried away to hide from the audience as they came into the hall after the show. In retrospect, she realized they probably wouldn't have hurt her—but at the time she felt sufficiently menaced to hide in another room until they were all out of the hall.

Stuart Fischoff described his last TV appearance as an expert, which took place on Geraldo's "Women Who Marry Their Rapist." The guests presented extremely complicated situations, involving very painful feelings. Fischoff was not introduced until just before the final commercial break. During that break, Geraldo turned to him and said, "You have thirty seconds." Fischoff said, "At that point, I realized this was a joke and an information fraud for the public." There clearly was no opportunity to say anything meaningful on that topic in that format.

Why Go On?

Like all the other participants, experts have their own reasons for wanting to appear on Talk TV. Like the guests, they receive expenses, limousines, and occasionally reimbursement for lost wages. But typically they are not paid for their appearances. If they appear frequently, they must join the American Federation of Television and Radio Artists (AFTRA). Once they have joined the union, they can earn money from other television appearances. But the rationale for why an expert wants to appear on a nationally syndicated talk show varies.

I Have a Message

As we have seen, many of the experts who appear on these shows have information that they genuinely believe the public needs.

Ellen McGrath served as a national spokesperson for psychology in the media and has appeared often on *Today, Good Morning America, CBS This Morning, The Oprah Winfrey Show, Donahue, Nightline, Sally Jessy Raphael,* and *Sonya Live.* McGrath sees Talk TV as "having tremendous potential to reach people with important information they would not otherwise be able to obtain." She explains that "many people can't afford middle-class therapy" and therefore rely on other sources like television to find answers for problems in daily living. Aware that Talk TV has both the potential to inform the public and the constraints of media entertainment, she points out that Talk TV "can be both helpful and harmful to your health."

Leslie Accoca, a licensed marriage and family counselor who has extensive experience with women in prison, said, "I feel so frustrated that these women and girls are people with no voice. Their struggles need to be heard." She feels a deep commitment to communicating their problems, so when Rolonda Watts's producer called her to appear on the show, Leslie thought it might just be the opportunity she was looking for. Her experience on Talk TV was very frustrating, however—she was seated in the audience, never given time to provide the information she came prepared to present, and furthermore was horrified at what she saw as the mistreatment and misrepresentation of the guests. Nonetheless, she would be willing to try again. Her rationale for doing so is not at all unlike that expressed by many guests. She stated that she believes society needs to be informed about women and girls in prison and that TV talk shows provide the largest possible audience for her ideas.

Likewise, Nancy Steele is another committed professional who feels that she has information that would be important for the public to have. She ended up on *Sally Jessy Raphael* doing a show on "Wives of Rapists." She explained her reasons for doing so: "As the victim movement grew and as there was a 200–300 percent increase in the incarceration of sex offenders, I felt someone needed to get accurate information to the public about these people."

Selling Books

When authors publish popular psychological or self-help books, Talk TV producers are interested because the authors might attract viewers. The authors, and their publicists, are interested because the show might attract consumers. Thus, both participants are looking to benefit, but the results are mixed.

Gayle Delaney has been appearing on talk shows since 1979, when she first appeared with Oprah on Baltimore's *People Are Talking*. At that time, she and Oprah appeared on stage together, without other guests, and took questions from the audience. Oprah had read Delaney's book and talked to the audience about how much it helped her to understand her own dreams. Oprah's early endorsement as well as Delaney's numerous other appearances may have contributed to her success. But while talk show publicity may have enhanced sales in the past, Delaney no longer sees the shows as having that power.

Likewise, Charlotte Kasl was contacted by the shows following the release of her book on *Women, Sex, and Addiction*. She appeared on *Donahue*, *Sally Jessy Raphael*, *Geraldo*, and many other local talk and news programs. However, she did not feel that her appearances drew attention to her book or to her as a potential resource for more Talk TV. Her experience was reiterated by Laurel Richardson, author of *The New Other Woman*, who also did not feel that Talk TV helped book sales.

On the other hand, in 1979, Harry Waters of *Newsweek* magazine reported that *Donahue* had replaced *Today* as the most effective "let's meet the author showcase." He estimated that a single appearance on *Donahue* was worth fifty thousand book sales. The shows' perceived power to turn books into best-sellers simply by discussing them on air has only continued to grow. Oprah Winfrey has been credited with the success of Marianne Williamson's *A Return to Love* and Robert Waller's *The Bridges of Madison County*, not to mention *In the Kitchen with Rosie*, her own personal chef's cookbook.

But the marriage between Talk TV and authors is not always a happy one. Often it has been arranged to meet the interests of the show and the publisher, leaving the author feeling squeezed in between. Laurel Richardson described the pressure from publishers in this way: "Books get to audiences because of publicity about them. Publicity is accomplished though the media. My role as a trade book author was to meet the media over and over again."

As competition has increased and the shows have become increasingly bizarre, experts who go on primarily to promote books have been affected. Pulitzer Prize–winning author David Halberstam used to call *Donahue* "a televised Ph.D. course." Now he says that *Donahue* has "lost its soul." Likewise, Art Buchwald used to receive regular invitations to talk about his essays and books on *Donahue*. But now "Buchwald claims he can't get an invitation . . . unless he gets a sex-change operation."

Fifteen Minutes of Fame

The allure of national television is strong for some professionals as well. Charlotte Kasl talked about not really liking the title "Women Who Love Sex," which Donahue's producers proposed for her appearance, but said, "Hey, I wanted to be on *Donahue*. . . . This is a way to get to people 4 to 10 million at a time."

Stuart Fischoff, who has been on all the major talk shows, says "I enjoyed the glitter for awhile and then it wore off." He will now only do shows where he can control the information and so consequently avoids Talk TV, saying, "I don't do it anymore—it has become a very sleazy circus." Nevertheless, he understands the allure of TV and that professionals are not immune. Having experienced the seduction himself, he said, "Psychologists are so thrilled by the idea of being on TV they tend to suspend good judgment and good taste."

Moral Dilemmas for Professionals

Many of the professionals we interviewed felt some concern over what the shows want them to do and what they, as mental health professionals, know to be responsible practice. This comes as no surprise. From the outset, mental health professionals and Talk TV producers are guided by different professional priorities as well as different ethical standards. In attempting to work with the shows, experts often get involved in potentially compromising situations.

The shows' practices and procedures are driven by their interest in ratings. And as they have repeatedly stated themselves, the prevailing ethic is to do whatever it takes to get those ratings. This is hardly an atmosphere that fosters reflection about the moral dilemmas created by wanting to get information to the public while at the same time protecting individual rights to privacy and dignity. In fact, the producers are rewarded for disregarding those kinds of concerns. If they lie or manipulate to get what they want, they are rewarded by their profession with bigger contracts and more opportunities to do the same.

Mental health professionals are also rewarded. They obtain national recognition, increased book sales, increased demand for services, and invitations to appear on other shows. But such benefits are secondary to the real goals of the mental health profession and its codes of conduct. Prevailing mental health ethics have not come about in order to produce these benefits. Instead, the codes are designed to protect citizens and ensure appropriate care. Such codes govern mental professionals even when they enter the world of Talk TV, where a different code exists.

Certainly, the responsibility for adhering to accepted mental health practice lies with the professional, not the show. However, it is clear that left to themselves many professionals, even conscientious and reflective individuals, are having difficulty sorting out how to balance the two different sets of priorities and codes. And while it is clearly not Talk TV's responsibility to chaperon experts, it most certainly is the professions' duty to provide a clear framework for interacting with other professionals, including TV producers.

The pressure that many experts feel to both educate the public in the service of their profession and to conform to the shows' methods of operating is a subject mental health professionals need to confront. A wide range of dilemmas faces the individual professional, which in turn impacts the entire profession. There are existing codes of ethics that address many of these issues. We will discuss those professional codes and standards in detail in Chapter Eight, but want to outline here some of the problems created for a professional who agrees to be a Talk TV expert:

- Pressure to find and bring on guests from the expert's practice compromises the therapeutic relationship. The shows want guests with problems, and mental health practitioners are a ripe source. However, approaching current or former clients with a request to appear on television creates unique problems for both the client and the professional. It is assumed that recommendations and suggestions are devised to aid clients in solving their problems, so even the gentlest of requests to appear on Talk TV can only be received as beneficial advice. Even though the professional asks permission, the client is in a position of vulnerability established by the professional relationship. Therefore, the client is likely to acquiesce in hopes of benefiting either through self-improvement or by pleasing the therapist.

- Professionals may inadvertently or improperly release confidential information. For example, the professional may have obtained the guest's permission to discuss highly sensitive matters, but others involved with the client, who could be identified through association, may not have given permission. This is particularly troublesome if the others involved were also clients at one time. Since the profession relies on confidentiality as one of its core assurances, this dilemma is perhaps one of the most serious problems for the profession.

- Professionals are sometimes aware that a guest is troubled and in need of specialized help, which in their judgment will not be obtained through appearing on a TV talk show. Moreover, the professional may suspect that appearing on the show may actually worsen the problem.

For example, the professional may be asked to appear with a family in severe turmoil. After meeting with the guests right before taping, the professional could detect indications that the turmoil will only be worsened by disclosing painful secrets on the air. It could even appear that spite and revenge are the motivating factors, not seeking help. Without sufficient time for a thorough family assessment, however, it's impossible for the professional to confirm such suspicions. This leaves the expert in a position of making recommendations without an adequate assessment.

• Professionals are often aware that guests have been encouraged to have unrealistic expectations for help. With no real contact or relationship established, most professionals consider it unwise to offer specific advice on the air. Nonetheless, the professional is also often aware that the guest was promised on-air therapy.

• Professionals have no control over editing of the shows. They may realize later that editing has skewed the representation of guests or issues, or their own remarks, yet they have no influence or control over how the show is presented.

• Shows do not adequately describe credentials. Instead, they use labels that are often vague or misleading. This causes problems for viewers who do not have enough information to make distinctions about the qualifications of the expert.

• The shows encourage personal accounts to keep the atmosphere friendly but fail to distinguish such remarks from professional advice. The result is that casual comments not intended as professional judgments may be misconstrued as expert advice.

• After an appearance, professionals may be in a position of knowing that the guests need professional debriefing. This presents two separate but related problems. First, the professional may not have allotted sufficient time to follow up with guests and may therefore be unable to do so. Second, the debriefing may require professional expertise beyond the scope of the professional's practice and therefore it may be inappropriate to provide such services. Both cases, however, can result in professionals questioning what their obligations are in locating follow-up services for guests. The question of whose responsibility it is to get help remains trouble-some. Is it the professional who knows there is a problem? Or the show, which clearly wants to use the person? If guests do get help from the show, they are often asked to come back with the profes-sionals to give testimonials. This is an unethical practice if the tes-timonials are solicited by mental health professionals.

• Professionals are asked to render "sound" professional opin-ions, summations, and recommendations—but given virtually no time in which to do so. Attempts to provide information in a lim-ited amount of time can result in superficial, generic statements that ring of "common sense" and nothing more. This can leave viewers disappointed and the profession sullied.

These dilemmas and more are what mental health profession-als face when they step into an arena where they have very little control. In the next chapters, we will discuss in detail the problems created by Talk TV for viewers, guests, and the mental health pro-fession. These problems are inextricably tied to each other. All the problems created for viewers and guests also represent problems for the profession because of the role that experts take on when they accept offers to appear on these shows. The problems are not minor and it is incumbent upon the mental health profession to take a leading role in addressing them. Without such effort, the profes-sion must bear the burden of failed responsibility and diminished credibility.

Notes

P. 97, *"Television speaks with the voice of authority"*: Steele, J. "Why Do Television's Academic Experts So Often Seem Predictable and Trivial?" *Chronicle of Higher Education*, Jan. 3, 1990, p. B-2.

P. 98, *"Everybody can be a journalist, including moi"*: McDougal, D. "Don-ahue's Dilemma: Balancing Truth, Trash," *Los Angeles Times*, Jan. 28, 1990, California sec., p. 83.

P. 98, *About 70 percent of talk shows:* Timney, M. C. "The Discussions of Social and Moral Issues on Daytime Talk Shows: Who's Really Doing All the Talking?" Unpublished master's thesis, Dept. of Communications, Ohio University, Mar. 1991, p. 42.

P. 100, *for the Oprah Winfrey Show:* Ellen McGrath, personal interview, Sept. 20, 1994.

P. 102, *"other than stunningly boring":* Stuart Fischoff, personal interview, Sept. 21, 1994.

P. 102, *"I can help the producer with a hot topic":* Gayle Delaney, personal interview, June 22, 1994.

P. 103, *feels positive about using Talk TV to further his agenda:* Rob Freeman-Longo, personal interview, Dec. 7, 1994.

P. 103, *"These producers know how to manipulate":* Laurel Richardson, personal interview, July 7, 1994.

P. 104, *"That is where I should have quit"* (and other information from Steele in this paragraph): Nancy Steele, personal interview, Sept. 23, 1994.

P. 104, *"waiting for four hours":* Richardson, L. "Disseminating Research to Popular Audiences: The Book Tour," *Qualitative Sociology,* Summer 1987, *10*(2), 164–176; p. 173.

P. 104, *"extremely mistrusting and cynical":* Stuart Fischoff, personal interview, Sept. 21, 1994.

P. 105, *"Like an infant":* Richardson, L. "Disseminating Research to Popular Audiences: The Book Tour," *Qualitative Sociology,* Summer 1987, *10*(2), 164–176; p. 167.

P. 105, *"people are judged more on how they look and talk":* Richardson, L. "Disseminating Research to Popular Audiences: The Book Tour," *Qualitative Sociology,* Summer 1987, *10*(2), 164–176; p. 165.

P. 106, *"Looking at the dream-message"*: Richardson, L. "Disseminating Research to Popular Audiences: The Book Tour," *Qualitative Sociology,* Summer 1987, *10*(2), 164–176; p. 168.

P. 106, *received training in how to present himself:* James Windell, personal interview, Oct. 3, 1994.

P. 106, *transition to Talk TV shows:* Nancy Steele, personal interview, Sept. 23, 1994.

P. 111, *information from watching soap operas:* Lawrence Balter, personal interview, Sept. 26, 1994.

P. 111, *"Look, we haven't introduced you yet"*: Nancy Steele, personal interview, Sept. 23, 1994.

P. 111, *present their points of view:* Timney, M. C. "The Discussion of Social and Moral Issues on Daytime Talk Shows: Who's Really Doing All the Talking?" Unpublished master's thesis, Dept. of Communications, Ohio University, Mar. 1991, p. 42.

P. 111, *"or else you might never get to talk"*: Charlotte Kasl, personal interview, Aug. 29, 1994.

P. 112, *"It was TV at its best"*: (and other quotes in this paragraph): Ellen McGrath, personal interview, Sept. 20, 1994.

P. 113, *useful to the public:* Lawrence Balter, personal interview, Sept. 26, 1994.

P. 114, *the message she had intended:* Laurel Richardson, personal interview, July 7, 1994.

P. 114, *'I fight for what is mine'*: Richardson, L. "Disseminating Research to Popular Audiences: The Book Tour," *Qualitative Sociology,* Summer 1987, *10*(2), 164–176; p. 171.

P. 114, *"I thought the show was dreadful"*: Richardson, L. "Disseminating Research to Popular Audiences: The Book Tour," *Qualitative Sociology,* Summer 1987, *10*(2), 164–176; p. 171.

P. 115, *all out of the hall:* Barbara Schwartz, personal interview, Sept. 17, 1994.

P. 115, *"I realized this was a joke":* Stuart Fischoff, personal interview, Sept. 21, 1994.

P. 116, *Talk TV "can be both helpful and harmful to your health":* Ellen McGrath, personal interview, Sept. 20, 1994.

P. 116, *"I feel so frustrated":* Leslie Accoca, personal interview, June 23, 1994.

P. 116, *"As the victim movement grew":* Nancy Steele, personal interview, Sept. 23, 1994.

P. 117, *worth fifty thousand book sales:* Waters, H. "The Talk of Television" *Newsweek,* Oct. 29, 1979, pp. 76–82, p. 76.

P. 117, *her own personal chef's cookbook:* Lannon, L. "Oprah's Seal of Approval," *Detroit News and Free Press,* July 3, 1994, p. 1.

P. 118, *"Books get to audiences because of publicity":* Richardson, L. "Disseminating Research to Popular Audiences: The Book Tour," *Qualitative Sociology,* Summer 1987, *10*(2), 164–176; p. 165.

P. 118, *"gets a sex-change operation":* McDougal, D. "Donahue's Dilemma: Balancing Truth, Trash," *Los Angeles Times,* Jan. 28, 1990, California sec., p. 84.

P. 118, *"Hey, I wanted to be on Donahue":* Charlotte Kasl, personal interview, Aug. 29, 1994.

P. 118, *"I enjoyed the glitter for awhile":* (and other quotes in this paragraph): Stuart Fischoff, personal interview, Sept. 21, 1994.

5

Problems for Viewers

"Panem et circenses!" Ancient Romans believed that people were satisfied as long as they had bread and circuses. And their circuses were both gruesome and popular. On the first day the Colosseum opened in A.D. 80, nine thousand animals were slaughtered as part of the show for a crowd of eighty thousand cheering spectators. Gladiators fought to the death with these beasts and with one another. Christians, a disposable minority, were thrown to the lions for entertainment. And the crowds came back for more.

Two thousand years later, the crowd yelled, "Why don't you cut his balls off?" and "Kill, kill, kill!" These people weren't at the Colosseum, however, they were in the audience of a TV talk show. The transfixing power of sudden devastation runs deep throughout human history. Our desire for that particular blend of terror, amazement, and awe that we can get only from the deep suffering of other people is just as strong now as it ever was, even if our "circuses" are less fatal.

Tabloid character assassinations have replaced public executions (though Phil Donahue tried to offer the real thing, unsuccessfully suing for the chance to broadcast a recent execution). The Christians have been replaced by the emotionally wounded or the socially outcast. "Psychic demons" stand in for the lions. And while the show is less bloody, the crowd is bigger than ever and roaring for more. The seating capacity appears to be unlimited. All one needs to do, in any bus station, airport, bar room, dorm room, or living room, is tune in Talk TV.

Shows that give viewers a chance to watch trouble and strife, from murderous teenagers to sisters who sleep with each other's husbands, are enormously popular. Talk TV also brings fairground-style freak shows into every home, and viewers lap them up. It seems that viewers only want to see and hear about problems. Most of the shows that have attempted to focus on positive topics have either dropped in the ratings or gone off the air completely. It is clear that viewers will tune in if there's trouble. What is not clear is what happens to us individually and collectively as a result of so many millions of people watching so many thousands of hours of troubled talk.

The early years of Talk TV accomplished some very important tasks. Information that was previously taboo or accessible only to those who had already sought professional help was suddenly made available to the general public. This made it possible for many people to finally understand that they were not alone, that help was available, and that differences could be respected by talking and listening.

Phil Donahue and Oprah Winfrey have performed an important public service by helping unveil many of America's best kept secrets. Naomi Wolf, the author of *The Beauty Myth*, and *Fire with Fire*, explains their contribution this way: "[Talk Shows did] something absolutely unique among our cultural institutions: that is, they treat[ed] the opinions of women of all classes, races, and educational levels as if they mattered . . . That daily act of listening, whatever its shortcomings, made for a revolution in what women were willing to ask for; the shows daily conditioned otherwise unheard women into the belief that they were entitled to a voice." Enormous credit for providing a platform for the voices of so many who needed to be heard belongs to these two hosts. We can all thank them for raising the American consciousness on many important topics, including domestic violence, child abuse, and other crucial problems.

But those pioneering days are over. As the number of shows has increased and the ratings wars have intensified, the manner in which issues are presented has changed. The shows now openly encourage conflict, name calling, and fights between the guests and the audience. Producers set up underhanded tricks and secret revelations. Hosts instruct guests to reveal their anger with "Let's fight it out!" The camera and our attention is turned to conflict, not resolution.

Consequently, it is our contention that in its current form Talk TV creates more problems than benefits for viewers. As we have seen, the more dramatic and bizarre the problems the better it is for the shows. The mental health experts are brought on to legitimize the discussion and offer "professional" advice about resolving the problem. But since all of this takes place in an entertainment-driven, one-hour format, problems are exaggerated to heighten the drama and solutions are simplified to squeeze into the final moments of the shows. Consequently, mixed messages, distorted representations, inaccurate information, and unrealistic solutions often result in problems for viewers.

Millions of people tune in every day, many of them perhaps intending only to be entertained. However, all of them, no matter what their motivation for watching, absorb some part of the message. And even though the stated goal of Talk TV is informing the public, the amount of inaccurate information they give us about our own and others' problems is staggering.

There are a wide variety of ways in which the shows can cause problems. Essentially, these problems are the result of three broad categories of ill-conceived tactics:

- Providing bad lessons in mental health
- Offering bad advice and no resolutions for problems
- Reinforcing stereotypes rather than defusing them

Bad Lessons in Mental Heath

There is nothing inherently wrong with wanting to shock viewers, or with providing disturbing information about problems we wish would go away. But when we are given information relating to mental health that is directly or indirectly supported by representatives of the mental health profession, the information should be valid. Viewers ought to be able to trust that they are not being deceived. Admittedly, one of the problems of trying to provide mental health information on television is the difficulty of keeping it manageable while still attempting to provide something of use. Unfortunately, the clichés, exaggerations, and inflated statistics that Talk TV provides do not achieve that balance and often seriously misinform viewers.

The primary focus of Talk TV has always been to entertain and to do so by using sexual, familial, and personal problems. This leads to a predictable distortion of events, emotion, and truth. Producers claim viewers want shows that sizzle—so that's exactly what they produce. But all that sizzling means something's getting burned. And that something is mental health information.

Distorting Normality

Although Talk TV shows are all about problems, they also indirectly present viewers with a picture of normality. The shows set themselves up as reliable sources for information about what's really going on in America. And, in fact, they often cover what sound like common problems with work, love, and sex. But the information presented about these "normal" problems is skewed and confusing. Routine problems are exaggerated almost beyond recognition and extremely unusual problems are presented as though they are common. Common problems such as depression and anxiety are rarely presented, yet these disorders affect millions. On the other hand, more exciting but less common problems involving sex-change operations and serial murders are presented so often they become clichés.

When ordinary problems *are* dealt with, they are transformed. Work problems, supposedly common to us all, become "fatal office feuds," "back-stabbing co-workers," and "financial disasters." Problems concerning love, sex, or romance become "marriage with a fourteen-year-old," "women in love with the men who shoot them," or "man-stealing sisters." The hosts' constant reminders that the guests are "average" people with "common" problems certainly have the potential to create confusion for viewers. The lines between what is bizarre and alarming and what is typical and inconsequential are blurred.

Talk TV shows suggest that marrying a rapist, having a defiant teen, or discovering a cross-dressing neighbor are catastrophes about to happen to everyone. On an episode of *Sally Jessy Raphael* titled "Wives of Rapists," for example, Sally said to the woman on stage, "How would you ever know that this quiet man was a rapist? He could be anyone." As Sally described him, we were shown family pictures of him with his children. The wife cried as she described the quiet and angry withdrawal that preceded his rape of an eighty-year-old neighbor. Sally responded, "My husband withdraws when he is angry too."

This episode involves a number of potentially dangerous elements. First, the manner in which the topic is presented suggests that women are generally at considerable risk of marrying rapists. And while it is true that many rapists are married, it is not true that most married or marriageable men are rapists. Additionally, while it is true that wives might have a difficult time determining if they are married to a rapist, there was little discussion of what factors, other than being quiet and angry, might have been present to indicate that the man had a problem. Moreover, the implication that "quiet and angry" husbands might actually be rapists in disguise is of little use other than to inflame already strained relationships.

Day in and day out, the shows parade all the myriad traumas, betrayals, and afflictions that could possibly befall us. What can follow is the creeping sense that America is not the home of the brave, but of the depraved. And it is this sense that things are bad all over, not in terms of world politics but in terms of home and hearth, that is one of the most damaging messages viewers get from Talk TV. Normality is lost in an artificially crafted sea of problems. Viewers can be left with the notion that everyone is really quite sick—another related problem we think Talk TV creates for viewers.

Exaggerating Abnormality

Talk shows exaggerate abnormality in two different but often simultaneous ways. The shows suggest that certain problems are more common than they actually are, thus exaggerating their frequency. The shows also embellish the symptoms and outcomes of problems, thus exaggerating their consequences. Both of these distortions serve to inflate the problems' significance in the minds of viewers and serve the shows' desire to "make it sizzle."

In actuality, relatively few people are likely to be abducted as children, join a Satanic cult in adolescence, fall in love with serial rapists, marry their cousins, hate their own race, get sex changes in midlife, or become strippers at age eighty. But these unusual problems are presented over and over again in the endless stream of Talk TV, repeated so often that the resulting familiarity suggests that they are, in fact, quite likely to occur. Average viewers can't help but come away with very distorted notions about the frequency of mental health problems.

Sally Jessy Raphael, for example, did a show about incest during which she informed viewers that there are forty to sixty million survivors of incest in the United States. By definition, incest does not include survivors of nonfamilial sexual abuse. Yet even without those figures, Sally's estimate indicates that one in four Americans has been a victim of incest. The actual figure is debated in mental health journals, but it was presented to viewers as if it were an indisputable fact.

Shows also present generic information as though it were definitive. Quite often lists of symptoms meant to help viewers identify problems are presented without clear explanations. Viewers are informed, for example, that the indications of sexual abuse include overreacting to change, leg and back pain, sexual dreams, memory loss, seeking approval and affirmation, taking oneself too seriously, and fear of sexual involvement. While many survivors of sexual abuse may experience these symptoms, such symptoms are also likely to stem from a wide variety of more common problems.

Exaggerations of frequency, coupled with vague definitions, prime viewers to believe that the mildest of hints of a problem forewarn of something very serious and potentially disastrous. Considering the shows on incest alone, the potential for harm is alarming. The insufficient explanations may leave fathers thinking they shouldn't engage in normal caregiving tasks, such as bathing their baby daughters. Wives may be encouraged to become suspicious of husbands who want time alone with teenage daughters. Young adults who are appropriately anxious or confused about their first sexual encounters may conclude they have hidden incestuous histories. And parents who are fighting legal battles over child custody may be tempted to cite the same vague symptoms heard on talk shows as evidence for their cases.

Perhaps the best example of how Talk TV has taken a relatively obscure, even questionable phenomenon and transformed it into a standard household feature is *multiple personality disorder*, MPD, more accurately called "dissociative identity disorder."

When most abnormal psychology textbooks discuss multiple personality disorder, they include descriptions of the early childhood conditions that could produce this problem—but they also point out the possibility of *iatrogenic illness*. Iatrogenic illnesses are produced by the very treatments used to "cure" them. And in fact, it is very rare to find people who think they have multiple personalities who have not also been treated with hypnosis. Hypnosis requires a high level of suggestibility, and once hypnotized, such people are even more open to further suggestions. As a result, many professionals believe that it is the process of hypnosis that actually creates the condition. Other professionals claim hypnosis is the cure. The media's interest, in addition to the suggestible nature of the individuals, is also cited as a potential cause for the overdiagnosis of this disorder. Textbooks also point out that when there is the potential for "secondary gain," such as getting out of jail or some other dilemma, MPD is very appealing because patients can claim to have no knowledge of actions they would rather not admit to because "someone else" did them.

These issues, however, are not what makes MPD appealing to Talk TV. An exceedingly different picture of multiple personality disorder takes shape in the hands of Leeza Gibbons, Sally Jessy Raphael, Geraldo, and Oprah.

Leeza Gibbons invited actress Roseanne Barr and writer Trudy Chase to appear. Both women claim to have MPD. Roseanne reported that she has twenty-one personalities and Trudy claimed to have ninety-two. Roseanne presented a positive characterization of her disorder, stating: "It's a gift that allows you to be multiply gifted." She pointed out that "sometimes they [the personalities] change and sometimes their names change, but I'd never do anything weird or frightening." With Trudy, it was very difficult to understand how she managed to keep track of her ninety-two personalities long enough to count them, not to mention write a book.

Oprah Winfrey aired a show called "MPD: The Syndrome of the '90s," during which she "informed" her viewers that "we used to think that it was rare, but it's not rare. It's not any rarer than child abuse, which isn't rare at all." While she is correct that child abuse is not rare, the frequency of MPD does not parallel child abuse, nor was the controversy around the MPD diagnosis reported on her show. Geraldo did bring on an expert to briefly discuss the controversy about MPD for "Investigating Multiple Personalities: Did the Devil Make Them Do It?" He introduced his guest, however, as a "professional naysayer." Apparently Dr. Underwager had earned this title because he had the audacity to question the diagnosis of Kayla, who claimed to have four hundred personalities, and Kathleen, who claimed to have eight hundred. Sally Jessy Raphael "informed" her followers that "Most multiple personality disorders, unfortunately, go undiagnosed. So this could be someone you know." Her show also included warnings about how children have it but go unnoticed and how therapists "really don't catch on."

These shows were all very dramatic and entertaining, but from a mental health perspective also quite disturbing and dangerous. Viewers were not adequately informed that there is considerable controversy over this diagnosis. The possible reasons for the shows' oversights are disconcerting: either the shows didn't know that the disorder is controversial, didn't care that it is, or even worse, assumed that because of the tongue-in-cheek manner in which the guests discussed their disorders no one would take it seriously anyway. It is interesting to note how these shows work to create interest in a disorder, present it as an exciting eccentricity, and then tell viewers that anyone could have it. The subtle mockery of mental health problems is a serious concern, which we will discuss later on in this chapter. Let it suffice here to state that these particular shows, like many others, present a clear example of multiple problems but not multiple personalities. Perhaps if MPD is indeed the "syndrome of the 90s" we can all thank Talk TV for helping to make it so.

In much the same way that information concerning MPD has been presented in a sensationalized yet oversimplified fashion, information about other serious problems is likewise dangerously generic. It can be so generic, in fact, that viewers can come away with the impression that any fluctuations in mood, memory, or life satisfaction are signs of deep-rooted problems rather than the ordinary experiences they generally are.

Additionally, Talk TV presents all issues with the same level of seriousness, concern, and interest. Regardless of the frequency of a problem, very little information is ever provided to help viewers place the problem in perspective. The result can be that regular viewers come away thinking that people are more disturbed, unbalanced, or troubled than they really are.

Over thirty years ago, in *The Myth of Mental Illness*, Thomas Szasz outlined the dangers of psychiatrists persuading the public that behavioral excesses are diseases. More recently (in 1986), he and two colleagues noted the role that Talk TV plays in furthering that myth. Specifically, they objected to Donahue's comment that "we have an awful lot of people out there who are suffering biochemical disorders of the brain for which they have no responsibility." They described several of Donahue's early shows about the "disease" of addiction. The overuse of the term *addiction* bothered them, particularly when it was used to talk about sexual behavior, gambling, working, exercise, and shopping—all of which had been labeled as addictions on talk shows. They also raised serious concerns about encouraging the public to believe that any problematic behavior could and should be excused by attributing it to psychological problems beyond a person's control. In other words, nearly ten years ago there was a warning against the growing trend on TV to encourage people to deny responsibility. Unfortunately, producers did not listen.

Denying Responsibility

With their incessant focus on individual problems, television talk shows are a major contributor to the recent trend of elevating personal concerns to the level of personal rights and then affording those "rights" infinitely more attention than their accompanying responsibilities. In other words, Talk TV helps maintain "A Nation of Whiners" (the title given to a *Crossfire* episode)—a nation in which everyone is entitled but no one is obligated.

Every day, we see guest after guest elaborate the ways in which their rights have been violated. Without a doubt, many of the guests have indeed been wronged, often seriously. But almost none of the guests ever talks about responsibility and rarely are the guests asked to do so. In order to give the appearance of being tough on responsibility, guests are brought on who have committed villainous acts (most often against other guests). Such guests serve as the token whipping boys and allow the host and audience to gratuitously "confront" the offenders about their wrongdoing and responsibilities. But these tirades never lead to an understanding of accountability; instead, they only serve to heighten outrage and defensiveness, which in turn leads to more excuses that offset any real culpability. Little to no time is devoted to discussing responsibilities or how to fulfill them.

Furthermore, the alleged offenders almost always refute their accountability with revelations that they too were previously wronged or "victimized," and therefore are not responsible. On *Sally Jessy Raphael*, a man appeared on stage with roses for the daughter he had sexually molested. To explain his wrongdoings, he revealed that he had been homosexually molested when he was five. He summed it up with, "I'm on this show too! I need help; I'll go through therapy." His revelation was met with a round of applause from the audience, which only moments before had been set up to despise him for his behavior.

His sudden turnaround was not unusual. In fact, viewers rarely see guests admit error early in the show, but a reversal often occurs with just a few minutes remaining. This works well for the shows because they need the conflict to move steadily to a crescendo before the final "go to therapy" resolution. But before that, and for most of the show, viewers are treated to lots of conflict and a heavy dose of pseudopsychological explanations that are actually nothing more than excuses, and often lame ones at that.

This elevation of rights over responsibilities is problematic for viewers in a number of ways. It encourages viewers to focus on what others have or have not done as the source of their problems: *other* people are responsible. While this approach to resolving problems might initially seem appealing and comforting, it can actually increase feelings of despair and helplessness. When responsibility is completely lifted and shifted to others, the power to do anything other than complain goes with it. So while the shows might suggest that having the right to point the finger at others is the way to feel better, claiming one's share of responsibility may be more likely to produce useful change.

Cloning Pathology: The Copycat Syndrome

According to an old saying, "A little learning is a dangerous thing." It means that when situations or circumstances are complicated, attempts to handle the whole thing when only part of it is understood can result in real trouble for all involved. As we have seen,

Talk TV attempts to blur the line between the problems the shows depict and the ones likely to trouble viewers. This creates problems for viewers in two important ways. First, people who do have mental health problems are burdened by the sensationalized images created on Talk TV. Second, people who have mild problems are invited to exaggerate and sensationalize them, by copying problems "as seen on TV."

Many people who watch Talk TV have suffered from the same or similar problems as those depicted on the show. Michelle, a viewer who wrote to us, described how she discovered that other people had experienced events similar to those she had suffered as a child. She said, "I discovered from watching The Phil Donahue Show that there is a name for the general experience I had as a child. I was watching one afternoon as several women discussed their father's sexual abuse of them. . . . I felt a kinship with people who examined what had happened to them in order to understand who they were . . . for a long time I kept watching talk shows hoping to have that experience again. I never did. Instead, after several years of watching talk shows I began to feel that my own experiences were being denigrated by the gratuitous descriptions of the sordid details of the lives of quite often very disturbed people. I was sexually abused as a child, but I do not have multiple personalities, and I do live a relatively normal life. What happened was horrible and I feel depressed and sad and even angry, but I am also okay. No one who sees me at work or on the street or in a restaurant knows that I was sexually abused and that is the way I like it . . . These shows make a joke out of the intense pain of being hurt."

All viewers are given distorted information about the problem of incest, but the distortion can be particularly painful for those who have survived it. Watching Talk TV can lead survivors to believe that they will go on to abuse their own children, that good relationships are out of the question, and that at best they can hope for years of therapy with little hope of adequate coping. Michelle, for example, having generated expectations from watching the shows, was surprised that she could cope, that she had friends, and that she wasn't a multiple personality. In fact, there were even times that she questioned whether or not she was really abused because she was not like the women presented on television.

On the other end of the spectrum are viewers who could benefit from professional help but who decide to maintain their "quirks" because they've been legitimized by television. Mike, a young man who is sexually masochistic, described to us (under the assurance of anonymity) how he watched *Donahue* and *Geraldo* and on both programs saw a dominatrix, a prostitute who humiliates men for their sexual pleasure and her profit. Mike was relieved to discover that he wasn't the only one who enjoyed such behavior and so decided he should pursue his interest even though he had identified many problems it caused in his real-life sexual relationships. He came away from the shows with only one regret: that he had not taped them to use for masturbation fantasies.

In addition to troubling some viewers and offering misguided absolution to others, Talk TV can also inspire people to develop problems they don't already have. In other words, the shows may encourage viewers to copy the syndromes that are presented. A "copycat syndrome" may occur when viewers find the depictions of problems compelling enough to believe that they have the problem(s) presented, or to purposefully mimic the problem for secondary gain.

People quite naturally identify with painful situations when they appear to be similar to their own circumstances. Identification can produce reactions such as, "Wow, that's me!" or "I feel just like that." Troubled people often long for names for their problems. There is an illusion that "if I can name it, I can solve it." More importantly, people can believe that if it was named on TV then it is a "real" problem. And because it was named and discussed on TV, people may believe that others will be more accepting of the problem.

The attention garnered for the sensationalized problems presented on Talk TV makes the problems more acceptable and more interesting than more common problems such as depression, anxiety, or chronic substance abuse. Dysthymia, a mild form of depression, results in low self-esteem, worrisome thoughts, a blue mood, and loss of interest in activities. Dysthymia affects millions but doesn't make for interesting Talk TV. Further, it's not nearly as popular a self-diagnosis as MPD.

Friends and relatives may also collude in the copycat syndrome because the problems as presented on TV talk are far more engaging, traumatic, funny, or attention-getting than ordinary, real-life problems. The shows, of course, contribute to this relabeling or reframing of problems.

Sally did a show called "Teen Stalkers," which was supposedly about teens who are stalked by other teens. It was an attention-grabbing title but not really what the show was about. The alleged stalking problem looked much more like a bad disagreement between former friends, which hardly makes for great show titles ("Teens Who Had an Argument" or "Juvenile Squabbles"). On the show, the "friends" exchanged vicious insults of stalking on the one side and beating up little children on the other. Eventually everyone was screaming and Sally said, "I can't tell what's going on here!"

Sally then brought out the expert who informed viewers, "Well, maybe this wasn't stalking but . . . It could lead to stalking." Sally continued to fan the flame by throwing out hyperbolic statistics about the dangers of stalking. The only real danger on this show, and many others, was the risk of glamorizing and therefore encouraging mundane and petty conflicts that would have faded away if they weren't overblown and given the status of a trendy label.

A similar problem occurs when viewers assume they can diagnose friends and family. Armed with the inaccurate information provided on Talk TV, wives can label their husbands as "obsessive-compulsive" because they are finicky. Children can misunderstand a father's bad mood as manic-depressive illness. Parents can come away thinking ordinary restlessness is actually an attention deficit disorder. Mental health professionals routinely hear reports of erroneous information that led to inaccurate self or family diagnosis.

Viewers learn from these shows that some problems get more

attention and reaction than others. It isn't surprising that some viewers figure out that copying the problem is useful. A "shopping addiction" is more excusable to an angry spouse than careless over-spending. Multiple personality disorder elicits more understanding and patience from family members than simple moodiness. "Chronic fatigue syndrome" can serve to justify missing work or coming in late. And a disinterest in sex can be attributed to being the child of an alcoholic rather than acknowledged as a sign of a bad relationship. There are endless reasons for developing a copy-cat syndrome.

In many people's view, Talk TV has great power to confer status and absolve responsibility. The desire to gain that status and be given that absolution appears to have no limits. Gian Luigi Ferri opened fire with two assault weapons in a San Francisco law office, killing eight and wounding six others. He had hopes of going on a talk show after his killing spree. In a rambling, four-page letter found on his body, he described a list of the shows he was consider-ing. We can only wonder what pseudopsychological, "victim-based" interpretation would have been offered up to viewers. While the shows may offer appealing and even successful excuses, the excuses do not offer useful explanations. Further, the advice provided for "solving" these inflated problems is similarly vague and impractical.

Bad Advice and No Resolution

Talk shows claim that the purpose of airing all sorts of problems on national television is to benefit viewers. The central selling point is that both guests and viewers will benefit if we "break the silence," and at long last acknowledge what has been wrongly hidden. Air-ing problems is great for entertainment value but is marketed to viewers as if it is the only legitimate way of seeking resolution. The hosts remind viewers that frank talk about horrifying or embar-rassing details is needed so that we can all collectively generate solutions and then feel better for it. What actually happens is that the problems are often compounded for both viewers and guests.

Because the problems that are "uncovered" are layered in distortion, the suggestions offered about how to resolve them are also twisted. Typically, there is only a superficial nod to offering help in the last five minutes, after plenty of bad advice has already been relayed. Absorbing that advice directly and indirectly places viewers at risk for adopting some seriously misleading and potentially very harmful strategies. Viewers are given the impression they should always talk about their problems, saying whatever they want whenever and wherever they desire, confronting people who upset them, and exaggerating their problems if it pays to do so. Finally, they can justify their actions with pseudopsychological gibberish and solve it all with quick and easy fix-'em-up therapy.

Getting It All Out

On Talk TV, the guests present their problems, the hosts encourage them to do so with concerned questions and occasional self-disclosures about their own troubles, and the audiences frequently get in on the act with their own testimony. After all this public talk about private matters, viewers may question the value of privacy—after all, the guests sure are getting a lot of attention for their disclosures.

In fact, however, the kind of revelations that currently take place on Talk TV have previously been considered inappropriate and were actively discouraged, perhaps because we were "uptight" as a nation and unprepared to deal with what we might hear if we let people talk. But perhaps the prohibitions weren't completely self-serving. Perhaps they also recognized that sometimes privacy allows us personal dignity, that intimate disclosures build kinship with friends but can result in disgrace among strangers.

On today's Talk TV, anything and everything goes. Disclosures of every kind are encouraged by the hosts, who suggest that guests who are willing to share their stories are laudable because their "courage" helps us all. The implication is that those who talk are somehow more honest and noble than those who prefer to keep their secrets to themselves. The hosts also pull the audience in by asking for applause for some of the most gut-wrenching disclosures.

Viewers are sold the idea that people should come on national television and say that they have fathered children with women other than their wives, that they have been sleeping with their sisters' husbands, that their fathers were abusive, that they have had sex-change operations, or that they have been raped, all revealed for the first time on national TV. The reigning motto is "secrets keep you sick" and guests as well as viewers are basted in this advice—although it hardly prepares them for the roastings that follow.

Jerry Springer, for example, did a show about confronting secrets. Jerry introduced a couple and told viewers that the husband had a secret he wanted to reveal. What the husband revealed was that he had been having an affair. Not only was the unsuspecting wife humiliated and speechless, Springer upped the ante by bringing out the mistress who kissed the husband and informed the wife that she loved them both. Conflict predictably ensued, and viewers were told this was a good idea because now the problem was in the open.

When Ricki Lake did a show about confronting people, she hammed it up by wearing a silly Sherlock Holmes outfit as she "solved mysteries." The outcome, however, was far from light-hearted. On the show, a man explained to his very surprised roommate that he had "finally" informed the roommate's mother about a secret the roommate was hiding from his family. The secret was that the roommate was gay.

No time is spent considering the potential negative consequences for self or others of such disclosures. In fact, simply referring to these premeditated catastrophes as "disclosures" softens their edges and affords them a kind of legitimacy they do not deserve. No warnings are sounded that once these things are said they cannot be taken back or that when the show is over the conflict generated will have only just begun. In fact, the pain and anguish generated by these divulgences is concealed from viewers as the credits roll by and everyone is encouraged to "keep talking" and to "get therapy."

The advice to talk is not as beneficial as it might appear. Sometimes talking doesn't help. If productive ways of managing are not also a part of the conversation, talking can make problems worse.

People may only feel their pain more directly and intensely. Mental health professionals understand that talking about some problems intensifies the anxiety and depression. Another problem is that talking by itself, no matter how much or how often, will not alleviate some problems. Furthermore, releasing pent-up emotions can be quite harmful if the situation is not controlled and the newly released emotions lead to violence or other vindictive behaviors.

Another very dangerous piece of talk show advice is that confrontation is a good way to deal with problems. Daily, for the drama of it all, people are confronted. Women confront their thoughtless husbands. Husbands confront their unfaithful wives. Children confront their neglectful or embarrassing parents. Everyone from wedding disrupters to old lovers to rapists gets the same sort of tongue-lashing on Talk TV. All this confrontation is orchestrated to entertain but is presented as therapeutic.

Credible therapeutic practice aimed at catharsis or confrontation is quite different from the bastardized Talk TV version. Unlike TV talk shows, where people are encouraged to tell all for the first time in front of millions, therapeutic "disclosures" occur under well-constructed contracts between the client and the counselor in a safe, supportive, and confidential environment. If confronting others is ever going to be part of the resolution, it is responsibly done after careful consideration of, and preparation for, its probable consequences. But in the combative arena of Talk TV, everything is laid bare without consideration. Viewers may be encouraged to follow guests' examples, believing that this is all very helpful. It is understandable how this could happen. Day in and day out the hosts and guests extol the benefits of getting it all out: Sally admonishes, "You've got to let her vent!" Oprah implores, "Please, talk to me!" Donahue chides, "Hiding your feelings is a white male problem, come on, tell us."

The message from Talk TV is that anger should never be concealed. Jealousy, rage, frustration, and bitterness should come out and come out now! In reality these feelings are sometimes used as weapons in attempts to control other people. Intensely negative feelings are often vented as a way for the guest to feel better or to retaliate, but rarely does the release help bring about reconciliation. These shows present the on-air battles as if they help solve conflicts. In reality, such confrontations may create more problems. This is particularly problematic for vulnerable viewers who may have difficulty protecting themselves, such as the "Children of Violent Parents," or the families of "Vengeful Men" or the "Women [Who] Accuse Their Sisters of Neglecting Their Children."

Not only is "getting it all out" potentially a very bad idea for some guests, it also opens the door for a whole host of rude and inappropriate comments. When there is no privacy, everything is open to review and the boundaries between what is anyone else's business and what is not are lost. Which brings us to the second problem created by the bad example set by Talk TV's approach to problem solving: "get it all out" is really an invitation to "fight it out," and that invitation is also extended to viewers.

Saying Whatever It Takes to Win

The "getting it all out" approach to problem solving depends on the mistaken and juvenile belief that having the final say is the way to feel better. The flaw of such thinking is perhaps best captured in the phrase "won the battle but lost the war." That is, guests and viewers may feel vindicated by the sharp words that are tossed at those who have caused pain, but those barbs are of little real value in solving problems. And since all guests are encouraged to operate in the same mode of "saying what it takes to win," there is little opportunity for any guest to listen to another point of view. The disclosures of some guests provoke counterdisclosures from others and the battle for the last word begins.

In the course of these revelations, guests resort to rude and offensive tactics, which are only bolstered by the host and audience. Insult is added to injury and the supposed attempt to resolve the problem quickly turns into a shouting match between guests. No one is ever told they should not say something because it might be inappropriate or hurtful. On the contrary, the more outrageous and spiteful the comment the better, because it keeps things lively. Unfortunately, what makes for lively television rarely helps solve real problems.

A recent *Sally Jessy Raphael* program about bigamy illustrates how guests were set up and encouraged to say whatever it took to win. While this on-air battle for the last word might have amused viewers, it was not harmless fun. Sally invited two women who had been married to the same man at the same time to appear on the show. The man was also on the show via satellite and in disguise. His daughter (one wife's child) appeared as well. Not surprisingly, this combination of guests yielded a terrible fight over who was guilty of the most deception.

The truly unfortunate part of the show was that the nineteen-year-old daughter, Cindy, sat on stage while these women and her father tore each other apart. Sally and the audience encouraged the fight with "oohs" and "ahs" and rounds of applause at the ever-increasing accusations. Cindy had undoubtedly witnessed many of these fights before appearing on Sally's show, but she was further drawn into the conflict when she was asked to get in her own last words. And the audience's fervor over the situation only escalated the conflict. The "expert," identified only as a "relationship therapist" with a Ph.D., was brought on to do the postmortem. Her most notable warning was that all this turmoil could turn Cindy "to women," presumably meaning that Cindy could become a lesbian.

The scenario was almost too absurd for words, but it was just one more show like so many others: founded on stereotypes and capped off with clichés. From the orchestrated catfight to the no-good father, from the eternal triangle to the archaic explanations of homosexuality—cheap thrills and bad advice were dressed up like information and expertise. Furthermore, the show's concern about the consequences of arguing viciously in front of offspring were grossly distorted. The more probable outcomes—such as the loss of parental connection, lowered self-esteem, confusion about loyalty and love—are less titillating than the possibility of a teenager driven to homosexuality, and therefore were ignored.

Without a doubt this kind of dialogue never leads to increased empathy and understanding. And the problems it does create are rarely discussed. If viewers accept this as a model for communicating it will only encourage the kind of self-centered and thoughtless behaviors that produce problems, not solve them.

Masking It All with Psychobabble

Getting it all out in an attempt to win is often legitimized by the use of pseudopsychological explanations, otherwise known as psychobabble. This "no talk" talk is the fine art of offering an explanation that sounds as if it elucidates a subject when it clarifies nothing. Psychobabble obfuscates any problem. Its "explanation" is gibberish, simply stringing together words that sound good but actually mean very little.

Psychobabble is particularly useful on Talk TV, where people are encouraged to behave badly but told to do so in the name of mental health. The shows are rife with situations in which people are called upon to explain or justify questionable behavior. They certainly aren't likely to say, "I am acting like this so I could be on TV," or (even worse) "I have no intention of changing." Psychobabble allows guests and viewers to sound well-intentioned when in fact they are not. It helps remove responsibility. In other words, it is the language of excuses. Rather than acknowledge selfish, excessive, or aggressive behavior, we can now "disclose" our struggles with our "inner children," our "addictions" to nonchemical substances, or our "unresolved traumas" that need "venting."

Often psychobabble is used as a disclaimer or a prelude to nasty revelations: "I've relapsed and my wounded child acted out . . . so I slept with your sister." Other times it is used as a justification: "I try to be powerful by giving it all away." Still other times it is used for retaliation: "Your shame-based attack on me demonstrates how emotionally unstable you are."

Psychobabble is also used as a new and more sophisticated form of old stereotypes: "Men are cognitive, not emotional" and "Women are nonhierarchical in their conversational patterns" or "Adult children are overly responsible" and "Abused women draw abusive men to them." Sometimes psychobabble is simply a proud proclamation of otherwise rude behavior: "I'm an aggressive listener," "I need to be really honest," or "It's unhealthy for me if I don't express myself."

Talk show hosts are experts in psychobabble. Oprah calls for guests and viewers alike to empower themselves. Geraldo encourages men to get in touch with their maleness. Sally implores us to move beyond our codependency. While these statements may sound supportive, with the guests' or viewers' best interests in mind, they actually work to the shows' advantage by increasing "disclosures." Further "exploration" and drama is encouraged with fairytale assumptions: "Hug her, she'll forgive you!"—"Say you're sorry!"—"Don't worry about it!"—"Forgive and forget!"—"Get help!"—"Tell her how you feel."

This pseudolanguage also leaves viewers with nothing more than platitudes to explain problems and clichés to resolve them. Like all sound-bite advice, psychobabble lacks two important ingredients. First, it does not adequately or accurately explain the nature of the problem. "Codependency" and "wounded children" might sound like diagnoses, but in order to qualify, the words must identify distinct and well-defined problems. Otherwise, they remain popular labels that convey the message "I was hurt" but provide little substance beyond that. The meanings of such terms are not clearly explained for viewers. Instead, lists of qualities that are actually applicable to most people some of the time are provided. The lists may sound professional or scientific when in fact they are about as academically advanced as horoscopes and palm-reading.

Second, psychobabble never equips people with practical methods for changing their circumstances. People with enormous conflicts and long histories of resentment and betrayals are instructed with platitudes about "tough love" and "setting limits" and listening to their "inner voice"—when many of them indicate having no understanding of what it would entail to put those clichés into practice. The nodding heads in the audience and the tearful embraces captured by the camera leave viewers in a position to believe it will work. Viewers may then be left chastising themselves when they can't make their own lives work because they can't get their husbands to stop drinking, or their fathers-in-law to stop complaining, or their children to be more appreciative.

Also, "steps" or "programs" are often described in a language so vague as to be virtually meaningless. The "four steps to get rid of your anger" may sound straightforward and easy enough to implement but what this kind of ready-made solution fails to acknowledge is that not all anger is the same, and certainly not everyone's anger needs the same treatment. Sometimes, for example, anger is a protective signal to people that they are being hurt, exploited, or taken advantage of.

The primary problem with psychobabble is that it creates the illusion of understanding. Rather than encouraging discussion, exploration, or further understanding, psychobabble shuts it off. With only a phrase or two, we can believe that we know what is being summarized. We can believe that we understand all the related issues. And we can assume that what we are thinking is what everyone else is thinking. Guests confess that they have "toxic shame" or that they are "codependents" or "enablers." Hosts encourage "healing," "empowerment," and "reclaiming of the inner spirit." In turn, viewers can nod a knowing nod without really knowing at all. Finally, once we've all agreed on the pseudopsychological nature of the problems, only one step remains: to "get therapy."

Fixing It Quick with Therapy

Having talked it out, fought it out, and explained it without really explaining it, we have a lot of bad advice that culminates in the admonition that therapy will solve it. This advertisement for mental health is a double-edged sword. On the one hand, it might help cut through lingering stigma associated with mental health problems and may encourage viewers to seek needed professional help. On the other hand, it suggests that therapy is a singularly effective resolution applicable to any and all problems, as if "therapy" were a "one size fits all" technique applied the same way by all clinicians to every problem. What viewers aren't told is that not only is this solution expensive, it may not be available, it isn't always easy, and certainly it doesn't "solve life." Similar to the bad lessons and bad advice, this notion of "getting help" is flawed and does not hold beyond the most superficial examination.

From watching Talk TV we may come to believe that we can say anything to anyone and then "go to therapy" to have our problems fixed. The shows demonstrate over and over again an easy four-step plan to problem solving: attack, confront, hug, all done. Of course, we don't see the guests after the show. We don't see that "happily ever after" is not always the outcome of therapy. What is lost to viewers is the often lengthy and painful—and sometimes unsuccessful—attempts at change that many people struggle through when they do go to therapy.

Therapy comes in many complicated variations. But Talk TV makes it seem as though the very trip to the therapist's office is the solution to everything from rape to attention deficit disorder. Further, Edward Liska, M.D., a psychiatrist in practice for over forty years and the former medical director of the Edgewood Children's Center in San Francisco, pointed out that viewers of Talk TV "come to expect a cure rather than maintenance. . . . Therapy is presented with vague allusions and no clear responsibility for both the therapist and the client as co-participants in a complex experiment."

Therapy, moreover, is not available to all who need it. The average cost of one day of inpatient hospitalization is $1,000. Outpatient day treatment can run $200 to $300 per day. One hour of psychotherapy with a licensed mental health professional averages between $75 and $125. Lower prices can be found, but typically only by seeking assistance from professionals with less training. Many viewers do not have insurance—and even for those who do, the cost is passed on to consumers in the form of the premiums they pay.

The medications used to treat many mental health problems are also very expensive and must be taken under close supervision to be effective. Prozac (used to treat depression) costs about $70 a month, Haldol (used to treat variety of problems) costs about $260 a month, Clozaril (used to treat schizophrenia), which also requires a weekly blood test, costs $650 a month. All of these treatments must be monitored by physicians, which also adds to the cost.

For those who don't have the financial resources for therapy with a private practitioner, there are frequently long waiting lists. Mental health clinics are often staffed with competent but over-worked practitioners. When President Kennedy originally proposed the development of community mental health centers to replace large mental hospitals, the recommendation was one center for every hundred thousand people. To achieve this goal, we would currently need 2,415 centers rather than the 1,000 currently in operation.

Mental health centers are often so busy supplying services to emergencies and seriously disturbed individuals that there is little time available for anything other than very limited contact. Session limits instituted by social policy and the availability of resources also dramatically reduce the availability of services. In the final analysis, therapy is really governed more by economics than by the needs of the patients. This fact is ignored by Talk TV, which presents "therapy" as a readily available cure-all waiting for anyone who will partake.

Viewers also aren't told about the importance of investigating practitioners' credentials, which include both academic training and licensing. Licensed mental health professionals have passed examinations and must abide by the ethics codes of their profession.

These codes are designed to protect consumers and ensure the quality of care. The shows like to use people who will be good on TV—and often these are not licensed professionals and therefore not governed by the profession's ethical code. Such freedom allows them to diagnose on the air, offer treatment and advice to callers, and most importantly to mislead viewers about the nature of the mental health profession and its services.

Bad Results: Maintaining Stereotypes

Many, many Americans rightfully believe that they have been excluded and discriminated against, or that their concerns have not been on the national agenda. Those feelings have generated a strong desire for a public forum in which to call attention to their issues. TV talk shows have built a reputation on providing that forum. In fact, these shows have become the primary source for airing problems that other media don't cover and in ways that supposedly allow people to speak for themselves.

But now Talk TV falls sadly short of its previous claim to fame. Rather than allowing new voices into the conversation in a way that produces understanding or change, the conversation on Talk TV further solidifies the existing social and political arrangements. Vicki Abt, Ph.D., a professor of sociology and American studies at Penn State's Ogontz campus, has pointed out how talk shows rely on the poor and already exploited as the major source of the guest pool. The shows are appealing, in part, because they rely on strongly held stereotypes about virtually every segment of the population they present. Minorities are depicted as violent and irresponsible users of social resources—victims who are ultimately responsible for their own problems. Homosexuals are presented in the most outlandish fashion possible. Regardless of whether or not the stereotypes are consistent, they provide viewers from the majority with the illusion that they understand "them" because the evidence can be found on TV to justify entrenched and prejudicial views.

But it's not just "them"—it's everyone. There are extremely

inflammatory portrayals of men and women in general that draw on the worst stereotypes of both. Not surprisingly, men are presented both as overbearing and power-hungry cheats and as dependent, immature creatures who rely on women to take care of them. Women are portrayed both as caring, helpless souls and as angry, bitter casualties.

Stereotypes have long held appeal: they help simplify complicated subjects to the point where they appear easily and quickly understood. Although they are typically contradictory and do not contribute to understanding, stereotypes offer comfort and reassurance to viewers in easily recognized images. The stereotypical images gain power as we take them on as truth. Although the shows can't be held responsible for the prejudices that preceded them, they can and should be held accountable for their significant role in supporting and reinforcing them.

As with most stereotypes, the stereotypes on Talk TV disproportionately affect certain members of our communities. And because of its power and reach, Talk TV further entrenches existing stereotypes like no other single factor in our culture. So Talk TV not only fails to produce the changes that many who go on hope for, it actually contributes to the problems of the groups most likely to be looking to it as a forum for addressing their concerns.

Gender Wars

The "war between the sexes" is a powerful explosive, loaded into TV cameras and fired at viewers daily. This is nothing new. Yet programming targeted primarily for women has not yielded the kind of improvements some might have hoped for. While the problems that face women get more air time, the topics are presented in ways that are not likely to produce change. In fact, the very same stereotypes that have plagued both men and women for centuries are in full force. Instead of encouraging changes in sex roles, the shows actually solidify them. Women viewers are given a constant supply of the worst images of men, all the way from rapists and murderers to garden variety liars, cheats, con artists, and lazy good-for-nothings. The depictions of women are no better.

Most women on Talk TV are perpetual victims. Women are presented as having so little power that not only do they have to contend with real dangers such as sexual or physical abuse, but they are also overcome by bad hair, big thighs, and beautiful but predatory "other" women. The "Women of Talk" are always upset, always traumatized, hormonal, and in need. The "bonding" that occurs is invariably centered around complaints about men or around the worst stereotypes about women, as if claiming those stereotypes will somehow remove their stigma.

But of course this is the heart of Talk TV: in order to be a part of the sisterhood, women are required to be angry with men and dissatisfied with themselves. We need not look further than the titles of the programs to recognize the message. Shows about men bring us a villain for every offense: "Stalkers," "Chauvinistic Sons," "Lascivious Fathers," "Vengeful Men," "Hated Sons-in-law," "Men Seeking Virgins to Wed," "Gay Police Officers," "Condemned Man Who Wants His Execution Aired," "Men Who Won't Commit to Women."

More often, the shows provide a forum for women to complain, confront, and cajole. Such programs might be a welcome release, but because there is never any change as a result of the letting-loose, the shows are simply setups to reinforce stereotypes and outrage. The shows support the mistaken notion that women's complaints have no weight, that the only power women have is to complain, and that they cannot make real changes.

By bringing on offensive male guests who do nothing but verify the grounds for complaint, the shows are reinforcing several self-defeating propositions. Ideas such as "women should direct their energies toward men" rather than looking for solutions in themselves are conveyed daily. And even when the audience chastises such behavior, nothing changes, because only arguments and justifications follow. Certainly the assumption that men will not be responsive to women's concerns is given plenty of air time. Women appear helpless to do anything about it other than complain. Of course, a long-standing stereotype about women is that they are all whiny "bitches" (typically defined as women who voice complaints). Viewers who are inclined to believe that stereotype will find ample support on Talk TV.

A recent *Jenny Jones* illustrates how the gender war is fought on Talk TV. Jenny introduced a woman whose label read "no longer has sex with husband because saw him with a stripper." Viewers got to hear how the stripper "put her boobs in his face" and then kissed him. Upon hearing the complaints, the husband predictably defended his callous actions, "At least I didn't tongue her. I didn't know this was going to happen." The next few minutes proceeded with insult upon insult, with the audience exclaiming and applauding. When given the chance, the audience asked for more, refueling the argument and keeping the show hot. To top it all off, viewers were informed that the offense in question occurred at the husband's thirtieth birthday party, which his wife arranged, stripper and all.

The result is that both parties were discredited. First viewers were lathered into a rage about the husband's behavior in order to get them to side with the victimized wife. Then, however, it was revealed that the wife set this up. This revelation allowed those watching to distance themselves from her because "it was her own fault." As a consequence, viewers could come away thinking that men are untrustworthy but that women bring it on themselves, an attitude that certainly presents a real problem in other situations.

The show wasn't over, however. It went on to reveal how the wife had only had sex twice in the last five years, an unsatisfactory situation she blamed on the stripper incident. Then, in the last few minutes of the show, a psychologist pointed out the couple wasn't wearing rings and didn't seem committed. She suggested that their fighting might be related to some other problem. Her comments seemed reasonable enough until she suggested that the wife might really be trying to get her husband to rape her. Where this idea came from is hard to know, because there was no explanation or discussion. Jenny cut to a commercial—not an altogether bad idea—

but the comment was already made. Ignored or not, it certainly called up some of the most absurd and destructive ideas imaginable about men and women and their relationship to one another.

After the commercial, a new problem was added to the stage. A husband whose label read "seeing prostitute for 2 years" was confronted by his wife. She cried as he tried to defend himself. The wife, predictably, got lots of audience support and the husband got thoroughly flogged. Since the wife was too distraught to say much, the audience served as a quick understudy.

In both cases, the situations were never explained well enough for viewers to understand what was going on between these hapless men and women. Instead, viewers saw only the familiar and emotionally loaded images of angry women suffering at the hands of their cheating, self-justifying men. Producers expect that the situations are inflammatory enough that the audience will be off and running without needing any more details. And they are right.

But if there is a man for every offense, there is certainly a woman for every trauma. A quick trip through the shows' titles provides a glimpse of what Talk TV thinks about women: "Custody Fight," "Women Who Love Ex Boyfriends," "Voice Makeovers," "Lusty Husbands, Indifferent Wives," "My Daughter Is a Stripper." Even when shows are meant to be positive, such as Oprah's "Intrepid Women" and "Mother-Daughter Truces," there is always a problem at the root of it. There are endless portrayals of virtuous women who claim that their only flaw was loving too much the men who hated them in return. Stereotypical images of struggling women are also reflected in the many makeover shows, and the countless battling sisters and feuding mother-daughter teams who catfight over everything from stolen lovers to bad hair.

It is not that women and men don't find lots of ways to disappoint each other, or that some men and some women don't act and think like the men and women on the shows. The problem is that Talk TV inflames the gender war with endless portrayals of vicious acts, overboard retaliations, and outrageous justifications. Viewers already predisposed to believe the worst about men and women, or even those wondering about their real motives, are pumped full of the ugliest nastiness news from the front.

People of Color

When issues affecting people of color are dealt with, the stereotypes about race are layered on top of the stereotypes about gender. Since most of the shows pivot around issues related to sex, violence, and relationships, the shows tend to get people of color who reflect stereotypical images. They bring on guests who have illegitimate children, are supported by welfare, fight viciously, and have complex and unsolvable problems. While there certainly are less-than-flattering depictions of white people on such shows, white viewers have the luxury of belonging to the dominant group, and therefore are more often presented in the media in positive ways.

The titles provide graphic examples of stereotypical themes: sexual power tied to race—"When Your Lover Leaves You for a Different Race," "Interracial Gay Relationships," "Sexually Molested Women Turn Racist," "My Daughter Dates Another Race;" the consequences of interracial dating—"Mother of Two Biracial Children Confronts Grandmother Who Favors White Grandchildren;" or from the child's perspective—"I Don't Know Who I Am," "Mom's White, Dad's Black," "White Parents Raising Black Kids;" or intraracial discord—"Is the Black Woman Bringing the Black Man Down?" "Black Men: An Endangered Species," "Harassed for Dating White Women." Together these titles run a wide range of stereotypes about African-Americans: impoverished, angry black women with illegitimate children; oversexed, promiscuous black males who act violently, or irresponsibly date white women and then hurt them; mixed-race kids who are all confused and needy; gracious white families who come to the rescue and then need to build more prisons to house these violent people.

Not all of the shows are destructive, however. Some even attempt to break down stereotypical images. Oprah, for example, invited Jane Elliott, who taught classes in race relations, to conduct a consciousness-raising activity with the audience. Audience members were divided by the color of their eyes and then treated poorly if they had blue eyes and treated well if they had brown eyes. The show resulted in a useful discussion of prejudicial treatment that allowed the audience to get involved.

Most of the shows, however, focus on problems, emphasizing chaos and ignoring positive adjustments and coping strategies. Oprah's "White Parents Raising Black Kids," for example, depicted the African-American guests who were reared by white parents as troubled, despite the guests' attempts to explain how well they were coping. Oprah probed for turmoil by asking questions such as "Tell me when you noticed there was a problem?" or "When did you realize that you were not like your parents?" When the guests explained that they were happy or that they had found ways to adjust, Oprah refocused the attention to their problems and away from their strategies for coping.

Even when professionals try to break down stereotypical images, they often find themselves at odds with the show's agenda. Richard Majors, Ph.D., a senior researcher at The Urban Institute and president of the National Council of African-American Men, welcomed the opportunity to appear on Talk TV. He hoped to provide statistics that would counter some of the stereotypes of black men, which he feels "make black men the sacrificial lamb and then poster child for all of society's ills." He appeared on a show about black men and black women that, in his opinion, could have turned into a "dog fight." The woman he appeared with accused him of favoring white women because he had written a book with a white female coauthor. The audience, stacked with his fellow guest's friends, attacked him.

Majors said he was in a very difficult position. If he fought back and countered the arguments, he would have fed the stereotype that black men and women can't get along, so he avoided the fight and elected to say little. He was then concerned that he was not able to adequately represent his issues. He felt the fight would have made for more exciting TV, but would have prevented him from doing what he had intended: provide information that breaks down stereotypes. He was particularly disturbed that this show, like so many others, devoted most of its time to stirring up trouble instead of discussing solutions. Majors stated that he learned from this experience to be more careful in setting up show arrangements. Like many other competent professionals and guests looking to inform viewers, he worried that he had participated in something that contributed to the very problem he had hoped to address.

Shows that give racists the opportunity to champion their views are just another setup for conflict. Such guests allow the host and audience to come down hard on racism while still reinforcing negative stereotypes. Shows with titles such as: "Skinheads," "Hate Group Member Involved in Murder," "Whites Blame Blacks for Nation's Ills," and "Racist Teens" signal viewers to tune in to the hate-fests the shows are bound to turn into. In one example, Sally brought on two white women who angrily expressed concern about black women on welfare. Also on the stage was a black woman who felt blacks are entitled to welfare as a form of "payback." Next to her was a man who had gone to the United Nations to appeal directly for reparation from slavery. There were more angry guests on the show and the group of them provided Sally the opportunity to appear to be the only reasonable person involved. Viewers should realize, however, that she was the one most responsible for setting up the unavoidable conflict. It would not be hard to argue that little of use is accomplished by giving a national voice to marginal racists. All such shows end up doing is to keeping alive the racial conflicts that divide our country.

The possibility for doing better with Talk TV is often reiterated by leaders in the African-American and Hispanic communities. Cecilia Garcia, with the Congressional Hispanic Institute, says that Talk TV "aims at too low a standard. For Hispanics, that image reinforces the stereotypes of low economic status, overly dependent on public assistance." She worries that Hispanic viewers internalize the message and then don't see other options for themselves. The only balance for such images comes from the hosts and the audience. Geraldo likes to talk about his Puerto Rican heritage and could serve as a role model to some viewers, but he does little to counteract stereotypical images on his show. Hispanics are invited when their participation confirms some existing stereotype.

Likewise, there are now three African-American talk show hosts: Oprah, Montel, and Rolonda. Thomas Parham, Ph.D., president-elect of the Association of Black Psychologists and director of the Counseling Center at the University of California, Irvine, pointed with pride to those hosts' accomplishments and their influential positions. He also pointed out, however, that "because of their ethnicity they have a larger responsibility on their part to right some of the wrongs."

Parham has extensive experience with the media, having been involved in many news shows and documentaries, but he has not appeared on Talk TV. "I wouldn't agree to go on a talk show because it is very hard to present an intelligent position. . . . They do not present normalized images of culturally different people. Instead, they find the wildest, most diseased people hanging out in the margins. . . . I am quite disgusted with the TV talk shows I have seen. They do little to allay society's fears; most of society learns what they know from TV. And nobody is stepping up to the responsibility, which is too much like the right thing to do, instead they step up to do more sensational stuff."

Courtland Lee, Ph.D., professor of Counselor Education at the University of Virginia and the past president of the Multicultural Division of the American Counseling Association, expressed similar concerns about Talk TV in general and the depiction of people of color in particular. He described Talk TV as the "cesspool of TV," stating that the shows "are freak shows that parade pathologies before the public, sensationalizing issues and creating shock value. There is really no socially redeeming value. We need to pull the cord on these things." More specifically, he pointed to the *Ricki Lake* show as one of the worst offenders, because "she brings on young blacks and Hispanics with limited education to fight it out on air."

A recent *Ricki Lake* program about women who sleep with their friends' boyfriends provided a vivid example of Lee's concerns. The guest panel consisted of mostly African-American and Hispanic women who put on a such flamboyant show of screaming and fighting that people of color and their allies who witnessed it could only feel heartsick. The profanity was so extreme that many of the words had to be deleted. Viewers could understand, however, that one of the guests, Tracy, was upset with another guest, Ava, who had said, "Sure, I'll sleep with anyone I want." The fighting got so heated that Ricki had to stop the show because Tracy yanked off Ava's wig. But the "time out" did little to change the situation; once back on stage, this time without the wig, Tracy and Ava continued to shout insults and accusations. Such loud, uncontrolled, and incoherent public displays of hostility play into almost every major stereotype about black women while doing absolutely nothing to help the guests or viewers understand the legitimate rage that many African-American women feel. Further, for viewers living in predominately white communities, these are the images that form their beliefs about minority populations.

Asians and Native Americans rarely appear on Talk TV. But when they do, they encounter the same stereotypical attitudes that African-Americans and Hispanics face. When Cathe Che appeared on *Donahue* with the label "lesbian movie critic," she told viewers that "basically I happen to be queer, so anything I say I think is from a queer perspective." Viewers were also alerted to the fact that she is Asian-American. Donahue did at least address the stereotypes by remarking that, "We have significant numbers of Americans who do not see an American when they see an Asian person. And then you add that to the fear and ignorance that abounds in some communities regarding gay people, you got yourself some real kind of challenge here, girl." She answered, "I am very aware, though, that there are more space aliens on television than Asian-Americans." The audience laughter indicated a recognition of the truth in her response.

Geraldo's people failed to demonstrate any understanding of

minority concerns with their show, "Fatal Family Feuds." Producer Lora Wiley wanted Marvin (a Native American) to do a phone interview from a reservation to verify the violence of another Native American, Kevin, that resulted in one member of his family being shot and another one rolled up in a carpet and set on fire. Marvin was hesitant, saying, "My folks is really upset. They don't want me to go on television and say anything." Marvin's parents' concern was not unfounded. Lora Wiley cleverly persuaded Marvin to "share" his story, then referred to his family's situation as "fucked up family murders" in an interview with New York magazine in December 1994. Her comments are hardly reflective of the racially sensitive attitude Talk TV claims to have. In fact, it is difficult to imagine how Wiley, with that kind of attitude, could produce a show that did anything other than reinforce the most negative of beliefs—which is what many of the shows typically do, not only with gender and race, but also with sexual orientation.

Sexual Orientation

Early on, Talk TV helped bring issues of sexuality into the mainstream. By addressing the prejudices that lead many homosexuals to remain closeted and by discussing the risks of coming out, the shows raised the awareness of many viewers who otherwise might never have considered such issues. While societal attitudes have indeed continued to advance, the shows themselves have failed to progress. In fact, the shows have regressed, resorting to calling on the very stereotypes and hostilities they used to lobby against. By re-presenting outdated and exaggerated issues, bringing on hostile and backward opponents, and inviting fringe representatives of the gay community to appear, the shows help sustain and entrench prejudice against homosexuals.

The shows' titles signal what viewers will be in for: "Gay Worker Charged with Sexual Harassment," "Where Gays and Lesbians Get Babies to Start a Family," "Black Preacher Says He'll March with the KKK Against Gays," "Men Who Star as Drag Queens in

Movies," "Female Cop Becomes Macho Man on Police Force," "Loves Husband But Would Rather Make Love to Women," "Gays Turning Straight," "I Blame Myself for My Child Being Gay," "My Husband Has a Gay Lover," and "Three Gays and a Baby."

Viewers are left with images of drag queens getting makeovers and transsexuals' surprising transformations blended together with normal adolescent development. The distinctions between these very different groups are lost. Additionally, there is typically a backdrop of conflict created by members of the Christian right and the Family Defense Council reminding viewers that all homosexuals belong, at the very least, back in the closet—or at best transformed into heterosexuals. The overall picture of homosexuals created by the shows is that of confused, dysfunctional, and predatory people in need of change.

It appears that when the shows want to highlight the strangeness of homosexuals, they feign interest in presenting legitimate issues. Guests are selected who will undoubtedly show themselves to be unusual and the hosts have to do nothing more than give them a forum with a false title. Jerry Springer, for example, aired a program titled "I'm Confused about My Sexuality" in which all the guests repeatedly stated that they were not confused about their sexuality. Clearly, these people did not view themselves as confused about which sex attracted them. Equally clear, however, was the chaotic and unusual nature of their circumstances.

What they revealed and how they were presented was probably so out of the ordinary for most viewers that Springer's assessment that the guests were confused about sexuality was bound to win out. The array of guests included a wife who revealed for the first time a crush on her brother's wife; a "heterosexual" couple who revealed that they were both actually homosexual and so decided to split up; a woman who claimed to be lesbian but appeared with her boyfriend, who turned out to be a man who stated he was a "dike-lesbian"; and a man in drag who had crushes on both another man in drag and a woman. With some of the guests dressed in drag and others with spiked mohawk hair styles, lip-rings, and glitter in their hair, the show attracted more attention to the guests' grooming and personal habits than to the issues of sexual confusion. Along the way the show highlighted personal conflicts as well as disagreements about breast implants and the use of hormones.

Likewise, a *Donahue* program titled "What, Another New Talk Show? Yes, a Gay Talk Show" supposedly informed viewers about a new talk show featuring gay hosts. Linda Simpson, whose label read "Transvestite Talk Show Host of Party Talk," appeared with her co-host, Brad Lamm, whose label read "Gay Talk Show Host." By billing the show as a program about a gay TV talk show, viewers were left with the inaccurate impression that all transvestites are gay. In actuality, most transvestites are not gay but rather obtain sexual pleasure from dressing in women's clothes. Likewise, information was not presented about the fact that most transvestites are heterosexual and do not dress in women's clothes to attract men. Nor were viewers alerted to the fact that most homosexuals do not derive sexual pleasure from cross-dressing. A small segment of the gay population enjoys dressing in drag but rarely does that signal confusion over sexual orientation. While Donahue's show was not necessarily intended as an educational program, as Springer's was, it still presented just enough information with no explanations to result in confusing the uninformed and perpetuating stereotypes.

Another common technique that perpetuates stereotypes is the constant parade of worn-out ideas such as the desire of gay people to convert heterosexuals and the ability of homosexuals to change their orientation if they so decide. On the same show mentioned above, Donahue spiced things up by bringing out Howard Hurwitz, Ph.D., whose label read "Says Gays Should Not Impose Their Beliefs on Others." This is a typical ploy used by Talk TV to spice up the conflict. On this show Donahue pointed out that Hurwitz "want[ed] the audience to know you don't hate gays, but you feel this kind of television does what?" Hurwitz answered, "Well first, I want to draw a distinction between homosexuals and gays. Gays did not come into the vocabulary of the country until 1953 and as late as 1986 the *New York Times* wouldn't use the word 'gay' in its publications." (Lamm interjected, "You still call blacks Negroes.") Hurwitz continued, "Gays are radical homosexuals and they have a political agenda, and their agenda, and I am an educator and experienced . . . they want school children to learn that homosexuality is normal, healthy, viable, and an alternative to heterosexuality . . . that is what we oppose unalterably. But the individual homosexual, we don't want to interfere with his life, that's his behavior, let him have it." Talk TV got another hour of controversy.

Tim Fisher, the director of the Gay and Lesbian Parents Coalition, is alarmed by shows such as Donahue's. He worries that provocative issues such as "choice" and strategies for "changing" sexual orientation predominate the discussions, but are not the concerns that most homosexuals struggle with. Fisher has refused all of the many talk show invitations he's received, not only because of the potential for public ridicule and his desire to protect his family's privacy, but also because of the deliberate recruitment of gay-bashers for the audience. He's learned from his organization's members that on-air confrontations only lead to more discord and negative images. The pressure to counter the many harmful images and messages, however, is great.

Paul Cameron, for example, makes the rounds of talk shows with preposterous, derogatory stories to feed viewers' suspicion and fear of homosexuals. He tries to get people to believe that gay men eat feces, have urine sex, and are infected with lice. Joshua Gamson, Ph.D., a professor of sociology at Yale University, was asked to appear on Donahue but refused. He stated, "The structure would not be mine and you can't really control how the discourse is used, and besides I would have missed teaching my classes, where I can educate." His decision was reinforced when he learned that Paul Cameron was scheduled for that show. Gamson teaches classes entitled "Sexuality and Social Change" and "Mass Media and Mass Culture." He states that Talk TV often draws on stereotypical presentations of homosexuals as "limp-wristed florists, gym teacher lesbians, suicidal everything, and really the butt of everyone's joke."

Despite the negative images often portrayed on Talk TV,

Gamson realizes that homosexuals are caught in a classic dilemma: "be invisible or be stereotyped by the media." Because the shows need some spontaneity to make them work, they must also hand over some control to their guests, and thus "talk shows provide a very limited, compromised and often dangerous opportunity to self-represent." Nonetheless, he states, "While stereotyped images are damaging, at the same time even stereotypes may be mobilizing for young people." As with many other marginalized groups, many homosexuals recognize the problems inherent in appearing but also realize they have few other opportunities to reach so many Americans at once.

The shows have been a mobilizing force for Amy, a young college-educated lesbian activist. In a letter to the authors, she said, "My life is lived in the shadow of talk shows. Because I am an incest survivor and a lesbian, I worry about how these two groups of people are represented on TV in general and talk shows in particular. For me, it's an issue of representation—who is representing me. I still think that any representation adds to visibility, but I wonder at what cost. I've seen a few talk shows on lesbians—enough so I know that I do not want these people representing me." She believes that if talk shows represent lesbians as "women who just haven't met or slept with the right man," then "the talk shows are only expressing what people have been saying about us all along."

The much-needed public forum that early Talk TV provided for silenced or marginalized groups has been turned over to hate groups who effectively use the programs as a vehicle to express their hostility. In exchange, talk shows get an hour of conflict and tension. Resolution and understanding are sacrificed for ratings. Skills related to listening, understanding difference, and coexisting without rancor are lost.

Reinforcing Invisibility

Talk TV producers are only interested in those individuals and groups who will make for entertaining shows. Often the criterion is that there are already existing stereotypes or myths about the group to draw viewers. Consequently, some marginalized groups receive very little attention. Informational programs are rarely provided on the deaf, the elderly, the multiply handicapped, or the mildly retarded. If there is any way to make a group sensational, Talk TV will do it. But if the group is not sexy, pitiable, or violent, it will probably not be represented.

"Talk shows aren't calling us to find out about issues for disabled veterans," says Ron Drach, the national employment director for Disabled American Veterans. "Now during the 70s, we saw disabled vets portrayed as walking time bombs, baby killers, drug addicts, and villains, so maybe it is better not to get that kind of recognition." Drach also pointed out that there is still a lingering stereotype that veterans are trained to kill and that if talk shows were interested, they would probably be after the sensationalized aspects. "I lost a leg in Vietnam, but I have had a good adjustment. I would be glad to talk about important issues like capping pensions on veterans who were wounded and are disabled. But they don't call about that."

Catherine Odette, the director of the Disabled Womyn's Education Project, watches a lot of talk shows. She identifies herself as "a wheelchair user with disabilities who is also fat." She is a regular viewer of Sally, Geraldo, and Montel in the morning, followed by Oprah and Phil in the afternoon, and Jerry Springer when she can't sleep at night. "It is important to watch the audience reaction, because that is where the masses are. It tells me what I have to deal with . . . I am aware that the audience of the talk show represents what is out there, opinionwise, and it isn't very hospitable, in my opinion." Odette believes that if she were to appear, the audience would be torn between its two most common responses: pity and disdain. She maintains that her handicap would foster pity, but that her obesity would provoke condemnation. She points to shows in which audiences scream at guests and tell them they need to do something with themselves, that no one would want to have sex with them in their current condition, and that they need to get some control. "With both issues, I know the audience sees me as pitiable and as out of control about fat."

Another group that is growing in numbers and is certainly representative of a large number of daytime viewers is the elderly. Despite the group's size, however, its members are not seen by potential advertisers as desirable targets and therefore are rarely the focus of TV talk shows. Talk TV makes much more money if it is marketed to groups who are establishing their buying habits: younger viewers. The success of Ricki Lake attests to this recipe for ratings and power. But Ricki Lake is no maverick. Producers of early talk radio screened out the voices of older callers because they believed younger listeners would be repelled by them. Similarly, even the audiences of daytime talk shows that are marketed to older viewers contain few elderly people. The most common way for an elderly person to be included is to play into the stereotype of dirty old man or sexually starved old lady. The issues facing the elderly are transformed into issues for the young, as was done with "Eighteen-Year-Old Pregnant by a Sixty-Two-Year-Old."

Thus, producers want only certain groups with readily apparent differences to create scenes that will be emotionally touching to viewers. Consequently, viewers really don't learn much about the world most people inhabit. The disabled, some minorities, and the mildly retarded remain as invisible as ever. The few images of the disabled are presented to reflect stereotypes of misshapen, asexual, heartbroken, strong-spirited invalids.

Creating Future Trouble

If talk shows teach viewers bad lessons in mental health, and add to it bad advice on how to deal with those problems, the results are quite predictable. Viewers are left with clichés and reinforced stereotypes. These images are made more objectionable because they are marketed as education.

We've seen how inaccurate and dangerous information is likely to have a disproportionate impact on certain segments of the population. Those most affected are apt to be the ones who have limited access to other credible sources of information. For the most part, our comments have focused on adult populations, but without a doubt, the most vulnerable of viewers are young people. With limited experience to draw upon and immature capacities for reasoning and discriminating ideas, children are highly susceptible to the chaotic, intrusive, and hostile quality of the shows. Clearly, the younger the viewers, the less likely they are to be able to assess the value of the information or the consequences of show-biz advice. Further, the more likely they are to be caught up in the "you did it, no I didn't" fights that parallel those so often seen on playgrounds.

Given their popularity with adult viewers, it is not surprising that children are exposed to Talk TV, but the actual number of child viewers is alarming. In 1990, there were 448,000 children and 742,000 teenagers watching Oprah, 400,000 viewing Geraldo, and another 500,000 apiece tuning in Sally and Phil. Even with overlap, these numbers make it clear that millions of our country's children are soaking up the same doses of pathology, perversity, and interpersonal aggravation that their adult counterparts tune in to every day. And for every problem the shows create for adult viewers, there are other and more serious troubles for children.

Perhaps young viewers are able to read the responses of adult viewers or pick up the tongue-in-cheek tone of the shows enough to grasp that some of what is presented is not intended to be taken seriously. Nonetheless, impressionable youngsters are exposed to all sorts of traumatized people screaming about betrayals and abuses, lobbing rude and offensive remarks, and even at times resorting to physical violence. The continual uproar over anything even remotely connected to sex certainly sets the stage for yet another generation of sexual hang-ups.

Whether or not certain behaviors are presented as "outrageous" on the shows, there is certainly the potential for children to learn that there are plenty of ways to get attention. Histrionic behavior— wearing shocking clothing, screaming when you want to be heard, pumping out crocodile tears, and blaming everyone else—are all part of the repertoire of strategies that children see modeled on Talk TV. In other words, children may be learning how to act, either to resolve conflicts or get attention, from what is presented on the shows. As Americans struggle with problems of civility all the way from common courtesy to respect for personal property, indoctrinating the nation's youth with such images is hardly likely to help. While the actual consequences cannot be accurately predicted without good research, it is clear that the shows create the potential for problems that need to be better understood and addressed.

Although it would be hard to know it from what currently remains, Talk TV initially had great potential as a vehicle for disseminating accurate information and as a forum for public debate. But because the goal of Talk TV has become sensational entertainment that will increase ratings, that potential has been lost. We are left with cheap shots, cheap thrills, and sound-bite stereotypes. Taken on its own this combination is troubling enough, but when considered against the original opportunity for positive outcomes, what Talk TV delivers is truly disturbing.

Notes

P. 127, *On the first day the Colosseum opened:* Wiedemann, T. *Emperors and Gladiators*. London: Routledge & Kegan Paul, 1992, pp. 20, 60.

P. 128, *"something absolutely unique among our cultural institutions":* Wolf, N. *Fire with Fire: The New Female Power and How to Use It.* New York: Ballantine, 1993, p. 9.

P. 131, *damaging messages viewers get from Talk TV:* Howard Rosenberg, personal interview, Nov. 16, 1994.

P. 132, *forty to sixty million survivors of incest:* Goodman, W. "When Even Victimizers Say They Are Victims," *New York Times*, Mar. 28, 1994, p. C-14.

P. 133, *overdiagnosis of this disorder:* American Psychiatric Association. *Diagnostic and Statistical Manual of Mental Disorders.* (4th ed.) Washington, D.C.: American Psychiatric Association, 1994, p. 487.

P. 133, *the potential for "secondary gain":* Holmes, D. *Abnormal Psychology.* New York: HarperCollins, 1994, p. 156.

P. 134, *"I'd never do anything weird or frightening":* "People," *USA Today,* Sept. 30, 1994, p. D-2.

P. 135, *that behavioral excesses are diseases:* Szasz, T. *The Myth of Mental Illness: Foundations of a Theory of Personal Conduct.* New York: HarperCollins, 1961.

P. 136, *addictions on talk shows:* Vatz, R., Weinberg, L., and Szasz, T. "Psychiatry and Television: An Unhealthy Alliance," *USA Today,* May 1986, pp. 53–55; p. 53.

P. 137, *"I'm on this show too!":* Goodman, W. "When Even Victimizers Say They Are Victims," *New York Times,* Mar. 28, 1994, p. C-14.

P. 138, *She said, "I discovered":* "Michelle," letter to authors dated Sept. 1994.

P. 140, *Dysthymia affects millions:* American Psychiatric Association. *Diagnostic and Statistical Manual of Mental Disorders.* (4th ed.) Washington, D.C.: American Psychiatric Association, 1994, p. 345.

P. 141, *going on a talk show after his killing spree:* Rabinowitz, D. "Talk and Consequences," *Wall Street Journal,* July 12, 1993, p. A-10.

P. 150, *"Therapy is presented with vague allusions":* Edward Liska, personal interview, Dec. 30, 1994.

P. 151, *a licensed mental health professional averages between $75 and $125:* Holmes, D. *Abnormal Psychology.* New York: HarperCollins, 1994, p. 577.

P. 151, *costs $650 a month:* Holmes, D. *Abnormal Psychology.* New York: HarperCollins, 1994, p. 577.

P. 151, *rather than the 1,000 currently in operation:* Holmes, D. *Abnormal Psychology.* New York: HarperCollins, 1994, p. 573.

P. 152, *"talk shows rely on the poor and already exploited":* Vicki Abt, personal interview, Nov. 14, 1994.

P. 158, *"make black men the sacrificial lamb"* (and the rest of the quotes in this paragraph and the one following): Richard Majors, personal interview, Nov. 21, 1994.

P. 159, *"aims at too low a standard":* Cecilia Garcia, personal interview, Dec. 15, 1994.

P. 160, *"because of their ethnicity"* (and quote in following paragraph): Thomas Parham, personal interview, Nov. 17, 1994.

P. 160, *"cesspool of TV"* (and other quotes in this paragraph): Courtland Lee, personal interview, Nov. 21, 1994.

P. 162, *"fucked up family murders":* Burns, C. "Next on Geraldo," *New York,* Dec. 5, 1994, pp. 100–109; p. 102.

P. 165, *on-air confrontations only lead to more discord:* Tim Fisher, personal interview, Dec. 14, 1994.

P. 165, *are infected with lice:* Walter, D. "Paul Cameron," *Advocate,* Oct. 29, 1985, pp. 29–30, 33; Cameron, P. "The Gay Agenda," *American Sociological Newsletter,* 1987, p. 11; Pietrzyk, M. "Queer Science," *New Republic,* Oct. 3, 1994, pp. 10–12.

P. 165, *"limp-wristed florists"* (and quotes in following paragraph): Joshua Gamson, personal interview, Dec. 6, 1994.

P. 166, *"My life is lived in the shadow of talk shows":* "Amy," letter to authors dated Dec. 12, 1994.

P. 167, *"better not to get that kind of recognition":* Ron Drach, personal interview, Dec. 13, 1994.

P. 167, *"a wheelchair user with disabilities"* (and other quotes in this paragraph): Catherine Odette, personal interview, Dec. 13, 1994.

P. 169, *the actual number of child viewers is alarming* (and statistics that follow): *Nielsen Station Index,* July 1990, pp. 1415 (Oprah), 693 (Geraldo), 1582 (Sally Jessy Raphael), 503 (Donahue).

6

Trouble for Guests

Viewers are drawn to guests' problems for much the same reason a traveler's gaze is riveted to an accident on the side of the road: wreckage, flames, trauma. Talk TV producers strive to create similar reactions because they want to draw viewers from one channel to another. To be successful, they must find the "Parents [Who] Learn Their Daughter Is a Stripper," or the children of "Spouse-Stealing Parents," or the "Woman Married to a Man Who Used to Be a Woman," or the children of "Mothers Who Kick Out Pregnant Teens." And since many of these people have very real trouble, the potential for real harm, not just staged harm, is great.

When people in trouble move full speed ahead into an intersection lined with eager, greedy producers who want to capture a collision on camera, serious wreckage can result. The bigger the spectacle, the larger the crowd—so an ordinary fender-bender will not do. The damage is aggravated by throwing in more than was expected: close-up angles of pain, shots of crying spectators, and more flaming cars in the guise of relatives and adversaries who want to add more dents and destruction.

Once the collision has occurred, viewers must be instantly distracted by another, so the intersection is quickly cleared. The fire hoses wash away the evidence, and the next scene is set to roll. The people and their pain are quickly gone. Or at least they appear to be.

Talk show guests, unlike the people trapped in cars on the side of the road, are especially easy to forget. They are brought to us as comical, pathetic, dismissable creatures who are not quite real. They *are* real, however, and whatever troubles they are experiencing certainly last longer than the fifteen minutes captured on TV. In fact, after their appearance, they are often faced with new troubles. Their treatment by the shows before, during, and after taping creates another kind of trouble, and these wounds are uglier because they're deliberate.

The public, however, hears very little about what goes wrong for guests. The general impression is that guests' experiences on Talk TV are highly positive. That impression is crafted by the shows. Returning guests are brought back to invariably report that the shows transformed their lives, that they've enjoyed their newfound status from having been "seen on TV," and that they are loyal, adoring fans of the host. The hosts also routinely read letters from viewers and guests about the benefits of the shows. On the rare occasions that the hosts read letters criticizing the shows, there are always members of the audience who are quick to negate such comments.

Undoubtedly, many people enjoy the shows and even benefit from their participation. But that is not the whole picture. It's important to remember that the same publicity machine that creates the image of the hosts is at work with guests. The shows decide who will be invited back on and whose letters will be read aloud to millions of viewers. It is unlikely that they're interested in bringing back guests who are unhappy with how they were treated, dissatisfied with underhanded tricks or surprises, or left shell-shocked after their talk show experience. Nor are they likely to tell us about the catastrophes that resulted in lawsuits and serious emotional harm. The injured remain silent. Thus the picture looks good but isn't complete.

It's easy to dismiss concern about what happens to publicity-seeking individuals who willingly bare all on national television. After all, they asked for it. But what exactly are they asking for? The chance to gain visibility? Yes. The chance to advance their cause? Probably. The chance for help? Perhaps. The chance to be unexpectedly humiliated, labeled as sick, or forced to disclose more than they intended? Not likely.

The shows defend themselves by discrediting their guests with the very characteristics that led to their selection in the first place: problems and exhibitionism. Thus, if a guest complains, the shows can simply claim that the guest is "troubled" or just after more "press." There are almost no limits to what the producers feel they can do, and rarely do they report regret or remorse for their actions.

Tom O'Neill, an investigative journalist, summarized the problem: "The producers walk a fine line and cross it with increasing ease, telling themselves that these people ask for it and get something out of it." As an indication of the callous attitude they've developed, one producer described his reaction to dealing with guests by stating, "I go home at night to take a shower, and I have to wash off the guest grease." This careless comment reveals an underlying contempt for guests that foreshadows the potential for harm.

Setting the Stage for Trouble

We are not suggesting that the shows be held accountable for the mistaken, grandiose, or delusional beliefs of would-be stars or troubled exhibitionists. Bad judgment on the part of guests, however, does not remove culpability on the part of the shows. In fact, in some cases it increases it. Some guests are enormously troubled, with few skills for coping with stress, and the producers don't merely recognize their vulnerability—they want them because of it. Consequently, they design their production priorities in specific ways that are potentially damaging to guests.

No Mental Health Screening

Guests with the hottest problems create the shows with the highest ratings. So producers go in search of extreme cases. In some situations, they actually use those severe stresses and wounds to help convince guests to participate. For example, when producers spotted an article in the newspaper about an unemployed nurse, Laura Thorpe, they were in hot pursuit. She had such immediate appeal because she'd removed her own breast implants at home with a Bic razor.

Despite the fact that she had no phone, that her still-infected wounds were oozing silicone, and that no one had determined why she slit open her breasts, *The Maury Povich Show* had her scheduled to appear less than two weeks after the incident. Before the Povich staff could get her out of her trailer park, however, producers from *Sally Jessy Raphael* tracked her down and had her on a plane to New York with the jars containing the remains of her silicone implants in hand. Her unemployed husband and three of her children were brought along to help fill in the details.

Two producers for Sally's show took Laura and her family out for Easter dinner, then took the jars for safekeeping. They weren't as careful with the actual guest. Left alone at the hotel, Laura was a sitting duck for the *Povich* producers. Convincing her that they wanted only to talk, Maury's people took her out of the hotel and to their offices. Her husband and daughter never realized she was gone from the hotel. Less than one hour later, Laura was being taped for the *Povich* show.

Heavily medicated and with a spreading infection, Laura was introduced to the audience and viewers by Maury Povich. "Just two weeks ago, at one A.M. in the morning, in the privacy of her bathroom, she took a razor blade, just like this one, and attempted to perform surgery on herself. I mean, we can't even imagine—I mean, the audience is breathless, and so am I. I mean, we want to clutch ourselves. Why would you want to do such a thing?" The question was spurious and designed only to draw out more details of the gruesome scene. Maury's introduction implied that the guest seated before him was rational, that she was an ordinary woman driven to extreme behavior for reasons viewers needed to understand in case they found themselves in a similar situation.

Laura was clearly in no condition to explain her problem. When she tried, Maury kept redirecting her because her explanations were meandering. Her first attempt went like this: "I felt I was going to die. And my husband, on March 13th, had a grand mal seizure in our car and broke his back—he had an accident. And then I ended up, ten days later, in the hospital with gangrene in my fingers. I've been in orphanages and foster homes all my life. I did not want my children to end up like that, so I had to make sure they had—when my husband got home, I said—The only way—I called doctors. I asked them could they do it pro bono."

Thorpe's answer should have brought up additional concerns, not only because of its content but also because the thoughts were so loosely connected. But Povich ignored those cues and continued to focus on her implants. He asked for descriptions of her self-inflicted operation: "What did you do?" Once again, her answer reflected her confusion. "Well, I took the razor and, I mind you it had shaved about ten sets of legs. I feel bad for guys, I really do." She was wandering again. So Povich tried again to focus: "Forget them, we're interested in you." Ms. Thorpe answered, "And so I smashed it open. And see, you have to remember, I've been in the military and trained for all kinds of situations if you're in the jungles, how do you get out. If you're going to die, if you don't do something, you've got to do something, and this is the way I felt. If [I] had to die, and I also had to protect my children. My children are very, you know, much to me. They're—they are my life." The interview was clearly in trouble, so Povich asked the obvious, "You wouldn't recommend this procedure would you?" "No, No," she said, finally able to provide an understandable answer.

Ten minutes into the show, in a weak attempt to acknowledge how disoriented Ms. Thorpe sounded, Povich asked, "Now you sound like you've got—it sounds like you're on medication. You're talking slowly, you know, maybe there's a slight slur. So you've got to be on medication still, two weeks later." She replied, "Yeah, I am taking a pain medication, right now because I, yesterday was so unbearable, just gobs of silicone was coming out again." Povich: "Still coming out?" Thorpe: "Yes, it's still coming and that way the wounds are opened they're big and they're opening and they're draining all the time."

As Povich continued the interview, his chief tactic was to play up the fears of breast implants that many women in America were experiencing at that time. This way, Povich could be successful no matter how incoherent his guest was. The show's suggestion was clearly that perhaps she had done this as a result of "autoimmune disease." Maury had a plastic surgeon in the wings who explained that doctors will do operations on a pro bono basis and that this procedure was not necessary, which only increased the impression that "something" had come over her to make her do this to herself.

The "something" was never explained and viewers were perhaps left feeling almost as confused as Ms. Thorpe appeared. The show, however, accomplished just what it was designed to do. It teased viewers with details about a truly bizarre act and justified the routine by calling it public education.

The possibility that Laura Thorpe might have been suffering from a psychotic break either at the time of her actions or of her appearance on the show was ignored, as was the possibility that she might have limited ability to adequately explain the situation to viewers. The story of a woman cutting open her breasts and squeezing out silicone was so sensational that little or no consideration was given either to her physical condition or to her mental state.

According to Tom O'Neill, Laura's daughter had been considerably traumatized as well. It was she who found her mother, semiconscious on the bathroom floor. She also helped her mother finish the operation by assisting in squeezing out the silicone. Such an event would no doubt be highly traumatic. But there was as little regard for her as there was for her mother.

Because Laura did not appear on the show, Sally's people refused to pay the $2,027 hotel bill or return airfare. The producers were smarting from the loss of a really hot guest. If they needed consoling, however, they could find it in their new trophy: the jars containing Laura Thorpe's silicone, which were on display in the office.

The *Povich* producers said Laura's wounds were "still seeping, dirty and gross and she had to be hospitalized after the show." Indeed, she needed to be hospitalized for medical concerns. Had a psychological assessment been conducted, however, it is likely that she might have been hospitalized for psychological disturbances either stemming from the incident or from preexisting conditions that could have produced it.

A clear description of Laura's problems would require an understanding of her situation, but that was clearly absent. Based on what was presented on the show, it is impossible to determine whether or not she was psychotic, suicidal, depressed about having cancer or being poor, or any number of other possible contributing factors. It was also impossible to ascertain which, if any, of her concerns had been alleviated. The show, however, was billed as "Breast Implant Horror," a misleading title that simultaneously worked to reduce her problems and inflate viewers' fear.

After being released, Laura made the rounds on a few more shows. Each time, her personal tragedy was turned into a public spectacle for an hour. Then, for all intents and purposes, it was over—over for the shows, anyway. Tom O'Neill reported that he talked with Laura quite some time after the shows and that "she was still ranting and raving" over the producers' treatment. She felt angry and betrayed because they had promised to return her calls but now only haggled over her bills. Convinced she had both lupus and multiple sclerosis, she wanted to go on talking, but the producers were occupied with new guests.

The lack of established procedures that would ensure mental health screening of troubled guests prior to the show is problematic in two important ways. First, vulnerable guests may not be aware of, or have access to, other options. Further, they may not have the skills to choose the route most likely to result in improvement. The caution and reconsideration that seem called for, however, would be at odds with the goals of the shows. What would happen to the thrill, the rush, the drama if the most volatile guests waited until their situations stabilized? It would be diminished, of course. If guests like Laura Thorpe had some help to sort out problems, and proper medication, their stories would sound different. They would be flatter, less conflicted, and less unusual.

The second problem resulting from not conducting mental health screening is that there is no way to confirm the nature of the problems being presented. A self-diagnosis of multiple personality disorder, or false memory syndrome, or autoimmune disease has the potential to be very misleading to viewers. The quality of information would improve dramatically if there were some reliable, credible basis for it, such as a thorough diagnosis conducted by a qualified professional. The primary sources for screening and selection, however, are the young, eager producers who typically can neither assess the accuracy of mental health information, nor determine the degree of risk for potential guests.

One young producer put it this way, "We're not trained psychologists. We don't really know what's going to happen to this person. You go home and deal with next week's show, they have to go home and deal with their lives."

Preshow Pressures and Setups

Not only are guests not screened for mental health problems that could be exacerbated by appearing, they are often pressured into going on because of those very concerns. Laura Thorpe was not given enough time for her wounds to even begin to heal before she was swept off to Talk TV. For others, old wounds are reopened for the benefit of the shows. The need for excitement and conflict has even resulted in new problems for people who were unexpectedly set up.

Mary Duffy, a *Montel Williams* producer who credited herself with having created "conflict talk," described how she put together a show about mistresses that introduced this new way of producing shows. She wanted to demonstrate the conflict by bringing on not only the angry wife but the wanton mistress as well. In pursuit of her goal, she went after the guests. "Seventeen phone calls later, I got her, it was amazing television. One of our highest rated shows ever." If it took seventeen phone calls to get the cheated-on wife, doubts and all, the producer's goal of top TV ratings clearly took precedence over the guest's reservations.

Such pressure has even more potential to be damaging when those involved are children or adolescents. Children often get involved in Talk TV when family issues are discussed. Even with "family" topics, the producers want vivid stories of conflict, so they push the guests to reveal things that may be upsetting to other members of the family and play up every issue that has even the smallest potential to be a problem. That is exactly what happened to Jenny Sayward and her children.

Jenny Sayward is the director of Lavender Families, an association for families with lesbian mothers. The association is quite popular with Talk TV; they receive anywhere from two to six requests for appearances per month. After watching the shows and hearing about other members' experiences, Jenny was very cautious about appearing herself. She was concerned about "being exploited, publicly harassed, and sensationalized." She personally had refused many offers from other shows but considered *Gordon Elliott* partly because it was so new that show tapes were not available for review. She eventually agreed because the producers successfully convinced her the show would be different and her family's individualized needs would be met.

The eager producers' promises turned out to be untrue. But by the time Jenny realized that, it was too late. "The producers are very skilled in sensing what will motivate different people to participate in talk shows and they use those motivations for the sake of the show, they manipulate the participants to promote the producers' own agenda for the show."

The producer told Jenny's son, who lives with his father, all about "the expense-paid trip, the 'luxury' hotel, the limousines." Jenny reported that the producer also "offered to provide hotel accommodations for a few extra days and personally 'show him all around New York' if we could extend our stay." He was assured that his face would not be shown on camera.

These offers did not appeal to Jenny and her daughter, so other promises were made to them. They were lured with "a forum to speak up about how prejudice affects kids of lesbian and gay families, and a chance to open some minds. [She] eased my daughter's worries about an unfriendly audience by telling her that a group of gay New Yorkers would be in the audience."

The promises worked to get the family there, but once Jenny and her children arrived, the situation quickly changed. Jenny said, "I was promised an all-expense-paid trip, including our airport parking fee, [but] I was never reimbursed for our $30 parking expense. The 'luxury hotel accommodations' were another horror story. My son did take her [offers of a full vacation] seriously and blamed me for depriving him of this experience." The promises of being able to address the issues of prejudice to a receptive audience turned out to have been illusory as well. "There were no gay people evident in the audience, and Joanne [the producer] just shrugged off her concern."

Further, the producers assured Jenny and her children that they would be able to tell their own stories in their own words. That isn't what happened, however. After being told to speak up and say what they wanted, Jenny and her children found that the host controlled the mike. When they interrupted to make points about prejudice in a predominantly heterosexual society, their comments were edited from the final broadcast. In one segment, taped while the mothers were off stage, the host misquoted Jenny to her daughter. Jenny reported that Gordon Elliott made it sound like "I had admitted to disliking heterosexuals, and then asked for her feelings about that." Her daughter was doubtful that she had said it and so didn't react with the emotion he sought. That section was also edited out of the broadcast version. At least five other incidents were cut from the final tape. Jenny suspects they were eliminated not because the point wasn't made but because no significant emotion was aroused.

In her assessment, "The show was a fiasco! Every one of us was exploited and trivialized to the point of caricature . . . I was cut off and my kids never had a chance to tell their stories. My kids were portrayed as troubled teens who 'have a problem with their mom being gay' without ever being allowed to say that their real problem was the bigotry, fear, and prejudices they had successfully overcome." The producers set them up.

"My family was left feeling manipulated, exploited, and betrayed." Her son threatened to sue because he had been promised that neither his face nor even his profile would be seen on camera. When his profile was displayed, the show claimed it was "an accident." Jenny's son was very distressed when he was ridiculed at school and lost friends over the appearance. Likewise, her daughter was fed up and angry over her and her brother having been labeled "kids who have problems with their lesbian mother." Her daughter felt her appearance was used to demonstrate something that she didn't feel was true: that she had personal problems because her mother is lesbian. She resented being characterized in this fashion and is now appropriately distrustful of the shows or anything connected with them.

This is an illustration of how "get the guests" tactics can lead to feelings of betrayal when what was assured is then twisted and denied. There appears to be no accountability. When Jenny complained, nothing changed.

Preshow "Preparations"

Once people have agreed to appear on the show, they are brought to the studio for preshow preparation. But the preparation is not to prepare guests for what they might encounter or how to protect themselves. Rather, the "preparation" is to prime them to tell all. Guests are instructed to "get their points across" and to "not be afraid to speak up, to tell it like it is."

The providers of most products or services are required to warn consumers of potential ill-effects. In the social sciences, if human subjects are going to be used, researchers must inform them of any possible benefit or harm that might result. This procedure is referred to as obtaining "informed consent." It means that anyone involved has been provided with reasonable warnings about the possible consequences of an experience, and sufficient time to consider them before they decide to participate. Doctors, therapists, and researchers are required to obtain informed consent before treatment. TV talk shows are exempt from this procedure and defend themselves by citing the importance of free speech, the benefits of open discussion, and the demands of viewers' appetites. Time and again they demonstrate that they want the credibility that comes from associating themselves with the social sciences, and mental health in particular, but that they want none of the accompanying responsibilities. The consent forms they use address the right of the show to broadcast the guests' appearances, and copies are not routinely provided to the guests who sign them.

If guests voice any concern or reservation about appearing, the producers go into overdrive to talk them out of their concerns. Any sign of hesitation is labeled as preshow jitters rather than explored as serious concern over the consequences of a national revelation of intimate information. The emphasis is not on the legitimate and protective nature of the concern or the consequences of ignoring it. The agenda is always focused on producing a sensational show. As a result, fast talking and instant intimacy are often required. Convincing troubled guests that they won't be seen as "freaks" (even if that is how the shows think of them) takes savvy and deception.

Immediately before a *Donahue* show was to air, for example, Lillian Smith, a producer, took one of the guests back to her office to get a pencil. The guest happened to look up and see the chalk board with the names of upcoming shows. The show on which she and her children were scheduled to appear was labeled "FREAKS." She knew that the label was intended for her daughters—Siamese twins who were attached at their heads. Understandably, she began to cry. Crying alone might not have been viewed as a problem by the producers, but the mother also informed them that she and her daughters would not go on any show that would list them that way. The producer admitted she "had to talk fast, with only minutes until air time," to convince the guest that the show wouldn't treat her or her daughters like freaks, even if they did recruit them for that purpose. The producer claimed that she talked this woman out of her concern by telling her that it would be good for the country to see that they were really just like everybody else.

Manipulating guests before the show does not end with simply encouraging them to "talk it up" or falsely reassuring them that "it will be okay." Every opportunity to fire things up is taken. If guests with opposing views or with painful conflicts are appearing on the same show, which is often the case, the producers will place them in different greenrooms. Guests might interpret this as another example of the producers' concern for their well-being. The producers, however, use it as an opportunity to run back and forth between the rooms telling the guests all the inflammatory remarks made about them by the other guests.

One producer for Richard Bey explained to Tom O'Neill that he went from greenroom to greenroom with a feuding family. He explained to one group, "Your sister-in-law says she is going to say you have really been a bitch." He then went to the next room and explained, "Your sister-in-law is planning to say that you are really screwed up." When these two groups hit the stage they were ready for war. The technique worked to build false allegiances and to thoroughly rile up the guests before they were brought on stage, where the collision that had been so carefully (or carelessly) planned finally occurred.

Trouble on the Air

The pressure does not let up once the show starts. After having been flown in, put up in a hotel, fed in the hotel dining room, escorted to the show in a limousine, and spotlighted on national television, guests can end up feeling obligated to produce the goods. Responses such as "No, I won't answer that question. It's too personal," or "That doesn't have anything to do with the topic," or even "I don't want to talk about that" are clearly outside of the limits of expected or approved behavior. Overwhelmed or unprepared, guests often feel they must respond to every question asked. And those questions may be more personal or hostile than were anticipated.

Producers probe for the most vulnerable aspects of guests' lives.

Prior to the show, they sometimes falsely assure guests that once on the air private information won't be revealed. Tim Fisher, the director of the Gay and Lesbian Parents Association International, is concerned over how some of his members and their children had been set up. These children wanted to assist their parents in breaking down stereotypes and were hurt when it backfired. He described one teenager who went on *Donahue* to talk about her relationship with her gay father. This teen was also gay but had wanted the privilege of telling people at her own pace and in her own way. She was particularly concerned about her grandmother's reaction. Producers asked questions about her sexual orientation prior to the show, which she answered, but she was assured that her sexuality would not be discussed during the show.

Once on the air, however, Donahue went right for it, asking this teen the very question she didn't want to answer. Caught off guard, she answered truthfully. She was very upset and concerned following the show and left with more problems than she came with.

The entire culture of the shows is based on "telling all." The hosts and audience feel at liberty to ask anything. This may make for good entertainment, but it can be big trouble for real life. Despite the devil-may-care approach to the fast-paced thrills and shocks, it's important for viewers to consider the consequences. The guests are not actors playing parts, they are real people who have real reactions to what is said and done. Their lives will go on after the "fun" of the show has ended.

On-Air Surprises

One of the increasingly popular methods of keeping the shows lively is to surprise guests on the air with some person, event, or revelation they did not expect. By catching them off guard, giving them no forewarning or opportunity to prepare a response, viewers get the thrill of seeing people squirm. Guests, in turn, get no chance to protect themselves unless they refuse to appear or walk off stage.

Some of the surprises are "good natured"—boyfriends propose, old high school sweethearts reappear after years, or friends play silly tricks. Other surprises are not so light-hearted: daughters confront fathers with sexual abuse; husbands reveal affairs; children tell their parents they are taking guns to school, dancing in a strip joint, or hiding their boyfriends in their rooms; and in some cases parents reveal that they are gay, and lovers disclose that they have had a sex-change operation.

The so-called preshow preparation cannot prepare guests in any meaningful way for surprises since the "surprise" would then be spoiled. Rather, guests are deceived as to the real purpose of their appearances. They are lulled into thinking something "interesting or fun" is going to happen, and as a result are left even more vulnerable to the attack that is about to bear down upon them. Such on-air surprises can quite predictably turn very ugly for the people involved.

Oprah Winfrey claimed she has had it with such tactics, and even claimed she was surprised when a husband revealed to his wife that not only was he still seeing his mistress, she was pregnant with his child. As we quoted in Chapter Two, Oprah said, "It was a very hard moment, I wouldn't do that [intentionally] to anybody." But she did do it. She knew the wife was vulnerable. She knew the husband had already hurt her. She owned the program, hired the producers, and asked the questions that led to the revelation that was certainly made more painful because it occurred on national TV.

Montel Williams is also no novice to such setups. He invited Jerome Stanfield and his sister, Sarah, with whom he was living, to appear on the show. Sarah was kept off stage until just the right moment: after Stanfield had "disclosed" that he was a serial rapist of ninety prostitutes. Then, after emphasizing that Sarah was unaware of any of this, that all she knew was that her brother had a drug problem and was HIV positive, Montel brought her out. "I know you have not been able to hear anything that Jerome has said on the show, but Jerome wants to tell you something."

Clearly, Sarah was completely unprepared to learn on national television—in front of an audience of strangers who found out before she did—that her brother was a rapist. The scene was not only terribly cruel, it was willfully so in the face of evidence that Jerome was lying. In fact, he later denied the charges and the police publicly reported that there was no evidence that Jerome or anyone else had committed the crimes reported on the show. Although this show might appear particularly troublesome, it is only one of Montel's on-air stunts.

In another stunning example, Yvonne Porter was invited to appear on Montel's show in 1993 with her sister, Kimberly. Yvonne agreed. What happened on the show left her so humiliated and angry that she sued both the *Montel Williams* show and her sister. Yvonne Porter reported that she was not told prior to the taping what the show was about, but was reassured by the producers that she would not be embarrassed or humiliated. In fact, she reported that she was told she was in for a "pleasant surprise."

Porter was kept in seclusion until her it was her turn to appear. Once on stage, she heard Kimberly tell Montel that she had been sleeping with Yvonne's boyfriend of fourteen years. Yvonne sat stunned and silent as Montel informed viewers that she was hearing this for the very first time. Then, as the show proceeded, Montel had the audacity to chastise Kimberly for doing this to Yvonne on national television, as if he, like Yvonne, had been caught unaware of Kimberly's plan.

As we've discussed earlier, these on-air blitz attacks gain a false legitimacy because the hosts frame them as attempts to resolve problems, not create them, a kind of "for your own good" evisceration. Montel, in keeping with the tradition, told Yvonne Porter that her sister had not intended to harm her, but needed to "make a public statement for her own self."

Mental health experts also help lend credibility to these vitriolic encounters by allowing themselves to get pulled into the fray. On this particular show, Jacqueline Rose Hott appeared and attempted to both console Yvonne and explain the situation in the few minutes the show allotted. Of course, neither was possible in that setting. It is unclear if Hott was in on the setup or was just as unaware of what was coming as Yvonne. We can only hope that she did not know, and unwittingly got pulled in. Unfortunately, there are times when professionals do more than get caught. Sometimes they condone the setups or even help to arrange them.

On-air surprises often involve unplanned, and unwanted, reunions. Actor Brent Jasmer agreed to appear on *Geraldo* with his adoptive parents to talk about his adoption. He specifically sought assurance that there would be no upsetting tricks. The producers were aware that he had been looking for his biological mother but had not found her and was not yet ready to be reunited. On the sly, Geraldo's producers arranged to have his biological mother on hand for a first-time meeting on national TV. This highly emotional event was not only upsetting to Jasmer, it was equally disturbing to his parents. Jasmer filed a lawsuit charging breach of contract, fraud, and invasion of privacy. "I'd been anticipating this moment for about twenty-six years, what gave him [Geraldo] the right to alter my life like he did?" Even the birth mother felt set up, having been reassured that this was in fact what Jasmer wanted. Producers lured her by claiming that the article she had read about Jasmer's reluctance to meet his birth mother was no longer true. The show claimed this was all just a publicity stunt by an actor who wanted even more attention.

In another horrible example, *Jenny Jones* producers assured Jonathan Schmitz that his on-air surprise would be the opportunity to meet a secret crush. He "came out on stage before a studio audience, and there was a woman sitting there that he knew," said Sheriff's Lieutenant Bruce Naile. "He figured she was his secret admirer and walked up and kissed her. But then they told him, 'Oh, no, she's not your secret admirer, this is'—and out walked Scott Amedure. The show was about men who have secret crushes on men. He was stunned," Naile said. "He had agreed to do the show, so he didn't know what to do or what his rights were. So he sat there and went along with it."

Schmitz later told police that his experience on the show had "eaten away" at him. And three days later, after finding an unsigned note at his home that he assumed was left by Amedure, he went to the other man's mobile home and killed him with two shotgun blasts to the chest.

Officials at *Jenny Jones,* of course, claimed no responsibility for Amedure's death. Their ethics allowed the producers to lie to Schmitz, subject him to what he felt was a publicly humiliating situation, and then wash their hands of the tragic consequences.

These incidents are just a few examples of "on-air surprises"— but, in fact, most of the shows involve situations that are potentially compromising for either the guests or their friends and families. Topics such as sisters who sleep with the same man, wives who work as strippers, or children who keep secrets from their parents are all of interest precisely because someone is doing something others probably think they shouldn't. The nature of the show is to expose life's dirty little secrets. It doesn't require much of a stretch of our imaginations to realize that there are probably harmful consequences, both for those who tell and those who are told on.

After the Show

Before the taping, shows are interested in people because they have problems. Afterward, the producers who were so attentive before aren't worried about those problems any more—or the ones they might have caused for guests. But their lack of concern doesn't mean that what happens to guests once the shows are over is of no importance. What happens to some guests, in fact, is often more troubling than what brought them to the shows to begin with.

Geraldo's people, undoubtedly, thought they had recruited the perfect guests when they invited Dr. and Mrs. Pierce to appear on the show. The husband was a psychiatrist and the wife was a nurse with two children. What made them of interest was that the wife maintained a private practice as a prostitute. Her husband reportedly encouraged her endeavor and they were on the show to tell everyone all about this arrangement. As one might suspect, however, all was not rosy. The couple had already been embroiled in divorce proceedings in which she accused him of cruelty, adultery, and drunkenness.

Their situation worsened quickly and dramatically. The *Atlanta Constitution* reported that after the show was taped, but before it aired, Mrs. Pierce shot her husband twice and killed him. Broadcasting this show pushed at the edge of acceptability. Without a doubt, the Pierces were already having serious problems and Geraldo cannot be held accountable for their trouble. But encouraging public disclosures of inflamed personal problems probably did not help.

Trouble of this sort is compounded by the fact that because the shows specialize in complicated, tumultuous events in the lives of troubled people, it is virtually impossible to know exactly what influence the shows have in how those events play out afterward. While we cannot determine the exact effect of the shows, we should not dismiss their role by simply attributing all postshow difficulties to preshow circumstances. Many of the guests are highly troubled, and it is easy to dismiss such tragedies as inevitable—that's "how those people are." However, such explanations, while inviting to the shows and their fans, are hardly fair to the guests, no matter what their problems are.

Earlier, we briefly described a *Sally Jessy Raphael* program titled "Wives of Rapists." What we did not discuss was the trouble the rapist had following his appearance on the show. He had completed his prison sentence, his treatment, and his parole. Emotionally, he felt equipped to handle Sally, the producers, and the angry audience. He agreed to come on the show in disguise with his wife. Despite the disguise, however, he was quickly recognized by neighbors. The neighbors then felt justified in trying to get him fired from his job and ousted from their neighborhood. They called his employer and also tried to cause trouble with his wife's employer. Her children, who certainly had no role in their stepfather's previous behavior, were hassled on the school bus with taunts that left them confused and upset. The local police even joined their efforts, calling the man in for questioning. Finally, the couple sold their home and moved away.

Nancy Steele, a supervising psychologist at the North Central Correctional Institution in Marion, Ohio, feels guilty about her involvement with this incident because she assisted in arranging the appearance. Based on her knowledge of him as a former client, she was confident that the man could handle the show. She had not anticipated the consequences that followed, however. She had thought it would be useful for the community and meaningful for her clients, but it turned out to be a disaster. Not only was the family harassed after the show, the man was not able get across the information that had led him to agree to appear: that some rapists can benefit from treatment. He described his talk show appearance as "one of the dumbest things I have ever done." Whether or not we agree with his assessment, it is certainly an indication of how unpleasant life became after his talk show debut.

Steele made every attempt to prepare her clients and to act in their best interest. Not all professionals have that opportunity. Some clients decide to appear on a talk show even though advised against it by a therapist. A Miami therapist, who requested anonymity, described a series of events in which one of his clients was badly taken advantage of not only by the Talk TV industry but also by his own physician. The client, Greg, was a seriously disturbed alcoholic with a history of troubled relationships. During the course of his counseling, he learned of a doctor who did penis enlargement surgery. Greg mistakenly concluded that his problems would be solved if he had this procedure. Against his therapist's warnings, Greg contacted a Dr. Samitier, who agreed to perform the procedure at no cost. There was one catch: Greg would have to appear on *Geraldo* to do a testimonial about the benefits of the procedure.

Greg appeared on February 24, 1994, and described how the operation enlarged his penis from three and a quarter inches to five inches in circumference. On the show he also explained that his therapist recommended that he work on accepting himself as he was, rather than trying to boost his self-esteem by increasing the size of his penis. Sounds reasonable. Samitier, however, countered with,

"A therapist recommended that he not do the procedure. And that's the only thing that therapist could do, was get you to accept the way you are. But if you feel different than how you look and you want to change that, and you can, we have the technology to do it, then it's okay to do it." Geraldo, in his usual form, went for the punch line, "The sky's the limit? . . . I mean, if you're. . . ."

Despite the fact that Greg appeared in disguise, his therapist explained to us that he was recognized by a stewardess on the plane trip home. She flirtatiously suggested a meeting, no doubt raising Greg's hopes that he really had taken the right steps to improve his lot in life. Then she stood him up. When it began to dawn on Greg that his life was not suddenly better, he disintegrated emotionally. He dropped out of therapy and resumed drinking. Meanwhile, Samitier ended up in jail after killing one of his patients in a botched operation.

Clearly, the show and the physician were unconcerned with anything other than their own success. They took advantage of an obviously troubled man with poor judgment in order to gain viewers and attract new patients. In the process, millions of viewers were exposed to skewed information about a highly controversial and dangerous procedure. The guest was treated like a disposable container. They used what they wanted and threw him out when they were done.

The maltreatment of guests is a serious issue and should not be dismissed simply because some guests demonstrate faulty judgment. On rare occasions, this fact will penetrate a few of the producers, but the insight is usually only a fleeting weakness. Debbie Mitchell, a producer for *Geraldo*, reported to Dan Collison on *All Things Considered* that she once thought she had ruined a man's life. The guest had admitted to sexually molesting his daughter and agreed to appear on the show. Shortly after appearing, he suffered from a nervous breakdown. Ms. Mitchell said, "I felt so guilty because I felt that I shouldn't have had him on the show . . . in the end it wasn't my fault. It really wasn't, but I felt very responsible."

During the same interview, Ms. Mitchell reported that she

once spent three months trying to convince a woman who said she was raped by her husband to appear on the show. Her standard procedure during preshow negotiations is to convince potential guests that their appearance will be therapeutic. If the appearance goes sour, a more laissez-faire attitude is substituted: Guests want to do it and the shows bear no responsibility for actively encouraging them to appear. It's a convenient and cost-effective change of heart right at the time when guests are most likely to be in need of additional services.

No Professional Follow-Up

Having just encouraged guests to emotionally disembowel themselves and those closest to them in front of millions of viewers, one might expect that the least the shows could do is to provide careful postshow debriefing and arrange for professional counseling for the guests. In fact, the shows would have us believe that they do so on a regular basis. The hosts often refer to counseling during the show, bring out experts to "work" with guests on air, and frequently report that they pay for counseling if it is needed.

The postshow services, however, appear to be as unimpressive as the preshow preparation. Some of the shows can point to incidents in which they did, in fact, pay for help following a show. More often, however, guests are in and out in rapid succession, with little or no debriefing or follow-up. Even in some of the most serious situations, when it is clear that the guests are troubled and in need of help, the shows unceremoniously dismiss them with the name of a hometown counselor and proceed full steam ahead to the next troubled guest.

Ruth Peters, Ph.D., a psychologist who appears regularly as an expert in child and family concerns, has also been working for the *Rolonda* show to find therapists who can provide services to the guests after their appearances. In the four years that she has been on retainer with King World, she has been asked "a handful of times" to locate aftercare for guests. Peters is quick to add that by no means does she believe that she is the only psychologist employed in this capacity—but, if her experience is any indication, the shows are not routinely providing postshow services.

In an attempt to determine what sorts of services are provided by Talk TV as part of the much touted "aftercare," and the frequency with which those services are provided, we called shows directly. The standard answer was that if counseling seems necessary, the shows will give the guests the name of a therapist and sometimes even pay for their treatment. It hardly sounds like a well-oiled machine. Who determines what constitutes "necessary?" What procedures are used to determine the appropriateness of the chosen therapists? What factors are used in deciding whether or not to pay for the services?

Some of Dr. April Martin's experiences support the suspicion that the shows don't do much to follow up with guests after their appearances. Martin is a psychologist who has appeared on *Gordon Elliott*, *The Oprah Winfrey Show*, *Sally Jessy Raphael*, *Donahue*, *Sonya Live*, and *The Maury Povich Show*, as well as numerous local shows. While Martin said that the *Donahue* and *Povich* staff treated her particularly well, her experiences with some of the other shows were not entirely positive. She explained that on both *Gordon Elliott* and *Sonya Live* she had "really painful and unpleasant" experiences yet received no follow-up services. She also feels certain that there were no services offered to any of the other guests.

Martin stated that although she appeared on *Sonya Live* in part as an expert—and clearly she is a high-functioning, resourceful person—she needed follow-up after the show because of harsh questioning from her opposition. She was invited to discuss issues related to gay and lesbian parenting but got no support either during or after the show. During the show, there were difficult call-ins, including a very threatening voice saying, "Get the queer off the air." Not only did the show's staff not respond to the caller in a manner that protected or supported their guest, they also failed to even comment on the incident following the show. Martin reported that she doesn't remember how she got onto the street; she remembers only that she was there, feeling horrible and dazed.

Similarly, Martin reported that for almost all of the programs on which she has appeared, no formal aftercare services have been offered. She stated that Donahue came in and spoke with her following a taping for his show but that none of the other shows' hosts offered to talk even briefly about what had happened on their programs. "It's out with you and in with the next one." Even in situations where the production staff had been highly responsive to her requests and suggestions before the show, as the *Oprah* staff had been, the responsiveness ended when the taping was done. The staff were busy with the next program and the next set of guests.

To highlight her point, Martin recounted that when she appeared on *Gordon Elliott,* the most positive guest had been a sweet young man whose mother had been murdered for being lesbian and whose father had recently died of AIDS. Martin stated that she was sure that the young man was hurting, but she was equally sure that he "was shoved into a limo six hours too early for his plane"—and that was his postshow service.

Clearly, services are not always provided when needed. When they are, however, one wonders if they constitute an improvement over offering nothing at all. The producers of *Sally Jessy Raphael* indicated that Gilda Carle, Ph.D., is their contact person for their aftercare program. If, in fact, Carle represents the top of the line in aftercare for *Sally Jessy Raphael,* there is considerable cause for alarm. Although both the producer of the show and Carle herself appear quite pleased with what they have going, it has little to do with providing credible, competent mental health services to troubled guests.

Carle describes herself as a "Relationships Therapist who mediates psycho sexual & professional issues." She "prescribes quick tools to become happier, healthier, and more successful." Her "motivational messages" range from "3 Steps to Anger-Busting (Frame it, Claim It, Tame It)" to "18-Second ConFRONTation" to "How to

Hook Him, Hug Him, Hold Him." Her doctoral degree is in organizational and administrative studies from New York University, and among the qualifications she lists on her résumé is the fact that as "a youngster, she danced and acted on stage." Her own accounts of her work provide the best description of the "mental health" services this kind of background and training yield.

She described the methods employed to assist a troubled couple that appeared on the *Sally* show. The husband had reportedly had affairs as well as physically abused his wife. He felt guilty and wanted to get rid of the guilt. The wife had become so distraught during the show that she walked off the set, then later returned. Carle's "intervention" was to hold the wife in her arms and soothe her. She reported that she "thinks" they went for some counseling in their hometown after the show. While this account is notable for all that it lacks, her most stunning description involved another show.

Carle highlighted what she felt was a poignant encounter on Geraldo's "Dissed to Death" program. The program centered around teenage murderers. We found her account equally gripping, but for different reasons. With great sincerity, Carle reported that "Killer" (one of the guests) was in disguise because he had "murdered someone the night before for sneaker stepping." She reflected that she had grown up in New York and therefore knew how to deal with this kind of kid. Feeling an instant yet deep connection with him, she reported that "I chose to do this, I didn't have to, but after the show I met with 'Killer' in his dressing room. I looked him in the eye and said, 'I have a big mouth. You and I have that in common. The difference is I use my mouth as a professional tool, you use yours to kill.' I could see by the look in his eyes that I really got to him. We would have never have met were it not for that show. I'd like to think I saved his life."

When asked if she followed up to see if her advice worked or what sorts of changes it might have produced, she explained "I could see it in his eyes. I educate and then plant a seed. No, I didn't see him again." Carle is apparently as certain about most of her "interventions"—she did not report following up with any of the guests she worked with in the weeks after the show. She informed us that "I heal for a living. I used to heal in classrooms but that was only a few. Now, I'm healing millions."

A Case In Point: The Story of Sally and Stephie

Certainly, many of these examples are troubling. Yet perhaps even more troubling are those that initially seem less severe because they are so routine. In her autobiography, Sally Jessy Raphael describes what she believes is one of her finest accomplishments: her interaction with a young woman named Stephie. She tells the story in a self-congratulatory fashion and proudly highlights the very aspects of the encounter that from a mental health perspective are the most questionable.

Sally tells the story as if her actions were solely motivated by a desire to help a troubled person. Readers are told that Stephie was an unemployed woman in her late twenties who turned to Sally with a problem that she had kept secret for fourteen years. She called Sally's radio show and revealed, for the first time ever, that she was date-raped at the age of fifteen and that now she was plagued by fears of going crazy. Too scared to say any more, she hung up. Later, however, she wrote indicating that she wanted to talk with Sally further because there was no one else she could trust.

Sally's response was to assign her top producer, Terry Murphy, to convince Stephie to appear on national television. Despite the fact that Stephie told Sally she could talk to no one but her, in a few weeks Stephie had confided in Terry as well. It took him several weeks to persuade her to appear but finally she agreed. Once at the hotel, Stephie was left alone in her room, became frightened, and had second thoughts about the arrangement. Terry was called away on a family emergency so Stephie went to the only person she felt she could trust—Sally.

Sally acknowledged Stephie's apprehension and reported that she was also torn about what to do. She knew that her show would be weaker without Stephie but wondered if she would be too afraid to appear. Sally then decided that Stephie must have really wanted to go on because she had continued to write to her about her problem and even came to the studio. Having decided that an appearance was what Stephie wanted and needed, Sally talked with her for several hours and finally Stephie agreed.

Stephie told the story of her rape, subsequent pregnancy, and abortion. She told how she felt such remorse that she vowed to punish herself forever. Following the show, however, Stephie was not better but worse. Her nightmares increased, she was plagued by fears of going crazy and was obsessed with the thought that her rapist would track her down and kill her for breaking her silence. Sally reported that what happened next was a "miracle." A "human behavior counselor" named Sandy Meyer, who had been abused herself as a child, saw Stephie's show. Readers are told that in a freak broadcasting of the *Sally Jessy Raphael* show to a location in which it otherwise does not air, a therapist happened to be turning the channel just as Stephie appeared. Not only did she hear her story but she felt immediately connected, knowing she could "help that person."

Sally went against production policy and paid for Stephie to fly to Rocky Mount, Virginia, to have two weeks of pro bono therapy with Sandy Meyer. She reported that within just three days of this "therapy" Stephie's nightmares ceased. In effect, she was completely "transformed" by the end of the week.

Sandy and Stephie were then invited to return to the show to broadcast the amazing results of her appearance on the show and her progress in treatment. As part of her vow to punish herself for the abortion, Stephie had also sworn to never have a child. After her second appearance on the show, however, she was so whole and complete that she got pregnant and named Sally the godmother.

Sally's analysis of this story is that it goes "to the heart of what I'm all about." She says that she genuinely loves meeting people like Stephie and that she can "relate to their pain. Maybe the reason is that like them, I'm a survivor."

If Sally had really wanted to encourage viewers who had been raped to get help, she could easily have gone to any rape crisis center and solicited someone who was no longer vulnerable. Such a person could better explain the benefits but also the often hard and painful process of getting help after being raped. This person would be less at risk to be retraumatized and could explain not only the benefits of treatment but also the hardships it involves. That isn't what Sally did. She brought on a vulnerable guest who exposed her pain and anguish graphically, which is always a ratings success.

The problems associated with convincing a vulnerable woman to come on national TV while she was actively suffering from having already been forced into behavior that she didn't want but that met someone else's needs apparently escaped Sally. Research, mental health practice, and personal accounts of rape survivors, however, bear out that there is a great deal of stigma and shame attached to such experiences and that the emotional traumas are deep and difficult to resolve. While talking about the experience can help, there is little to suggest that going on national television will facilitate recovery. In fact, too sudden a disclosure of long-held, shameful secrets is quite likely to produce more trauma. What was lost for Stephie was the opportunity to understand why she was silent for so long, and what steps needed to be taken to assure both her personal and emotional safety. She had no opportunity to understand her problems before disclosing them to a national TV audience. She was told that this would be good for her and for other people. It is not surprising that she suffered more nightmares and fears following her first appearance. Sally, however, gave only cursory acknowledgment to the problems and assumed no personal responsibility. She instead focused on the "miracle" that happened.

After hearing from Sandy Meyer, the "human behavior counselor," little emphasis was placed on whether or not this woman was qualified or appropriate for the situation. (We could not locate the Sandy Meyer Center in Rocky Mount, Virginia.) Instead, the fact that she heard Stephie in a freak broadcast and is a "survivor" herself was played up in order to suggest some mystical connection: they were meant to come together.

Further, the suggestion that—after fourteen years of trauma— Stephie could resolve her troubles within a week is ludicrous to those who know anything about these kinds of problems. And for those who don't know, it wrongly suggests that they could do the same. Viewers are deceived when Talk TV revelations are presented as an adequate way to deal with rape. The implication is that if someone has been exploited, they should be exploited again, only on TV, and that will somehow make it better

Stephie was reported to have improved. We don't question this. It is, however, quite common for highly traumatized people who truly want a problem to go away to undergo a temporary "flight into health" during which they suppress symptoms and act as if every-thing were fine. Given that Stephie had few resources, felt she could trust no one, and had been given lots of much-needed atten-tion and treated kindly by Sally and Sandy Meyer, it is not surpris-ing that she would feel that things had improved. But to conclude that all her problems were "cured" because she felt better at that time is premature and misleading to viewers.

Finally, there is the troublesome aspect of saying both Sally and Sandy understood the problem because they were "survivors." While surviving anything has the potential to produce compassion and concern, it can also lead to some fundamental distortions in understanding another person's situation. Assuming that another person's trauma is the same as one's own and that therefore the solu-tion should also be the same is a common error that mental health professionals are quickly disabused of. No two individuals are the same and no two rapes are the same. Pat resolutions, such as tell it all on *Sally Jessy Raphael,* only deceive viewers into believing that there are quick fixes for painful feelings. Further, when "experts" are presented as experts primarily because they have suffered them-selves, viewers may be misled into thinking that someone must suffer from the same problem to offer help.

The ways guests are currently recruited and treated before,

during, and after the shows is a serious breach of humane and therapeutic standards for dealing with troubled people. While the shows may be legally within the realm of acceptable behavior, ethically and morally they are well over the edge. The problems are compounded when mental health professionals get involved. Their presence generates the illusion that what the shows are doing represents professional care. That illusion has the potential to create serious problems for both viewers and mental health professionals. We move now to explore those problems.

Notes

P. 177, *wash off the guest grease:* Tom O'Neill, personal interview, Dec. 19, 1994.

P. 178, *Despite the fact that she had no phone* (and other details of the multipage Laura Thorpe story that follows): O'Neill, T. "Welcome to the Jungle," *US*, Feb. 1994, *193*, 78–81, 90–91; Tom O'Neill, personal interview, Dec. 19, 1994.

P. 182, *You go home and deal with next week's show:* O'Neill, T. "Welcome to the Jungle," *US*, Feb. 1994, *193*, 78–81, 90–91; p. 91.

P. 182, *Seventeen phone calls later, I got her:* O'Neill, T. "Welcome to the Jungle," *US*, Feb. 1994, *193*, 78–81, 90–91; p. 80.

P. 183, *The association is quite popular* (and quote in this paragraph): Jenny Sayward, personal interview, Dec. 20, 1994.

P. 183, *"the producers' own agenda for the show"*: Jenny Sayward, letter to authors dated Dec. 12, 1994.

P. 184, *eased my daughter's worries:* Jenny Sayward, letter to authors dated Dec. 12, 1994.

P. 184, *There were no gay people evident:* Jenny Sayward, letter to authors dated Dec. 12, 1994.

P. 184, *My kids were portrayed as troubled teens:* Jenny Sayward, personal interview, Dec. 20, 1994.

P. 186, *it would be good for the country:* Curry, G. "A Different Script," *Chicago Tribune,* July 26, 1992, Section 6, p. 4.

P. 188, *from greenroom to greenroom with a feuding family:* Tom O'Neill, personal interview, Jan. 16, 1994.

P. 188, *Donahue went right for it:* Tim Fisher, personal interview, Dec. 14, 1994.

P. 189, *Oprah Winfrey claimed she has had it:* Fisher, L., and others, "In Full Stride," *People Weekly,* Sept. 12, 1994, pp. 84–88, 90; p. 88.

P. 190, *there was no evidence:* Rosenberg, H. "Wanna Confess? Call Montel," *Los Angeles Times,* Mar. 25, 1994, p. F-1.

P. 190, *Yvonne Porter reported that she was not told prior to the taping:* Saunders, D. "Colosseum in a Box," *San Francisco Chronicle,* July 23, 1993, pp. 24–25; p. 24.

P. 190, *"make a public statement for her own self":* Rosenberg, H. "The Dropped Bombshell: Talk TV Hits a New Low," *Los Angeles Times,* May 11, 1994, pp. F-1 and F-9.

P. 191, *"I'd been anticipating this moment for about twenty-six years":* O'Neill, T. "Welcome to the Jungle," *US,* Feb. 1994, *193,* 78–81, 90–91; p. 91.

P. 191, *"So he sat there and went along with it":* Associated Press. "Fatal Shooting Follows Surprise on TV Talk Show," *New York Times,* Mar. 12, 1995, p. 11.

P. 193, *Mrs. Pierce shot her husband:* Foskett, K. "Sex, Drugs, Death—and All on Geraldo," *Atlanta Journal Constitution,* Sept. 29, 1991, p. D-4

P. 194, *"one of the dumbest things I have ever done":* Nancy Steele, personal interview, Oct. 17, 1994.

P. 197, *Some of Dr. April Martin's experiences:* April Martin, personal interview, Dec. 18, 1994.

P. 200, *"Now, I'm healing millions":* Gilda Carle, personal interview, Nov. 17, 1994.

P. 201, *"like them, I'm a survivor":* Raphael, S. J., and Proctor, P. *Sally: Unconventional Success.* New York: Morrow, 1990, p. 172.

7

Dilemmas for the Mental Health Profession

Just as guests enter a dangerous intersection when they come on Talk TV, so do mental health professionals. Preceding the intersection are enticing signs signaling great opportunities. But once in the middle, it's hard not to notice that the intersection is lined with deliberate wreckage. Talk TV "experts" are expected to make a contribution in two important ways: first to explain and then to resolve. But something is wrong. First, many of the "experts" aren't experts at all. Second, many who are experts are disabled by the shows. They are forced into standby positions and typically brought onto the scene merely to confirm that there has indeed been an accident at the crossroads.

The willing participation of mental health specialists raises important questions for the profession: What is their responsibility in these "accidents"? Should professionals agree to engage in situations where they cannot use their knowledge to prevent problems? What can the profession do when its members add fuel to the flames? And what is the public to conclude about such a group?

By inviting mental health professionals into their wreckage and then claiming to align with them, Talk TV generates two distinct but related problems; first in public image and second in professional practice. The first set of problems is cosmetic and as such is easy to identify. The second set of problems, however, is substantive but often hidden from the general public. Together these problems have the potential to change the nature of the mental health profession.

Adulterating the Public Image

Talk TV is not only a powerful force in the entertainment world, it undoubtedly holds great sway over the general public's perception of the mental health profession. There is no comparable source of mental health information for average Americans. There are numerous professional sources for information and services, but they are not readily known or accessible to the average person. Talk TV is.

Over fifty-four million hours of Talk TV are watched each and every weekday. Viewers are given numbers so they can call, write, and participate on a regular basis. Viewers also develop strong loyalties to the hosts that dull criticism and predispose them to believe what they are told. No professional organization commands such an audience or engenders such loyalty.

Not only does Talk TV cover topics people are interested in, it does so in a "personal" way. Talk TV appears accessible, direct, and unpretentious. It has become the primary public forum for discussing mental health concerns. As a result, public perception of mental health expertise is largely defined by Talk TV. The way expertise is handled on Talk TV generates a series of connected problems: Who is or is not an "expert?" Can "experts" be taken seriously? And what can one expect from "expert" care?

Who's an Expert, Anyway?

Talk TV relies on experts but makes no effort to inform viewers about differences in their training, experience, and credibility. All experts are presented in the same manner. They are brought on with fanfare, then given brief amounts of time to provide solutions for far more than they possibly could. Licensed and nonlicensed professionals, as well as self-appointed experts, are routinely asked to give opinions about what is wrong and what to do to fix it. This implies that they are diagnosing and providing recommendations ˙ ˙eatment.

˙ithin the mental health profession there is a wide range of ˙ and expertise, as well as of professional status. The profes- ˙ctually a constellation of related disciplines, ranging from ˙ to psychology, counseling, and social work, all of which ˙erned by professional associations and licenses. Each profession has established procedures for certification or licensure in order to have some control over individuals who present themselves to the public as legitimate members of that profession.

Consumers ought to know what kind of training, preparation, and experience professionals have had. This is particularly important for Talk TV, which uses a whole cadre of motivational speakers, book writers, "therapists," and communication specialists in addition to credible mental health professionals.

However, the key issue for Talk TV is that the public is *not* informed about the differences in credentials and licenses and what those differences mean. The shows trot out "relationship experts," "human behavior therapists," "dream analysts," "communication specialists," "psychotherapists," and "therapists," as well as "directors" and "founders" of all persuasions, without ever acknowledging that such titles are meaningless without some explanation of the professionals' training and experience.

In fact, all of the titles listed above are professionally meaningless because they are not restricted titles. In other words, they could be used by anyone regardless of training. Certification or licensure, awarded to professionals by particular disciplines, officially grants permission to use recognized titles, serves to bind professionals to accompanying codes of ethics, and provides an avenue for consumers to redress improper treatment.

Mental health licenses vary but essentially verify that the professional holding the license has completed the academic training and required professional experience, and has passed licensure examinations. Having completed these requirements, the recipient is then qualified to use the title associated with the profession and to perform its duties within the prescribed limits. For example, psychiatrists are professionally sanctioned to diagnose and treat medical disorders as well as to prescribe medication. Psychologists (and, in some states, clinical mental health counselors) can perform similar duties related to diagnosis and treatment of mental disorders but are not entitled to prescribe medication.

With adequate information, consumers can determine whether or not a professional is qualified to provide the services they are seeking. TV talk shows do not provide such information. Even for knowledgeable viewers, it can be impossible to separate the experts from the impostors because none are adequately identified. Unless viewers are already familiar with the experts' qualifications, which is unlikely, there is no way to make distinctions between the legitimate professionals and the self-serving hucksters.

Just being on TV or radio is often used as a credential in and of itself. Professionals include media presentations on résumés and the public generally assumes that any person presented by the media as an "expert" must be credible. Problems are compounded when media introductions not only omit relevant information on credentials but also disregard the importance of proper credentials. For example, Jerome Murray (a radio personality whose show, *For Lovers Only*, was heard in fifteen cities across the country) was recently indicted in Santa Rosa, California, for practicing psychotherapy without a license. Mr. Murray had had his license as a marriage and family counselor taken away in 1980, when he was found guilty of sexually exploiting a fifteen-year-old girl. Despite the fact that his professional association had ended his membership, he maintained the image of a credible professional by successfully hosting a radio talk show. The police chief who arrested him surmised, "Many people went to him possibly without knowing the status of his license. Some went to him because of his radio show and simply said 'he's on the radio so he's okay.'" The public may mistakenly assume an appearance on radio or TV confers respectability. But the credential "as seen on TV" or "as heard on Radio" is no credential at all.

In order for viewers to consider the advice given, they've got to have some context for evaluating it. Is the advice coming from a licensed family therapist? Is it coming from a writer interested in family problems? From a researcher who has studied problems such as those discussed on the show? Or someone simply with an opinion to offer? Any of those people is entitled to say what he or she thinks, but viewers would be in a better position to evaluate what was said if they knew the qualifications of the person doing the talking.

Unchallenged Expertise

Not only are many dubious consultants not questioned on the show about the validity of their claim to expertise, the information that they provide is likewise left unchallenged. To avoid questioning the experts is particularly extraordinary given that TV talk shows are all about finding out more. The contrast between the probing questions directed at guests and the trite, superficial queries posed to experts belies the shows' claim to be interested in expertise.

The shows routinely present "experts" who sum it all up in thirty seconds, then refer guests to treatment. What rarely happens is the kind of questioning that would expose the strength or weakness, depth or superficiality, of the expert's comments. Questions such as: How did you reach that conclusion? Where did you get that information? What experience do you have with this problem? Are there alternative ways of dealing with this? and How do you know if this treatment works? are all much needed and sorely missed.

When experts are questioned, the questions are often personal: Are you a rape survivor? Are you a battered woman? Professional codes of ethics make it clear that when making public statements professionals must be careful to distinguish between personal experience and opinion and professional observations. On Talk TV the two are often mixed and mingled with no effort to separate them.

Personal information regarding experts, in fact, is often given more attention and credibility than the accumulated years of study and professional experience. Robert Cabaj, M.D., an associate clinical professor in psychiatry at the University of California, San Francisco, has very extensive and impressive clinical and scholarly credentials. He holds a medical license, is certified in psychiatry by the American Board of Psychiatry and Neurology, and is also certified in Addiction Medicine by the American Society of Addiction Medicine. He was on the faculty at Harvard Medical School from 1974 to 1992. He is now a fellow of the American Psychiatric Association, and was recently appointed to the White House AIDS Commission. He has pages of publications and professional service. When he appeared on *Donahue*, however, to discuss the topic of using "therapy" to "straighten out gay people," the pressing question on Donahue's mind was "Are you gay?" According to Cabaj, it was at that point that the show "disintegrated into vitriolic exchanges." And even Donahue admitted after the show that he would have had more impact if that question hadn't been asked.

Likewise, Laurel Richardson was very frustrated with the questioning she received on tour for her book, *The New Other Woman*. She was rarely asked about her qualifications (she has a Ph.D. and is a professor of sociology), the methods she used to collect information, the validity of her inferences, or the conclusions she reached based on her research. Instead, she was continually asked whether she was the other woman or the scorned wife. Despite the fact that she was a researcher and not a clinician she was repeatedly questioned about what was wrong with someone's marriage or what an individual should to do about adultery. Equally frustrating and without her direct knowledge, Richardson's book publicist distributed a list of questions for interviewers to ask that suggested she be probed for just that kind of diagnostic and treatment information. Richardson felt that the lack of genuine questioning about her ideas and research limited her ability to provide the information she was there to provide.

Clearly, experts are open to the same invasion of personal privacy as are the guests. The host, by virtue of calling the shots and asking the questions, can either grant permission for professionals to function as experts or relegate them to silence. Once the host has determined what role will produce the results he or she wants, experts have few options.

Creating Unrealistic Expectations

For many informed viewers, Talk TV "experts" appear absurd. Viewers who know something about the mental health field are not likely to turn to Talk TV as their primary source of information. But for others, the images, advice, and models provided on the shows are powerful, especially for those most in need of information. Consequently, what the shows provide is an embarrassing parade of eager experts who may alter expectations about what the profession can and will do for consumers of mental health services.

Willard Gaylin, M.D., a psychiatrist and now chair of the board for The Hastings Center, an institution engaged in research on ethical issues in the life sciences, pointed out how Talk TV perpetuates misleading information in two fundamental ways. First, the shows imply that "knowledge informs conduct. . . . Second, that the same problem can always be cured with the same solution." Gaylin was referring to what most of us understand based on our own life experiences: that we can know something is wrong or harmful, but fail to make the changes in our behavior that would logically follow from that knowledge. Ask any smoker. The point is that sometimes "knowing" means nothing because it is impotent in the face of "doing." As Gaylin went on to explain, if knowledge informed conduct, then "philosophers would be more moral than mathematicians" because they are actively engaged in studying moral issues. But, he adds, "We all know that isn't true."

Most therapeutic methods are not based solely on educating the patient but on understanding the interplay of a variety of factors, of which knowledge is only one. The talk shows act as if they are completely invested in the belief that simply providing information to viewers will make a difference in their lives. Likewise TV talk shows specialize in pointing out the obvious as though it was novel and special. They pride themselves on presentations of "profound observations"—most often on the level of revealing that battered women should not be battered, that we ought not sleep with our friends' partners, and that children should not be abused. The need to rehash such obvious advice suggests that the shows are not as committed to bringing new information to viewers as they claim, and it helps prove that information by itself does not change behavior.

The second way shows perpetuate lies about the professions speaks more directly to therapeutic methodology. Willard Gaylin was critical of Talk TV for suggesting that mental health treatment is formulaic, meaning that once the problem has been identified and labeled, then all that need occur is the application of a preexisting "cure." He pointed out that "when there really is a cure in medicine there is usually only one." In the case of pneumonia, for example, there is one medically known cure: antibiotics. With other problems such as arthritis there is no single cure—instead, a wide variety of accepted treatments work to varying degrees with different people.

Mental health services are more like this second group of treatments. For example, panic disorders are routinely treated by many mental health professionals using a variety of techniques from psychopharmacology to biofeedback to talk therapy. All have a certain measure of success, but Sally brought on a Martin T. Jensen, M.D., and explained that he had *the* cure. His "cure" was a trial-and-error process of finding the right medication. Not only is this treatment not new, it is also not unique. It is a common practice of most psychiatrists. On Sally's show, however, his technique was presented as special and new. This "cure" produced a testimonial from a woman referred to as Ms. O'Grady, who later became Jensen's secretary, enabling her to continue giving witness to this "cure." While we would all likely agree that it is a good thing that Ms. O'Grady has both relief from her suffering and a new job, her testimony hardly constitutes scientific data.

Presentations such as these are highly problematic. Giving the public the idea that there are "cures" for mental health problems is not only a disservice to viewers, it contorts the entire profession. It falsely suggests that a quick and easy cure could be on hand for depression, anxiety, and substance abuse, which are the most common forms of mental health disturbance, but for which there are in reality no "cures."

The Expert as a Joke

Because legitimate professionals are mixed up with self-appointed experts, and because informed judgments are reduced to sound bites, then blended with unsubstantiated opinions, the entire profession can come off looking unstudied, unreasoned, and ill-equipped to assist people with their problems. But a careful examination of the shows' format suggests that this less-than-flattering presentation of mental health professionals is no simple coincidence. The shows routinely exclude professionals from the conversation until the last minute and then ask them to identify and resolve the enormous problems of numerous guests in the blink of an eye. It is no wonder that what the experts offer sounds generic and inadequate. It is. It has to be.

The result, however, is not that viewers think the shows should give the experts sufficient time, but rather that they are left with a vague dissatisfaction with the experts who appear. Beyond merely undermining the credibility of legitimate professionals, the shows also mock the entire profession by inviting as "experts" people who may or may not even be legitimate mental health professionals and who are nothing less than a major embarrassment.

Ricki Lake did a show recently about women who sleep with their friends' boyfriends. Interestingly enough, the focus on the show was not on the possible reasons for such behavior, but rather on how the betrayed women could prevent it. For the solution, on came an expert who had written a book about training your man as you would train your dog. She suggested strong words and decisive action followed by praise and pats on the head when directions were followed. She amused the audience from her stuffed leather chair with comments such as "Sit" and "Stay." One male got on the floor, looked up at her and said, "I don't think this will work." In keeping with her strategy, she completely ignored his resistance and went on offering the "cure."

This episode is so preposterous, it can only be taken as a joke. It is not the host, audience, or guests who look ridiculous, however, it is the so-called expert who is the butt of the joke. And in that sense, this hapless individual serves to bring the host, guests, audience, and viewers together while separating the "expert" even further. For a profession that relies on good relations, competency, and a sense of trust, such scenarios are no small matter.

Shows of a more serious nature can leave the "expert" in equally ludicrous positions. Supposed experts are routinely exposed as morons either by their own behavior or by the shows' deliberate setups. Consider, for example, the May 2, 1994, *Sally Jessy Raphael* show. Viewers were presented with the Theodore family. The twelve children sat on one side of the stage and announced that their father, who sat on the other side of the stage, had abused them all. The kids explained their version and the father defended his. When one of the children suggested forgiveness, Lillian Glass, Ph.D., the "relationship therapist" invited to serve as an expert, explained that his attempts were really only "denial" of the problem. "You are in denial!" she firmly informed him. The father began yelling and several of the grown children started yanking off their jackets, asking the father to go into the street so they could have it out. Then the show ended, but not completely.

On a follow-up show about 1994 guests, Sally explained that after the Theodore family appeared, she got the kids together and had the therapist and father removed. She never offered any information about what had already happened, only that there would be more updates. She did, however, reveal her attitude about her invited "expert." Her notion of taking care of the situation was to get rid of the very "relationship therapist" she brought on to solve the problem. Given the on-air assessments and recommendations offered, that might not have been such a bad idea. What was a bad idea was selecting a professional guest without making sure that guest was capable of helping, and then suggesting to viewers that such "expert professionals" should be quickly removed if problems are not easily resolved.

These kinds of presentations do nothing to support a positive image of the mental health profession. First, viewers don't know if these people are actually licensed to diagnose and treat mental health problems or if they have made their career in motivational speaking. Second, there is no professional association to which one can complain if concerned about the information provided. There is no board governing "relationship therapists" because anyone can use that title. But the impression is created that a "relationship therapist" is a legitimate profession within the mental health field—and that impression causes problems.

Most significantly, the public can end up believing that what occurred on the show is standard fare for mental health professionals; they buy choker collars for husbands and instigate horrible fights in troubled families. Such exhibitions not only cause public relations problems for the profession but raise considerable ethical dilemmas for those serious professionals who choose to participate.

Compromising Ethical Standards

Talk TV personnel are rewarded if they lie or manipulate to get what they want, winning bigger contracts and more opportunities to do the same. It is this world of fierce competition and general disregard for human dignity that mental health professionals enter when they agree to appear as experts. Although there are many impostors, there are also many legitimate, well-intentioned professionals who agree to appear. The challenges they face are formidable.

Typically, professionals are not adequately prepared for what is in store. They are often mistaken about what their appearance will accomplish. They have no control over what occurs in the studio, and are often caught up in fast-moving, highly questionable activities. Additionally, they have little opportunity to provide post-show assistance to guests or others. Finally, and perhaps most troubling, they may actually be rewarded for their participation, despite any ethical indiscretions, through increased requests for services.

We have discussed at length how the use of experts in this way benefits the shows while contributing to problems for guests and viewers. But the ramifications for the mental health profession are equally grave. Our intention is not to lay blame solely with Talk TV for any and all negative consequences. Nor is it to build a case for the innocence and naïveté of the mental health profession—the situation is far more complex than that.

We think that both of the following are true: the shows' standards of conduct are problematic, and the mental health profession is ultimately responsible for establishing and maintaining its own credibility and standards. It is the interaction of these two truths that we wish to explore.

Problems with Preparation and Supervision

Most academic preparation for mental health professionals does not include training in television performance. Ethics courses concentrate on matters related to research, supervision, and clinical practice, so that any coverage of the media is usually cursory. This leaves most professionals coming out of graduate school to learn their lessons about the media in the school of hard knocks.

What constitutes acceptable and responsible behavior with the media is a source of considerable debate within the profession. And perhaps it is the unresolved nature of this debate that has contributed to the lack of preparation. But regardless of that uncertainty, one thing is clear: significant numbers of mental health professionals are called upon to interact with the media. This has long been the case and the numbers are only growing.

Early in the development of Talk Radio, there were criticisms about mental health professionals engaging in "therapy" on the air. Likewise, self-advertising and the potential exploitation of callers were widely frowned upon. But even then, there were mental health professionals who chose to get involved, who argued that their participation was legitimate, and who countered that their critics were restricting their right to free trade.

Their arguments are supported and enhanced by the Federal Trade Commission (FTC). The FTC protects the right of free trade by prohibiting undue limits on the ways in which people legally earn money. It has pushed professional organizations, including mental health organizations, to loosen restrictions on advertising. One area of advertising that is of particular concern to any discussion of media involvement is that of testimonials. Testimonials as they apply to mental health services involve clients' laudatory comments about the help they have received.

Under earlier professional codes, testimonials were prohibited because of the power of the relationship from which such testimonials grow—that is, clients are particularly susceptible to the suggestions of their counselors. Testimonials are now permitted, however, as long as they are not solicited. But what constitutes solicitation within a therapeutic relationship is debatable. Many clients may express a desire to advertise their support of a professional who has helped them, but it's difficult to know exactly why they would wish to do so, and whether or not there has been subtle encouragement or pressure in that direction.

Questions about whether or not Talk TV testimonials can be considered unsolicited or not are further complicated by some of the tactics of the shows. Sometimes when the shows have arranged for "therapy" for guests, they invite the guest, and even the professional, to come on the show afterward to update the audience and viewers about all the positive changes that have resulted. When the shows have brought on troubled guests, chosen mental health professionals to provide assistance, paid their fees, provided airfare and hotel accommodations for the guests, and then "invited" the guests back to "tell us how it went," how can the testimonial be viewed as anything other than staged and solicited? The professionals may not directly ask for the public praise that follows but certainly cannot claim to be ignorant of the intense implication that it is part of the bargain.

The APA Media Psychology Division is devoted to assisting professionals in dealing with media-related activities. The division has been in existence for approximately fifteen years and is in the process of developing very useful guidelines for professionals. We will discuss those guidelines in more detail in Chapter Eight, but want to raise the point here that even this group looks upon the relationship between the media and mental health with a cautious eye.

The division, in fact, summed up the central problem of the partnership between mental health and Talk TV by suggesting that professionals must "walk the thin line between being entertaining enough to attract the broad audiences needed for survival, and remaining professional." With Talk TV, the potential for crossing the line is very high. Not only is it a matter of mental health professionals maintaining the standards of the profession, but they must rely on the shows to respect those standards as well. But because the producers are not bound to—and perhaps not even aware of—those standards, it is highly unlikely that they will do so.

Professional ethics dictate that professionals take reasonable precautions to ensure that the statements they make in media presentations are based on appropriate psychological literature and practice and are consistent with the ethics codes. It would seem that professionals clearly hold the responsibility to ascertain whether or not they are going to be able to offer information on the shows in such a way as to respect that dictate. Given that professionals are allotted only a few minutes at the end of the programs, during which time other participants will also be speaking, it is highly unlikely that they will be able to do so.

The potential problems for the profession are compounded by

the fact that it has limited ability to control what is happening on Talk TV. As noted earlier, there is the ongoing difficulty of impostor "experts." Because such people are not part of the profession, they are not governed by it, and therefore cannot be censured when their conduct is unethical by professional standards. They can go on masquerading as mental health experts, and conducting themselves in outlandish ways, while the profession has little or no opportunity to inform the public that they and their ideas are not professionally endorsed.

Even within the profession, however, it is difficult to monitor and respond to the ethical problems generated by Talk TV. Mental health organizations rely primarily on honor and training to guide members' professional conduct. After training and supervised experience, professionals are expected to have internalized a concern for humanity and a respect for their chosen profession's code of ethics. As many readers will no doubt already know, few ethical questions have clear answers. And the gray areas of responsible Talk TV practice are numerous and sizable. The profession is likely to censure only professionals who have clearly violated the ethical code. (The number of individuals censured for Talk TV violations to date is zero.)

Breaking Confidentiality

The core concept of the mental health profession is the power of concerned, confidential communication. Regardless of differences among disciplines, theoretical orientations, and therapeutic techniques, it is within the context of protected, private relationships that the work of the mental health profession always takes places. Central to the training of all mental health disciplines is development of a professional allegiance to a code of confidentiality. Both the profession's credibility and its effectiveness ride on the strength of that commitment.

The commitment to safeguard secrets carries with it an even greater responsibility: having achieved the role of confidant, the professional must not *in any way* use that position for personal or professional benefit at the expense of the client. The trust that allows clients to reveal the most intimate aspects of their lives is also the trust that makes clients vulnerable to the suggestions of their helpers. Consequently, mental health professionals must guard against any temptation to compromise that trust. Even the gentlest of requests to appear on TV can only be received as advice.

Most professionals recognize the serious problems that arise from soliciting clients as potential guests. Ruth Peters, Ph.D., who recruits professionals for TV talk shows, stated that many credible mental health professionals would be uncomfortable bringing on their own clients. She adds that only in special circumstances could she imagine that it would ever be appropriate to do so and, fortunately, she has found that most professionals operate under the same belief. Despite the obvious problems that arise from soliciting clients as potential guests, however, it is clear from watching the shows that many professionals are doing so anyway.

James Masterson, M.D., director of both the Masterson Institute and the Masterson Group, author of numerous books and articles, and internationally recognized authority on personality disorders, went straight to the heart of the problem. "Everyone wants to be on TV, but it is a risky operation." Masterson himself has been asked to appear on all the major talk shows to discuss his work with personality disorders. He has declined all invitations that also requested that he bring on his own clients. He explained, "I want to go on TV, but not at any price."

Other professionals, who are either somehow convinced that appearing will be helpful to their clients or to their own careers, do not negotiate the risk in a way that protects their clients or the profession. To have professionals appearing on national television with their clients in order to reveal a private professional relationship and its confidential content is in direct opposition to what the profession is about. Further, there is rarely any explanation about how the decision was reached or what circumstances might rationalize that appearance as professionally ethical.

Questionable Consent

TV talk shows frequently surprise their guests on-air with unexpected events or revelations. Often, producers make use of personal information about guests that was provided by family members or friends, sometimes without the guests' knowledge and frequently in the belief that the information will not be used on the air. As discussed earlier, the potential for harm is great in such situations. When mental health professionals participate in such on-air surprises, the problems are compounded. This activity not only has the potential for public humiliation for the guest, it also breaks the professional's code of ethics and misrepresents the profession.

Mental health professionals are ethically bound to "respect the rights of individuals to privacy, confidentiality, self determination, and autonomy." Honoring this directive precludes the possibility of providing a treatment intervention that a guest is unaware of prior to a show. Regardless of the "good" that a professional believes could come from confronting people about their behavior, on-air blitzes are unquestionably a violation of the established guidelines for professional conduct. Professionals are not to provide treatment that has not been mutually agreed on. Unfortunately, even highly qualified and skilled practitioners can get caught up in the shows' rationale for such events.

A psychologist who served as a consultant for the *Rolonda* show was asked to appear as the expert on that show's "Family Drug Wars," to work with a family who agreed to confront their adult sister, Sherrie, about her substance abuse. The psychologist stated that Sherrie was not aware that the intervention was going to take place on the show and added that, in all likelihood, Sherrie would not have appeared if she had known. In fact, Sherrie's sister Linda reported during the program that she had lured Sherrie onto the airplane by pretending that they were simply going to the show as audience members.

It is unclear, either from the psychologist's account or from the program itself, exactly what Sherrie knew before arriving on the set.

What is clear is that Sherrie was brought into the process under false pretenses. Already on a plane headed for the show with a sister who was determined that she appear, Sherrie was hardly in a position to freely agree or decline. Further, without even consulting Sherrie, the *Rolonda* staff had arranged inpatient treatment to follow her appearance on the show. The psychologist, serving as a consultant to the show, was aware of these arrangements and assisted in carrying out the plan for Sherrie.

During the program, her sister Linda and her brother-in-law Charles described their pain over having witnessed her self-destructive behavior. Sherrie's ten-year-old son was also present. When called upon and asked very leading questions, he told his mother, "I want you to get help."

The *Rolonda* staff deserve credit for presenting this situation in an informative manner. There was no shouting, no wailing confrontation, no hostile accusations or finger-pointing, and the outcome appeared positive—the woman agreed to go into treatment. Despite all that could be called upon to defend and justify the show, however, the inescapable fact remains that other people, including a mental health professional, largely decided for this woman what was best for her. And that decision included a public revelation of a very personal situation, with little or no time allowed for Sherrie to consider her choices.

Professionals commit to a code that places the well-being of those they work with first and that includes taking the least intrusive steps possible to assist them. There is no tenable argument that could describe an on-air intervention as nonintrusive. In fact, such family "interventions" are difficult procedures even in the privacy of a professional's office or the client's home. Surely, conducting an intervention on national television is not designed to enhance the treatment effect for the client but rather to benefit the show by playing to viewers' voyeurism. Undoubtedly, other measures could have been taken to assist this woman. As the controlling agent, the show required an exchange of services; they would arrange for treatment if the family appeared on the show. Interventions arranged under such conditions are not in keeping with the requirement that professionals refrain from using clients for their own or others' benefit.

In addition to breaking the commitment to privacy and autonomy, there are several other factors that make professional involvement in these kinds of situations problematic. Although viewers may not be aware of such obligations, mental health professionals are required to avoid multiple relationships or conflicting loyalties in their professional activities. The psychologist in this incident is a paid consultant to the *Rolonda* show and therefore has certain obligations as an employee, such as assisting the show to create successful programs. As a mental health professional she is also bound to those with whom she works, such as Sherrie and her family. When professionals commit to both sets of obligations, there may be times when their duties are in conflict. What is best for the show may not be what is best for the guests.

The ways in which an on-air intervention is troubling are numerous, but perhaps one of the most damaging aspects is the involvement of children. Mental health professionals are obligated to avoid causing harm through any of their activities. This requirement takes on special meaning when working with children because of their limited capacity to consent and their increased vulnerability.

Given the confused feelings that children of substance abusers experience, a nationally televised "intervention" could not be a neutral event. Sean's wide-eyed, quiet demeanor and his hesitance in responding to questions clearly signaled that he felt out of place. Although children his age do not have the capacity to understand all that was being discussed, they do experience shame and fear. Others involved in this program may have developed adequate defenses to shield themselves from the potential humiliation of national exposure, but it is highly doubtful that a ten-year-old child is capable of doing so. Unfortunately, the difficulty probably did not end when the cameras stopped. Repercussions from the family's appearance likely included increased exposure of the problem to community members, teachers, and schoolmates. Thus, not only did the show compromise the guests during the program, it ran the risk increasing their vulnerability and difficulties afterward.

Perverting Clinical Standards

When mental health professionals appear on Talk TV as experts, the impression is created that what they do and say is somehow representative of the profession. But in many ways it is not. On the shows, professionals are given little or no opportunity to do the things they are trained to do. They are also asked to do things that are in violation of professional ethics. In essence, they are invited as "experts" and then treated like understudies. The result is that on Talk TV, core aspects of professional functioning, such as screening clients, understanding and diagnosing problems, and assisting with the resolution of problems, are grossly distorted.

Inadequate Screening

Assisting people in managing mental health issues is always delicate work. Any credible professional begins a course of treatment by questioning whether or not the nature and scope of his or her expertise is appropriate to the client's needs. When it is, responsible professionals proceed with a careful assessment of any potential risk factors that might signal the need for extra precautions. This kind of screening, both of self and client, is essential to credible mental health practice. It rarely occurs in Talk TV.

Professionals are routinely misled about the nature of their participation on the shows or given inadequate time to assess the potential guests. Mental health professionals are, for example, often asked to comment on unexpected situations that arise during the course of the programs that are outside the scope of their expertise, or that they have not been given sufficient time to prepare for.

Professionals who are more skilled at dealing with the inappropriate demands of the shows are occasionally able to insist on the opportunity to screen guests before appearing, but most experts are not so successful. The result is that therapists and clinicians, acting in the capacity of "experts," are brought on the shows to deliver definitive statements about problems they know virtually nothing about.

Such impromptu commentary might be acceptable if professionals were being asked to speak in a generic fashion from their knowledge about broad categories of problems. That, however, is not what happens. Professionals are asked to address specific problems of actual people seated on the stage. In sum, they are asked to provide diagnosis and treatment on the air. Typically, they have met the guests only moments before—unless, of course, the guests are their clients, which is a whole other problem, as we've already discussed.

Such scenarios create the false impression that mental health expertise is a kind of "name that tune" wizardry, allowing professionals to sum people up with only a moment's notice. This is not how credible mental health experts operate. And the implication that they do insults the integrity of the guests, who are, despite how the shows present them, complex people with complicated problems. This presentation also disregards the evolving nature of the therapeutic relationship. The fact is, understanding people and their problems takes not only training but time.

Unsuspecting professionals often handle this dilemma by attempting to give answers that are more global and less specific. But on shows that want "Answers," the result is not that professionals appear sensible but inept. The experts are brought on, after all, to give "expert" answers, not generic, "anybody-could-tell-you-that" advice. Once again professionals are placed in a position where to do what their training and standards tell them to do results in looking bad, whereas to go against their training and standards yields praise and commendation.

The inability to screen potential guests can be problematic in others ways as well. Professionals sometimes discover that guests are in need of specialized help, which in their judgment will not be obtained through appearing on a TV talk show. Moreover, the professional may suspect that guests' appearance on the show may actually worsen their problems.

A professional, for example, may be asked to appear with a family in severe turmoil. The brief meeting with the family right before the show may suggest that their problems will only be worsened by disclosing painful secrets on the air. Without sufficient time for a thorough family assessment, however, it's impossible for a professional to confirm such suspicions. This poses the unfortunate dilemma of either making recommendations without adequate assessment or refusing to participate unless adequate time and information are made available.

No Time to Speak

The legitimate experts who are called to appear on TV talk shows will often have spent years studying and working with a particular problem. They understand the problem in a complex way and are in a position to offer useful advice that could make a meaningful contribution to the discussion. That is not, however, what typically happens.

Because the rigid, fragmented format for Talk TV is already established, there is very little room for the professional to offer ideas before or during the show. Before the show, it's the producers who guide the development and organization of the format. Typically, they will have spent only enough time on the problem to pull together a one-hour program. During the show, the host (who is likely to have spent even less time considering the issue than the producers) will dominate.

The result, again, is that what the "expert" is able to squeeze in is dangerously brief. It's not that professionals have nothing more to offer, or that audiences and viewers could not understand or appreciate more complete and complicated discussions. The shows simply do not allow for that.

Many professionals carefully prepare statistics, stories, anecdotes, and other relevant information that never make it into the program. Most are given a cup of coffee, groomed and styled, held in the greenroom, trotted out for a few words, occasionally thanked by the host, then shuffled back to the airport. Some are stuck in the audience because too many other "experts" have shown up. Others are not used at all.

Even if the professional manages to present information in a reasonable manner in a very brief amount of time, the problem of editing remains. Producers retain the right to edit what they tape in order to put the show together the way they want it. For even the most conscientious professionals, this final obstacle is virtually insurmountable. Despite any precautions they have taken to answer as fully as possible, to avoid making remarks that are not supported by research and practice, and to qualify any recommendations so as to keep from suggesting that their comments are applicable to any and all, the shows can edit the tapes in such a way that professionals appear to do the very things they have avoided.

Stuart Fischoff, wise from experience, talked about a TV show he assisted in arranging. A group of couples was to be taped talking about their relationships. Since Fischoff had a great deal of media experience, he was alert to the possibility that producers might edit the tape in a way that would exploit some of the comments made by a minority group participant. He specifically asked the producer to be careful about this possibility. Nonetheless, when the show appeared, a black man was highlighted making just the comments that Fischoff had hoped would be edited. The point here is not that Fischoff was looking to change the reality of the situation but rather that he knew his information and intentions would be lost to entertainment values because of the editing and that stereotypes would be reinforced.

Avoiding Responsibility

We've talked at length about how the shows contribute to problems for the mental health profession. They are not alone, however, in creating those problems. Mental health professionals who agree to appear must share at least a part of the responsibility. Likewise the profession as a whole is remiss for not preparing adequate guidelines for responding to the resulting difficulties. In fact, it's the willingness of mental health professionals, many of them credible, thoughtful clinicians, to get caught up in the glamour, excitement, and illusion of the shows that is perhaps most disturbing. Regardless of the extent of shows' transgressions, Talk TV itself is not a part of the mental health profession and cannot be held accountable to its standards. Some of the experts are and should be.

Jill Harkaway was, at the time of her appearance on the *The Oprah Winfrey Show*, the director of the Center for Family Studies and Northeast Psychiatric Associates at Brookside Hospital in Nashua, New Hampshire. She is one professional who was caught up in the fantasy of meeting Oprah and achieving fame before her appearance, then disillusioned and angry after it. "The biggest shocks were realizing how little control I had over what happened and how sensational everything was being made."

She was invited on as the expert about the role of weight in relationships. The show rapidly disintegrated, and Harkaway felt that the information she had to present was lost. She was concerned that couples with similar problems would have been confused by the brawl that ensued on Oprah. Viewers did not have the opportunity to hear Harkaway's conviction that weight is only a superficial problem that provides a means for regulating intimacy in a troubled relationship. Harkaway also worried that the tension between couples on the show was so great that full-fledged violence could break out. This is not surprising, since the audience started yelling, "Kill him, kill him!" in response to an insulting comment from one of the husbands.

Harkaway lamented, "I suddenly realized the enormity of both my naïveté and the difference between the world of therapy and the world of talk shows. As a therapist, I was attempting to protect this couple from their game and its consequences. Oprah was hoping to exploit it for its entertainment value."

Harkaway detailed how the show set her up and how Oprah

fueled the crowd mentality, then announced her own "guilty" feelings for participating in something "offensive and abusive." But rather than sounding like a genuine reflection on her own culpability, Harkaway's comments paint her as the victim. Certainly, the show set her up and did all the things such shows always do, but rather than merely point a finger at the shows, professionals need to calculate their own accountability.

What Harkaway and all professionals need to question is the strained naïveté of "experts" who agree to appear. In any other professional capacity, a mental health expert would be hard pressed to take on a duty, do poorly at it, place clients at risk as a result of it, and then declare ignorance as if that were an acceptable defense. If professionals are going to work with substance abuse, eating disorders, or any other problem, they are expected to understand what such work entails.

Certainly, the responsibility for adhering to accepted mental health practice lies with the professional, not the shows. However, it is clear that left on their own, many professionals, even conscientious and reflective professionals, have difficulty sorting out how to balance the two different sets of priorities and codes. And while it's clearly not Talk TV's responsibility to chaperon experts, it most certainly is the profession's duty to provide a clear framework for how to manage such an attractive nuisance.

Notes

P. 210, *sexually exploiting a fifteen-year-old girl*: Sonenshine, R. "Talk Show Host Pleads Not Guilty," *San Francisco Chronicle*, July 8, 1994, pp. A-2, A-21.

P. 211, *distinguish between personal experience*: American Counseling Association Ethics Committee. *Proposed ACA Standards of Practice and Ethical Standards*. New York: Hatherleigh, 1994.

P. 212, *"disintegrated into vitriolic exchanges"*: Robert Cabaj, personal interview, Dec. 1, 1994.

P. 212, *lack of genuine questioning about her ideas and research:* Laurel Richardson, personal interview, July 7, 1994.

P. 213, *"philosophers would be more moral than mathematicians":* Willard Gaylin, personal interview, Dec. 16, 1994.

P. 214, *"when there really is a cure":* Willard Gaylin, personal interview, Dec. 16, 1994.

P. 220, *"walk the thin line":* Broder, M. (chair). "Suggestions for Media Mental Health Professionals prepared by the Guidelines Committee of the Association for Media Psychology," 1983.

P. 220, *presentations are based on appropriate psychological literature:* American Psychological Association Ethics Code, Standard 3.04.

P. 222, *"I want to go on TV, but not at any price":* James Masterson, personal interview, Dec. 15, 1994.

P. 229, *exploit some of the comments made by a minority:* Stuart Fischoff, personal interview, Sept. 21, 1994.

P. 230, *"realizing how little control I had"* (and *Boston Globe* and Harkaway quotes in following paragraphs): Reynolds, P. "Are Talk Shows Bad for You?" *Boston Globe*, July 17, 1989, pp. 24–28; p. 28. Also from Harkaway, J. "A Night at the Oprah" *New Women*, July, 1989, pp. 49–52.

8

Recommendations

Talk TV still has the potential to be a much-needed forum for public discussion. Before the rapid expansion during the late 1980s, Phil Donahue and Oprah Winfrey encouraged communication—thinking, talking, and listening—about relevant, even controversial topics. Sadly, TV talk shows have degenerated to the point of covering bizarre issues so often and so outrageously that even those topics come across as irrelevant and stale.

To survive as anything more than freak shows, TV talk shows need to develop a new standard of operation. Having discussed the problems, we now turn our attention to what can be done about them. Everyone involved in the process can do something to help, including Talk TV personnel, mental health professionals, and the viewers themselves.

Suggestions for Production

The shows themselves, of course, hold the greatest responsibility for improving their own quality and are certainly in the best position to implement changes. They can accomplish most of what is needed if they choose to adhere to ethical standards already established for broadcast journalists, and return to their earlier mission of providing a stimulating alternative to daytime soap operas. To that end, here's what we advocate:

Guidelines for Producers

1. *Adhere to the ethical guidelines established by the media.*

Several broadcasting associations have established codes developed by peers to ensure both integrity and honesty in the production of information on television. The Society of Professional Journalists has a code of ethics, which speaks to standards of fair play and provides that journalists at all times will show respect for the dignity, privacy, rights, and well-being of people encountered in the course of gathering and presenting the news. There are warnings that news media must guard against invading a person's right to privacy, and against pandering to morbid curiosity about details of vice and crime. The code also provides that the media should promptly correct any errors that may occur.

In addition, the Radio-Television News Directors Association has a code entitled "Broadcast News Ethics," which we have included in the Appendix. The first tenet in this code states that members of the Radio and Television News Directors Association strive to present the source or nature of broadcast news material in a way that is balanced, accurate, and fair. To this end, they will evaluate information solely on its merits as news, rejecting sensationalism or misleading emphasis in any form. Most important is item three, which states that they respect the dignity, privacy, and well-being of the people with whom they deal. Additionally, there is a tenet stipulating that they promise confidentiality only with the intention of keeping that promise.

2. *Conduct orientations and staff training to establish limits on competitive tactics and to inform staff about the potential negative consequences of crossing those limits.*

Once the shows develop their own specific ethical standards, they have an obligation to instill those ethics in their staff. Producers may not necessarily be aware of how or when their recruitment, selection, and use of guests crosses the boundaries of fair treatment and moves into the realm of exploitation. Further, producers who are under intense pressure to "get the guests" currently have little opportunity or encouragement to reflect on the consequences of their actions—other than to consider the rewards of a "great" story.

Consequently, the shows should routinely conduct orientations for new staff and offer ongoing training for producers about ethical standards and how to apply those standards to daily practice. Without such training and reinforcement, the producers are likely to succumb to the pressures of competition and maintain the current mentality, valuing sensation over integrity.

3. *Determine the goal of each program.*

Prior to the organization of a program, the management of the show should require producers to determine whether the program is intended primarily as entertainment or as education. This step is not intended to suggest that one is superior to the other. Viewers benefit from both—but only when the two are not confused.

If producers are putting together a light-hearted program about the predicaments people get into when they spend too much money at the mall, when they are dishonest with friends, or even when they are disloyal to their spouses, they should stay true to the purpose of entertainment and not attempt to dress it up as education. Viewers are capable of understanding the lighter side of life's troubles and the shortcomings of humanity. And it is certainly not necessary to include a mental health professional on a show that is primarily entertainment.

If they are putting together a serious, educational program, they should likewise take care to select guests and experts who can make meaningful contributions. Viewers are also able to grasp the serious and complex sides of issues. When something is difficult or takes time to understand, viewers should not be led astray with oversimplified expertise or solutions.

The shows need to play it straight with viewers and not put the disingenuous mantle of concern on programs they regard as amusement. Likewise, when they cover an important topic, they need to find experts who really are experts on the topic and they need to cover the issues with respect for their complexity.

4. *Check information for accuracy.*

State-of-the-art information about mental health problems is not hard to verify. A host who is going to discuss statistics or serious information should either verify the accuracy of the subject matter through reading or, better yet, consult with a qualified professional—who can interpret complicated statistics and information. The shows generally claim to have research departments: let them search out accurate information rather than sensational tidbits.

5. *Avoid stereotypical portrayals.*

Talk TV likes to present that which is different, and this approach has the potential to break down stereotypes. When what is different is presented as usual, however, stereotypes are furthered. Scare tactics, innuendo, and sensational information mislead viewers. The shows need to take care to avoid stereotypical portrayals of guests. Likewise, they should try to balance the audience—or at least avoid stacking it—to avert the implication that the whole country has a single point of view on the issue under discussion.

Recruitment, Selection, and Use of Guests

1. *Avoid pressuring potential guests to appear or to reveal more than they should.*

Producers should be careful not to cross the line between invitation and coercion when attempting to secure guests. When they learn about people through newspapers or other media, they should first ensure that any gestures they make are in keeping with ethical guidelines about the fair treatment of potential sources of information. Additionally, they should judge each case individually and make special efforts to be especially cautious to avoid coercing traumatized or potentially unstable people into appearing. Guests should not be tricked or misled into believing that they have an obligation to appear, that they can only benefit from appearing, or that the shows will somehow maintain an interest in them after they have completed the taping.

2. *Carefully screen guests regarding the veracity of their stories and their ability to manage public disclosures.*

Producers should carefully screen all potential guests for their appropriateness for the shows—and proceed with caution when interacting with individuals who are overly eager to publicly disclose potentially damaging information about themselves or others. They should also take steps to verify potential guests' stories beyond merely conducting telephone interviews with the guests or a few of their friends.

Additionally, producers should assess whether or not potential guests are emotionally equipped to withstand both the inherent pressure of the taping and the subsequent national broadcasting of their disclosures. If producers are not adequately qualified to make such assessments, qualified mental health professionals should be contracted to do so. The Television Consultants Directory prepared by the APA Media Psychology Division has a complete listing of professionals who can provide this service. In addition, professionals who have an established allegiance to a show should not be presented to guests in the guise of a personal representative or therapist.

3. *Fully inform guests of the nature of their role and the content of the program.*

Producers and hosts should fully inform guests about the nature of the program they are being recruited for as well as their particular role within the program. Guests should never be caught off guard or misled about the title of the show, the wording of their own labels, the questions they will be asked, the revelations planned, or the identity of other participants on the show. Even ostensibly "good-natured" on-air surprises entail much too much risk of upsetting guests and eliciting unexpected emotional reactions to allow this practice to continue. Guests have no opportunity to protect themselves from the camera or from the audience and viewers and should not be exposed without their explicit, informed consent.

4. *Do not suggest greater concern for or interest in guests than actually exists.*

Producers and hosts should guard against statements or actions that might imply to troubled or needy guests that they have more than a professional interest in their stories and circumstances. Potential guests should not be persuaded to appear under the false impression that producers or hosts will maintain concern or interest in them beyond their involvement in the show. The suggestion that producers or hosts, who live in a very different world from most of their guests, will somehow become guests' friends or join their support system is not only misleading, it can also result in guests' compliance with potentially damaging situations. Guests should be reminded that all interactions are strictly a business arrangement and that any ideas they may entertain about personal attachments are unfounded. Guests should be directed to people and services in their own communities for such support.

5.   *Conduct a preshow orientation that focuses as much on how guests can protect themselves from potential harm as on how to create an exciting show.*

Producers should instruct guests not only about how to get their points across but also about the possible negative consequences of public disclosures. Because of their inexperience, guests may not be in a position to anticipate such outcomes. Therefore the producers and hosts, who know better what can happen, should bear the responsibility of providing warnings. To suggest through the deliberate omission of such information that only good can result from public disclosures is unethical and misuses the influential position the shows are in with their guests.

6.   *Retain the right and responsibility to cancel appearances that jeopardize any guest's well-being.*

Talk TV personnel should remain committed to protecting the well-being of guests throughout production. At any point during recruitment, screening and selection, preshow orientation, or taping, if a show's staff suspect that potential guests are not aware of, or prepared for, what their involvement in the program entails, they should remove such guests or cancel production of the program.

Likewise, if the staff suspect that guests will not be able to manage the consequences of their appearance, they should not air the program. Guests should not be in a position to have to threaten legal action to prevent a show from being aired. To proceed in the pursuit of profits with the knowledge that the guests will bear excessive hardship is unacceptable and should not be permitted by the shows.

7. *Provide guests with information about support services prior to taping.*

If guests are to benefit from information about support services, they should receive such information, verbally and in writing, prior to the shows. Adequately screened guests will be coherent and stable enough to understand and consider the information before anything upsetting occurs. Certainly, all steps should be taken to prevent traumatizing guests during the show. However, should trauma unexpectedly occur, its results will be less serious if guests received information about available services and assistance when they were calm and able to accept and understand it. Following the show, guests may be too upset to fully comprehend what is being recommended or too angry to consider it.

8. *Do not permit the production of vengeful or damaging on-air surprises.*

Talk TV personnel should be committed to ensuring safe, positive experiences for all their guests. To this end, production staff should never suggest or encourage some guests to "surprise" other guests with information they are unprepared to hear. It is never appropriate to maneuver a first-time revelation on national TV that a family is aware of a member's alcoholism, that a spouse is unfaithful, or that a child is homosexual. Shows could use guests who have recovered from such experiences to explain the problem without jeopardizing privacy with a surprise public exposure. They should also carefully screen to minimize the possibility that any guests might orchestrate such surprises without the show's knowledge. Further, Talk TV personnel should specifically inform potential guests that such "surprises" are neither condoned nor permitted.

9. *Keep the number of guests manageable.*

Production staff should make sure that each program can allow all the guests sufficient time to discuss their circumstances. Too many guests on the stage contributes to a superficial, fast-paced approach to issues that generates a lot of heat but sheds little light. Keeping the number of guests manageable also includes ensuring that guests appearing on the same program are appropriate to appear together, are prepared to do so, and are willing to cooperate and remain respectful even when they disagree with their co-panelists. Production staff should never set up guests to appear with their opponents if they are not prepared to do so, or to appear on programs if they will be greatly outnumbered or disgraced. Likewise they should not knowingly place people with a hostile attitude in the audience without informing the guests. (More on this point later.)

10. *Discourage the use of derogatory, rude, and stereotypical statements.*

During both preshow orientations and actual taping, Talk TV personnel should actively discourage the use of derogatory, rude, and stereotypical statements. Whether the purpose of the show is entertainment or education, guests should not be subjected to on-air attacks. Discouraging such remarks does not limit guests' ability to disagree with or challenge one another, it simply limits them to more productive, useful ways of doing so. In addition, shows should never condone—let alone set up—violent exchanges between guests.

11. *Interrupt invasions of privacy or on-air attacks.*

Even when guests are adults and are responsible for themselves, the host still has some responsibility for ensuring their safety and well-being during the show. If guests begin to attack one another or to invade one another's privacy, or if audience members do so, the host should interrupt such interactions. If the questions or comments are clearly intrusive or incendiary, the host should address that fact and redirect the conversation. If the host is uncertain, guests should be asked if they are comfortable responding and reminded of their right to silence. By doing so, the host not only protects guests but diminishes the likelihood that the conversation will turn into an on-air feud or intrusive interrogation.

12.   *Do not place children and adolescents in harmful situations.*

Children do not ordinarily appear without their parents' permission and in fact are more likely brought along to support their points of view. Nonetheless, this often places children in a position of having to go on public record with an opinion that may not be fully formed or that may be coerced. Likewise, they may not be able to anticipate the possible negative reactions of their peers. Hosts and producers should take care to inform children about what to expect in language that is appropriate to their ability to understand.

Children should never be placed in a situation on the air where they are caught between warring parents who are also on the stage. Likewise, they should never be asked to say negative things about a parent even if such statements are accurate. Such comments could leave the child vulnerable to the reaction of a potentially wrathful parent once the show is over. Finally, children and adolescents should be offered an opportunity for debriefing following any exchange that is upsetting or confusing.

Relationship with Audience Members

1.   *Do not prearrange audience composition.*

Talk TV personnel should make tickets for the shows available to the general public on an as-interested basis. The shows should refrain from recruiting specific group members or people with particular political or religious views to attend certain programs. Stacking the audience with opposing views or with preselected people misleads viewers and can make the show difficult for guests. If audiences are preselected, guests and viewers should be fully informed of that fact.

2.   *Foster an interest in discussion and understanding among audience members.*

Shows should establish and firmly maintain ground rules about audience participation. The audience warm-up should include strong statements about the show's commitment to a positive experience for all guests, and should encourage the audience to participate in the conversation in honest and respectful ways. Audiences do not have to agree with guests but should be instructed to listen to guests' stories and opinions and to question them in ways that are not offensive and not full of embellished emotion. And if the audience has been pumped up and told to react in certain ways, the show's introduction should include a warning to the viewers.

Use of Experts

1. *Ensure that professionals' credentials are clear to the general public.*

Shows currently trot out "relationship experts," "communication therapists," and many others with introductions implying that such titles designate genuine mental health professionals. This routine needs to give way to introductions that help the audience differentiate between titles that are reserved for people who comply with state licensing standards and are bound by professional ethical codes, and titles that are self-chosen and convey no protection whatsoever. Hosts should go beyond titles to sketch the "expert's" actual background and training. Clarifying what experts are qualified to do will help the public interpret the information they give and the suggestions they make.

Motivational speakers or relationship therapists should appear only in situations that don't involve serious medical or mental disorders and their treatment. Programs discussing organizational problems or providing general guidelines for polite behavior could use people who work in the field without formal credentials; programs addressing specific psychopathological conditions should not.

2. *Utilize professionals' skills throughout production as needed and appropriate.*

If the shows invite professionals to participate in programs, they should seek their expertise throughout production and not reserve it for the final moments of taping. Experts are in a prime position to offer suggestions regarding the recruitment of other potential experts, the organization of the show, and the screening of potential guests, in addition to providing expert commentary on the issues. Experts can also be of significant benefit after taping, when they can assist in debriefing guests and making appropriate referrals while Talk TV personnel move on to prepare for the next program. Experts' knowledge and skills should be more fully utilized to benefit not only the shows, but viewers and guests as well.

3.   *Carefully select professionals who understand and match the purpose of the show.*

In order to meet the goals of the program and provide viewers and guests with honest information or assistance, producers must choose experts to fit the programs on which they will appear. Talk TV personnel should carefully screen and select their professionals, which in no way indicates that only mental health professionals should be sought. There is a place on the shows for professionals from all disciplines, and for nonprofessionals as well. The point is that those asked to appear should be well-suited to their assigned roles and viewers and guests should be made aware of their qualifications and limitations.

4.   *Fully inform professionals of their role and the content of the program.*

Just as guests should never be caught off guard or unprepared for what is planned, neither should experts. Experts should receive a full description of the nature of the program and their role in it. Such information is essential if professionals are to be able to determine whether or not their skills and experiences are sufficient for what the show is requesting. Experts should never be set up with on-air surprises or "stump the expert" scenarios. In order to provide meaningful assistance, they must have sufficient information to prepare for their appearance.

5.   *Allot sufficient time for their comments.*

Experts should have enough time during the show to contribute to the discussion in meaningful ways. Any professional, regardless of media savvy and professional expertise, will be hard pressed to offer useful information if allowed to speak for the first time in the final few moments of the show. Hosts should routinely invite experts into the conversation early on, and allow them to contribute along the way with the same freedom afforded other guests and audience members.

6. *Question professionals' comments, interpretations, recommendations.*

Hosts should question experts about the meaning, source, reliability, and validity of their comments, and discourage them from offering quick summations and pat answers. Instead, professionals should discuss the complications of the topics presented as well as alternative methods for understanding and resolving problems. In this way, guests and viewers alike are encouraged to consider the complexity of mental health concerns, rather than being misled into thinking that simple answers exist if only they would pursue them.

7. *Hold professionals accountable to the recommendations listed below.*

This chapter offers a number of recommendations for individual professionals. Talk TV personnel are encouraged to examine those recommendations as well and to use them as part of their evaluation process in recruiting and selecting potential experts, regardless of professional background.

Suggestions for the Profession

Mental health professionals bear part of the responsibility to improve the quality of Talk TV, and they also have a responsibility to protect the integrity of their profession. Many professionals may not be aware of or concerned with what is happening on *The Oprah Winfrey Show, Donahue, Sally Jessy Raphael,* or *Geraldo,* but we think they need to be. Mental health professionals have an obligation to inform themselves of the issues and to support the development of strategies to work with the shows and with the public to reduce the problems the shows generate.

More than any professional organization, Talk TV has the public's ear—and is filling it with information that is not only inaccurate but potentially quite harmful. The responsibility to remedy this phenomenon lies both with professional organizations and with individual professionals. The recommendations we offer encourage both professional organizations and individual professionals to utilize existing resources, to share information, and to search for new information in order to redirect Talk TV in a more positive and useful direction.

For Professional Organizations

1.   *Use the media to inform the public and fight inaccurate information regarding mental health issues.*

Talk TV, like other media, is a tremendously powerful enterprise. With millions of viewers every day, it dwarfs the methods that the mental health profession has traditionally used to convey information: journals, workshops, community awareness projects, print media, and confidential services. Attempting to redress Talk TV's inaccuracies with traditional methods alone is comparable to trying to outrun a train; those methods simply cannot move fast enough or carry enough weight to make a difference. If the mental health profession hopes to convey accurate information and honest images about mental health issues to the public, it must be even more deliberate and skillful its use of available media.

2.   *Use more aggressive marketing strategies to distribute existing information to the public.*

Mass-marketing strategies should be sought to counter the false and damaging information that is currently so widely available. For example, the American Psychiatric Association's Division of Public Affairs has issued a series of Mental Illness Awareness Guides written for what they call "information gatekeepers," such as the media, educators, clergy, image makers, and film and TV producers and writers. They also have a series of fact sheets written to provide the public with information and to answer typical media questions. The fact sheets respond to various treatment issues and subjects that give rise to significant public misunderstanding.

For example, the *Insanity Defense Fact Sheet* came out before the Jeffrey Dahmer trial. Other titles include *False Memory Syndrome*, *Patient/Therapist Sexual Contact*, and *Mental Illness and Violence*. Thus, responses exist. The question is, are they being heard? The professions need to increase support for existing efforts to distribute accurate information to the general public.

3. *As needed, review and modify existing ethical codes to ensure that media interactions are adequately addressed.*

Existing ethical codes should be reviewed to determine whether or not they adequately cover current dilemmas facing professionals, such as those generated by the media. The work of Robert McCall, Ph.D., on ethical considerations for professional psychologists involved with television should be strongly considered as a beginning point.

In addition, the Media Psychology Division has been working to address media-related concerns for the profession since 1982. In 1983, the division issued its first set of guidelines regarding professional interactions with the media. These guidelines are currently being revised and will be available in 1996–97. These guidelines will specify the areas of the ethics code (1992) that apply specifically to media situations.

If professional groups do not have divisions to handle media issues, they should develop them.

4. *Identify media experts and sponsor professional training on a state and national level.*

If the mental health profession is to make the best use of the media, its members must know how to do so. This is unlikely to occur if professionals are left to learn only through the school of hard knocks. In 1994, under the direction of Ellen McGrath, Ph.D., APA Division 46 compiled the Television Consultants Directory (TCD)—a listing of mental health professionals who have media experience. This organization also provides opportunities for training and can direct interested professionals to reliable sources of information on media. Using resources such as this, professional organizations should identify media experts and sponsor professional training on a state and national level to increase the number of mental health professionals equipped to ethically and successfully interact with the media. From such training, more local training could occur and mentoring programs could be established to provide support and assistance to those who want to pursue working with the media.

5.   *Encourage the inclusion of media courses in graduate training programs.*

Graduate schools should likewise include courses offering students the skills to organize and present mental health material through more popular sources than mental health journals or clinical practice. Courses should help students anticipate the potential differences in values between the media and the mental health professions, and also prepare them for the differences among various media, such as print, broadcast news, and Talk TV. Students should be informed of their rights and responsibilities, before they find themselves being called upon to respond.

6.   *Encourage scholarly research and discussion regarding the impact of Talk TV on viewers, guests, and the profession.*

From the existing organizations and other interested professionals, a body of information regarding Talk TV is emerging. But the consequences of TV remain relatively understudied and therefore unknown. Professional organizations should support and encourage scholarly research and discussion regarding Talk TV. Jacqueline Bouhoutsos and Robert McCall are among the few who have written on media psychology and have given careful consideration to the important role professionals can play. Work such as theirs should be closely reviewed, discussed, and built upon.

For Individual Professionals

1.   *Regardless of the degree of direct involvement, become informed about Talk TV.*

Whether or not professionals believe they are likely to become directly involved with Talk TV, they should inform themselves about the nature of the shows, the possible influence they may have over the general public's perception of mental health, and more specifically how the shows might influence consumer perceptions and expectations. Without such information, professionals will be unable to counter the inaccurate information the shows generate.

2.   *If invited to appear, question carefully the nature of the shows and the proffered roles.*

Professionals should seek as much information as they can regarding the programs they are invited to appear on. Information can be obtained by watching broadcasts of the program, requesting tapes of programs the shows have produced on similar topics and with similar formats, and asking specific questions about what is the purpose and plan of the program.

3.   *Talk with other professionals who have appeared on that particular show.*

In addition to seeking information from the shows themselves, professionals should talk with other professionals who have media experience. Ideally, professionals who have appeared on the show in question should be sought, because the shows vary widely in their production strategies. In addition to concerns about how the program will be developed, professionals should ask trusted colleagues questions about the potential consequences of appearing both for their own careers and for the reputation of the profession as a whole.

4.   *Refuse to solicit clients as guests.*

Professionals considering a Talk TV appearance should review their professional code of ethics, particularly as it pertains to their relationship with clients. Professionals should refuse any attempts, by the shows or by clients, to get them to agree to appear with their own clients on the shows. This includes former clients, who are still potentially as vulnerable to the professionals' influence and suggestions as are current clients.

5.   *Require a preshow assessment with guests.*

Professionals should never appear on Talk TV with guests

whom they have not previously assessed. Professionals, by virtue of their appearance, confer approval on what happens. Without preshow assessment, professionals run the risk of appearing with guests who should not be on the show, whose concerns fall outside the realm of their expertise, or with whom they cannot effectively work. Preshow assessments also allow the professional to ensure the guests have appropriate expectations about what will and will not occur and about the professional's relationship to them, which is merely that of a co-panelist—not a therapist.

6.   *Refuse to appear if guests are at risk, volatile, or too numerous to manage.*

If, during the preshow assessment, there are any indications that the guests are at risk for negative consequences as a result of appearing, professionals should clearly inform the guests of such concerns and encourage them to reconsider their appearance. They should also provide guests with appropriate referrals at this time and should support them in their right to refuse to appear. If guests are unwilling to cancel the appearance, a professional who remains persuaded that there are problems should withdraw from the show. Above all else, professionals should remain committed to their obligations to provide assistance and to ensure they do no harm.

7.   *Make sure the show has arranged adequate postshow services.*

Before professionals agree to appear, they should insist that the shows arrange for adequate debriefing following the taping. Professionals should be cautious about agreeing to conduct such services themselves because that agreement may falsely imply to the guests that they have, in fact, taken them on as clients. Professionals should be willing to participate in such debriefings but are wise to allow other professionals to provide the actual services when necessary referrals for further help should be made.

8.   *Fully identify training, experience, and scope of expertise.*

Professionals should discuss with the shows the nature and extent of their expertise, as well as their professional limits, and should ensure that they will be properly identified on the show. During the taping, in addition to relying on the label provided by the show, professionals should clearly state their qualifications, their purpose on the show, and the limits of what they will be offering during the broadcast.

9. *Distinguish between personal and professional opinions and limit professional remarks to those that are clearly within the scope of practice.*

Professionals should take care to distinguish personal from professional remarks. They should remain alert to misunderstandings that could arise for viewers who have limited knowledge of the topic at hand and should never assume that viewers will be able to differentiate between personal and professional statements on their own. Whenever personal experiences or opinions significantly influence professional opinion or practice, professionals should indicate that connection and clarify the distinction.

10. *Avoid any behaviors or comments that might suggest establishing a therapeutic contract or an on-air diagnosis.*

Throughout the preshow assessment, taping, and debriefing, professionals should guard against making statements or engaging in any behaviors that might suggest they are establishing a clinical relationship with the guests. Professionals should remind guests that the preshow assessment is not for the purpose of diagnosis or treatment, but rather to ensure that guests understand what they are agreeing to and that they are able and prepared to appear. During the taping, professionals should also avoid any remarks that suggest they are providing a diagnosis or prescribing treatment.

11. *Maintain the integrity of training and the profession by refusing to oversimplify complex material.*

Professionals should insist on adequate time to discuss the topic of the show, to explain their comments, and to fully answer questions. Professionals should not permit the shows to squeeze them into a corner or pressure them into responding in sound-bites. Professionals should maintain the integrity of their profession and their training, and, if necessary, remind the shows that they were invited on as experts to provide informed opinions. If time does not permit a more lengthy explanation, professionals can indicate on the air that they do not have the time to answer the question.

12. *Decline offers that might involve questionable ethical practice, including kickbacks in the form of referrals.*

Professionals should guard against agreeing to any arrangements involving questionable ethics, particularly when guests or viewers are likely to be harmed or misled. Professionals should be firm about the limits of their role and should take care to avoid getting into dual relationships with the shows or guests. Professionals should not agree to provide services off the air in exchange for promotion on the shows. This places guests in the middle and may result in their feeling pressured to provide on-air testimonials.

13. *Do not use Talk TV videotapes for instructional purposes without explaining the production and entertainment values that dictate both the content and style of the presentation.*

Instructors should take special precautions in introducing videotaped copies of any of the shows into the classroom as training materials for future mental health professionals. While some of the shows could be useful in sparking discussion or providing examples, faculty must weigh these benefits against the problems of relying on Talk TV as a source of educational material. Since Talk TV portrayals of rare mental health problems are available, the taped show may appear to be a way to present certain types of problems that are hard to depict otherwise. Nonetheless, such media displays may be a result of self-diagnosis and also of embellishment for entertainment purposes. As such, these popular generalizations about trendy issues may be very inaccurate portrayals of real problems. The shows in their current form do not provide the realistic, detailed information needed by professionals in training. Further, faculty should take care to not perpetuate the false belief that Talk TV is a credible source for understanding mental health issues.

Suggestions for Viewers

Viewers can assist in reducing the potential for trouble by taking fairly simple steps to protect themselves from the damaging aspects of the shows. Whether viewers are looking for entertainment or education, they need to be informed consumers. They need to reject programs that do not provide what they are looking for or that offend their sensibilities. Our recommendations also encourage all viewers to reflect on their role in supporting and encouraging the current treatment of guests. The shows would not continue their current practices if they were not amply rewarded by viewers for doing so. Viewers have more influence than they realize and are encouraged to use it wisely.

The first step for all Talk TV viewers is to determine their reasons for watching. Carefully consider Ellen McGrath's warning: "Talk TV can be both harmful and helpful to your health."

1. *Clarify your expectations.*

Viewers seeking information from TV talk shows need to clarify what it is they hope to gain from the shows. Viewers who recognize that Talk TV is designed primarily as entertainment and not education, but are interested in hearing about different ideas, learning about other people's opinions concerning controversial topics, or even in discovering new self-help books, are sometimes able to satisfy those interests. Such viewers would be wise, however, to remember that the people appearing on Talk TV are not representative of average Americans of any sort—they have all been selected because they have unusual stories to tell.

Likewise, viewers who watch for fun need to remind themselves that the people who are providing their thrills are vulnerable to the criticisms and insults of others. Such viewers should be honest with themselves about their role in the exploitation of people with real troubles or bad judgment.

Viewers looking for definitive answers, solutions, or explanations for their own personal problems are much more likely to be disappointed and misled. The answers generated by Talk TV are simplistic bits of advice that have the potential to cause trouble, not to solve it. Regardless of the shows' claims and testimonials to the contrary, it is important to maintain a skeptical attitude about whether or not the shows provide helpful information.

2.   *Watch selectively.*

Viewers should carefully select among the different shows and their offerings. Review the options and choose only those shows that appear to offer the greatest opportunity to learn something useful or to provide acceptable entertainment. Retain the option of turning off shows that deteriorate into public lynchings, family feuds, or offensive stereotypes. Remain alert to changes in your mood or attitude about others that may be the result of frequent exposure to the hostility, trauma, and chaos of Talk TV.

3.   *Question the authority and legitimacy of so-called experts.*

Do not accept every "expert" as such. Listen carefully to the manner in which experts are identified and to the basis of their expertise, particularly as it relates to the topic at hand. If watching for information regarding a particular concern or problem, get acquainted with what sorts of professionals are qualified to offer "expert" opinions about that topic. Remember that while motivational speakers, authors, or nonprofessionals can offer sensible and inspiring assessments and advice, they are not licensed to provide either diagnosis or treatment of mental health problems. Because they do not have the training or experience to obtain the approval necessary for the license to provide such services, the information they provide should not be considered the same as that provided by a licensed psychiatrist, psychologist, counselor, or social worker. Be sure to understand the basis of the experts' comments and evaluate them accordingly.

4.   *Seek verification of alleged facts—particularly those that are of most importance or interest to you.*

Develop a skeptical attitude toward facts, statistics, and pat answers about controversial or complicated issues, especially when no information is offered about the source of such "facts." Often what is merely opinion can be stated with such authority that it comes across sounding as if it were established truth. A firm voice and self-assured manner may change the way a statement sounds while doing nothing to increase its accuracy. If information is presented that is of interest or seems compelling, seek further information from a local library or other community resources.

5. *Question the meaning of psychobabble and other catchy terms.*

Beware of the potential problems with Talk TV terminology. Question whether or not what is being described is actually a new "syndrome," "phenomenon," or "addiction," or whether it is simply behavior more honestly described as "predictable," "common," or "excessive." Decline the invitations to turn everything into a pathological problem and question whether the words being used are specific, defined, accurate, and applicable. And if they are not, ignore them.

6. *Consider what other explanations or strategies might exist.*

There are conflicting facts and figures regarding the causes and motivations of, as well as the solutions for, most human behaviors. Remember that Talk TV producers select their topics, guests, and experts in order to present the most interesting—that is, thrilling—shows they can. The views, opinions, and recommendations presented do not represent the full range of options. And more importantly, many do not even represent accepted perspectives. Always temper what is presented with a recognition that it has all been filtered through an entertainment screen. Consider how the presentation might be different if there were no viewers to be wooed.

7. *Avoid the temptation to apply other people's problems or solutions to your own life.*

Although the people, their stories, and their aspirations can all be quite compelling, do not assume that their predicaments are like yours. Despite the illusion of instant intimacy promoted by the hosts, there is no real connection between viewers and guests. If problems or circumstances that sound familiar are described, don't assume that indicates they are the same as yours. The shows provide only a small (and often distorted) slice of their guests' lives and problems. The recommendations they offer are likewise frequently generic and vague. Be careful not to overidentify with the strangers on the screen.

8. *Resist the temptation to "diagnose" friends or family members.*

Just as it is important to avoid overidentifying with guests, it is equally important to respect the complexity of family and friends. While the shows may provide information that is useful in identifying broad categories of problems, they are never sufficient to indicate what is wrong with someone else. Not only are such summations likely to be inaccurate, they are typically unwelcome. Armchair psychologists, supported only by "Oprah said so," can fuel more trouble than they resolve. Beware of this trap.

9. *Remain alert for stereotypes and biases.*

Observe how men, women, racial minorities, and marginalized groups are treated on the shows. Are racial minorities only present for certain topics? Are all guests asked about sexual orientation or is it only some guests for certain topics? Are men and women treated differently? Remember that the shows are primarily marketed to women and as such are often very critical of men. Remain alert to subtle forms of stereotyping, particularly with groups you are either unfamiliar with or inclined to hold stereotypes about. Ask members of those groups their opinions about how the shows depict their issues.

10. *Do not use the shows as a model for how to communicate—especially with friends and family regarding sensitive issues.*

Avoid modeling your own communication style after that of the shows. Guests may be rewarded for rude, intrusive, or outrageous remarks with applause and attention, but in real life such tactics are likely to produce angry arguments or sudden isolation. Consider how you might feel if such comments or questions were directed toward you. Consider the possibility that changes in your communication habits may occur that are not deliberate or planned but simply a result of frequent exposure to the shows.

11. *Do not dismiss preexisting concerns you have about your own behavior or circumstances because people on the shows appear worse off than you are.*

If you have concerns about some aspect of your life or behavior, don't override or ignore those concerns because the shows indicate that such circumstances are normal, or because so many other people apparently "have it worse." Consider your own circumstances independently of the shows and determine whether you feel satisfied or concerned. Remember, the shows and their hosts, guests, and experts will not have to live with any of the choices you make.

12. *Take action to resolve any concerns you have rather than believing that watching Talk TV will suffice.*

If you have concerns about your life or behavior, or have questions based on information from the shows, do not simply watch more shows in an attempt to address those concerns. Watching Talk TV will change little. Determine what actions might be helpful, identify a trustworthy person with whom to discuss options, and develop a plan. Avoid being seduced by the tube—it keeps you planted in your chair, immobile, often noncommunicative and preoccupied. Be alert to whether or not listening to people talk about personal concerns signals your own need for intimacy. Feeling more attached to the host or guests than to the people in your life is a signal that something is wrong.

13. *Identify and contact resources within your own community that could provide additional information or assistance.*

If the information presented on the show seems especially relevant or interesting, find out how you can learn more. Most communities have libraries, mental health centers, volunteer programs, or hot lines. Before drawing any conclusions based on what has been presented, read or talk with others about the topic. Doing so will put you in touch with the people in your community most likely to be of assistance and will provide a balance to the show's entertainment bias.

14. *If you are currently in counseling or are considering seeking help, remember that counseling is markedly different from Talk TV.*

Talk TV is not designed to be therapeutic. As a result, it bears little to no resemblance to counseling. Credible counselors are not likely to speak in sound bites, sum up your problems in less than five minutes, provide quick, easy steps to a new you, or jump on the bandwagon of denial and blame. Credible counselors will expect you to work, to examine your own problems and expectations in plain, honest language, and to accept responsibility for yourself. Be aware that the more difficult your problems, the longer they will take to resolve and the more painful it will be to do so. Remember that "talking" is usually not enough. Changes must follow.

15.   *Examine any books or materials promoted on the shows at your local library before you decide to purchase them.*

Be cautious about experts' claims that their books or materials are the definitive explanations. Their "rapid and painless cures for your problems" could result in more trouble. Remember that they benefit financially from your belief that their books, videotapes, workshops, or materials are the solution you've been looking for. Try to locate the materials in a library or lending center before you purchase them. Look at them closely and carefully in a bookstore. And ask yourself if purchasing a product is really the answer or just another trap that allows you to feel as though you're doing some-thing about your troubles when you're really not.

16.   *Consider how you feel during and immediately after the shows.*

The shows often address complicated, controversial, and upset-ting issues. They do so in a fast-paced, "go for the gusto" manner that frequently encourages hostility and disrespect while leaving the issues unresolved. The topics and how they are presented can also contribute to feelings that all is bad with the world and that there is nothing you can do about it.

Consider how you feel when watching. What was your mood before you started watching? What about during and after? When the show is over, do you feel better or worse about yourself? Your friends and family? How has the show affected your attitude toward the people on the show or others like them? Consider whether these shows lead you to understand other people or to ridicule and seek more distance from them.

17.   *Write the shows to support the aspects you appreciate and to inform them of those you do not.*

The shows continually report that they only do what viewers want, so let them know what *you* want. If there are shows that have been particularly useful or well done, or shows that were particularly offensive and destructive, write letters telling the hosts what you think.

Being a Thoughtful Viewer

As we've discussed, many of the ploys the shows use to boost their entertainment value put a subtle (or not-so-subtle) spin on the subjects they present. It could be helpful to take some time after watching a program to ask questions designed to clarify the usefulness of the information presented.

Useful Review Questions

Here are some sample questions that viewers might pose about shows they are likely to take "information" from.

1. How many times were stereotypes used or exacerbated? More specifically, how many times were:

   Women portrayed as petty, as whiny, or as victims?

   Women pitted against each other?

   Men portrayed as macho, as uncaring, or as perpetrators?

   Men pitted against women?

   African-Americans portrayed as criminals, addicts, unintelligent, or threats to Caucasians?

   African-Americans and Caucasians pitted against each other?

   Hispanics portrayed as aggressive and overly dependent on welfare?

   Gays and lesbians portrayed as immoral, hostile, or in need of change?

2. How many times were people interrupted while they were speaking?

3. How many times were rude or hurtful remarks made?

4. How many times were there invasions of privacy or pressure to reveal more?

5. Were the "experts" adequately identified and legitimate?

6. Were "expert" comments thoroughly explained and questioned?

7. Was "get therapy" the solution?

8. Did the advice sound too good to be true?

9. How many times did the host contribute to or exacerbate hostility during the show?

10. Was a diversity of guests and opinions sought and respected?

Implications

Based on your answers to the above questions, consider the following:

1. How useful is the information presented? And how do I know this?

2. How applicable is it to me or anyone I know?

3. Was there a solid basis for the information?

4. What might be alternative explanations or strategies and where could I get information about them?

5. What has watching this show done for (or to) me?

These suggestions are offered in the hope of making the educational elements of Talk TV authentic. The entertainment value of human dilemmas is undeniable, but it does not justify ignoring accuracy, maintaining hatred, and reinforcing stereotypical assumptions. If Talk TV is intended as a spoof of the human condition, then mental health professionals are not needed and the joke can proceed without their sponsorship. But even in a spoof, care needs to be taken so that people are not exploited for others' amusement. And if a host promises a serious attempt to both educate and amuse, then much more attention needs to be given to the accuracy of the information, the value of the advice, the substance of the expertise, and the treatment of the guests. Without this effort, all the features that make for such great entertainment only add to the harm the shows do.

Notes

P. 234, *Society of Professional Journalists has a code of ethics:* Mayeux, P. *Broadcast News Writing and Reporting.* Dubuque, Iowa: Brown, 1991, p. 404.

P. 234, *the Radio-Television News Directors Association has a code:* Mayeux, P. *Broadcast News Writing and Reporting.* Dubuque, Iowa: Brown, 1991, p. 404.

P. 246, *ethical considerations for professional psychologists:* McCall, R. "Ethical Considerations of Psychologists Working in the Media," in C. Fisher and W. Tryon (eds.), *Annual Advances in Applied Psychology,* Vol. 4: *Ethics in Applied Psychology.* Norwood, N.J.: ABLEX, 1990, pp. 163–185.

P. 247, *scholarly research and discussion regarding Talk TV.* McCall, R. "Ethical Considerations of Psychologists Working in the Media," in C. Fisher and W. Tryon (eds.), *Annual Advances in Applied Psychology,* Vol. 4: *Ethics in Applied Psychology.* Norwood, N.J.: ABLEX, 1990, pp. 163–185.

Appendix

Radio-Television News Directors Association Code of Broadcast News Ethics

The responsibility of radio and television journalists is to gather and report information of importance and interest to the public accurately, honestly and impartially.

The members of the Radio-Television News Directors Association accept these standards and will:

1. Strive to present the source or nature of broadcast news material in a way that is balanced, accurate and fair.
   A. They will evaluate information solely on its merits as news, rejecting sensationalism or misleading emphasis in any form.
   B. They will guard against using audio or video material in a way that deceives the audience.
   C. They will not mislead the public by presenting as spontaneous news any material which is staged or rehearsed.
   D. They will identify people by race, creed, nationality or prior status only when it is relevant.
   E. They will clearly label opinion and commentary.
   F. They will promptly acknowledge and correct errors.
2. Strive to conduct themselves in a manner that protects them from conflicts of interest, real or perceived. They will decline

gifts or favors which would influence or appear to influence their judgments.

3. Respect the dignity, privacy and well-being of people with whom they deal.

4. Recognize the need to protect confidential sources. They will promise confidentiality only with the intention of keeping that promise.

5. Respect everyone's right to a fair trial.

6. Broadcast the private transmissions of other broadcasters only with permission.

7. Actively encourage observance of this Code by all journalists, whether members of the Radio-Television News Directors Association or not.

Suggestions for Psychologists Working with the Media[1]

Psychologists who work with the media are required as psychologists to follow the *Ethical Principles of Psychologists and Code of Conduct* (APA, 1992). Various groups including Division 46, Media Psychology, have developed various editions of guidelines to assist psychologists working in the media. These ideas, which will be outlined in a separate document named *Suggestions for Psychologists Working With the Media* are currently undergoing the review process within the American Psychological Association (APA) and are formulated to provide guidance to psychologists working with the print or electronic media. The recommendations are intended to offer a structure for psychologists who work in the media to educate a wide audience, not where the media or platform is used in therapy or as a learning tool. These latter two areas are provided in the Ethical Principles of Psychologists and Code of Conduct (APA, 1992) in the sections covering therapy, education, and research.

These suggestions currently under review are intended to foster systematic development of psychology in the public media while also promoting a high level of professionalism among psychologists working with the media. The intention is to guide psychologists working with the media in meaningful ways without unnecessarily or inappropriately limiting their ability to exercise professional judgment or attempts for innovation.

The general guidelines for psychologists working with the media include the general principles of competence; integrity; professional and scientific responsibility; respect for people's rights and dignity; concern for other's welfare; solicitation of testimonials; social responsibility; and considerations of the differences between advertising and endorsing products and services.

It is hoped that these suggestions will have completed the review process of the American Psychological Association by 1996–97. Both the ethics committee of Division 4, Media Psychology and the Public Information Committee (PIC) will be working to update these recommendations over time. For additional information and clarification please write or call:

Public Affairs Office
American Psychological Association
750 First Street, N.W.
Washington, D.C. 20002–4242
(202) 336–5706

Division 46, Media Psychology
c/o Division Services
American Psychological Association
750 First Street, N.W.
Washington, D.C. 20002–4242
(202) 336-6013

The Ethics Office
American Psychological Association
750 First Street, N.W.
Washington, D.C. 20002–4242
(202) 336–5930

[1]The *Suggestions for Psychologists Working with the Media* include consideration of the 1991 APA's *Ethical Principles of Psychologists and Code of Conduct; Media Guidelines for the Psychologist* by Vasquez, Masters, and Pope, 1986–87; *Guidelines for Media Mental Health Professionals* by Broder et al., 1983; *Suggestions for Media Mental Health Professionals*, revised by Wachs et al., 1989; *Ethical Considerations for Psychologists in the Media*, Ethics Committee Task Force, APA, Strassburger, F. et al., 1983; *Ethical Guidelines for Media Psychologists*, Public Information Committee Subcommittee on Ethical Guidelines, Haber, S. et al., 1986–87; and Ethical Considerations of Psychologists Working in the Media in *Ethics in Applied Developmental Psychology: Emerging Issues in an Emerging Field* by McCall, R., 1990.

Adapted from Ethical Principles of Psychologists and Code of Conduct (APA)

We have included parts of the ethics code of the American Psychological Association because it is representative of the basic guidelines mental health professionals are to follow when they appear on Talk TV. The American Counseling Association, The American Psychiatric Association, and other professional groups have similar codes that guide the conduct of their members.

3.03   Avoidance of False or Deceptive Statements

(a) Psychologists do not make public statements that are false, deceptive, misleading, or fraudulent, either because of what they state, convey, or suggest or because of what they omit, concerning their research, practice, or other work activities or those of persons or organizations with which they are affiliated. As examples (and not in limitation) of this standard, psychologists do not make false or deceptive statements concerning (1) their training, experience, or competence; (2) their academic degrees; (3) their credentials; (4) their institutional or association affiliations; (5) their services; (6) the scientific or clinical basis for, or results or degree of success of, their services; (7) their fees; or (8) their publications or research findings. (See also Standards 6.15, Deception in Research, and 6.18, Providing Participants With Information About the Study.)

(b) Psychologists claim as credentials for their psychological work, only degrees that (1) were earned from a regionally accredited educational institution or (2) were the basis for psychology licensure by the state in which they practice.

3.04   Media Presentations

When psychologists provide advice or comment by means of public lectures, demonstrations, radio or television programs, prerecorded tapes, printed articles, mailed material, or other media, they take reasonable precautions to ensure that (1) the statements are based on appropriate psychological literature and practice, (2) the statements are otherwise consistent with this Ethics Code, and (3) the recipients of the information are not encouraged to infer that a relationship has been established with them personally.

3.05 Testimonials

Psychologists do not solicit testimonials from current psychotherapy clients or patients or other persons who because of their particular circumstances are vulnerable to undue influence.

About the Authors

JEANNE ALBRONDA HEATON, Ph.D., is a psychologist at Ohio University's Counseling and Psychological Services. She teaches part time in the Psychology Department and has a private practice in Athens, Ohio. In addition to her university responsibilities, she is a mediator for the domestic relations court in Athens County, as well as program coordinator for the board of Milestones, a therapeutic foster care network. She also serves on the Ohio Psychological Association's Peer Review Committee on Ethical Practices.

NONA LEIGH WILSON, Ph.D., is an assistant professor in counseling and human resource development at South Dakota State University. She earned her doctorate in counselor education at Ohio University, where she coordinated the campus sexual assault education and prevention program. She has ten years of experience working in the area of violence against women.

Index